6

SECRETS

TO

A

LASTING

LOVE

# 6 SECRETS

## *to a*

### *Recapturing Your*

# LASTING LOVE

*Dream Marriage*

## DR. GARY & BARBARA ROSBERG

TYNDALE HOUSE PUBLISHERS, INC.

*Carol Stream, Illinois*

Visit Tyndale's exciting Web site at www.tyndale.com

*TYNDALE* and Tyndale's quill logo are registered trademarks of Tyndale House Publishers, Inc.

*Six Secrets to a Lasting Love: Recapturing Your Dream Marriage*

Designed by Ron Kaufmann

Edited by Lynn Vanderzalm

Some of the names and details in the illustrations used in this book have been changed to protect the privacy of the people who shared their stories with us.

This book is adapted from *Divorce-Proof Your Marriage,* copyright © 2002 by Gary and Barbara Rosberg. Portions of Secret One and the diagrams in chapter 4 are adapted from *Dr. Rosberg's Do-It-Yourself Relationship Mender,* copyright © 1992, 1995 by Gary Rosberg. Portions of Secret Two are adapted from *The Five Love Needs of Men and Women,* copyright © 2000 by Gary and Barbara Rosberg. Portions of Secret Four are adapted from *Guard Your Heart,* copyright © 2001 by Gary Rosberg. All previously published portions are used by permission of Focus on the Family and Tyndale House Publishers, Inc., Carol Stream, Illinois 60188. All rights reserved.

**Library of Congress Cataloging-in-Publication Data**

Rosberg, Gary.
  6 secrets to a lasting love : recapturing your dream marriage / Gary and Barbara Rosberg.
    p. cm.
  Includes bibliographical references.
  ISBN-13: 978-1-4143-1210-1 (sc)
  ISBN-10: 1-4143-1210-5 (sc)
  1. Marriage—Religious aspects—Christianity. I. Rosberg, Barbara. II. Title. III. Title: Six secrets to a lasting love.
  BV835.R66 2006
  248.8′44—dc22                                                        2006020061

Printed in the United States of America

15  14  13  12  11  10  09  08
 9   8   7   6   5   4   3   2

For the sake of our next generation—

Sarah and Scott, Missy and Cooper.

And for the sake of our future generations—

Mason, Kaden, Lilly Anne, and Kia Marie.

We love you and promise to leave a godly legacy.

# Contents

# $\mathcal{A}$cknowledgments

We have had the opportunity to work on some great books with our friends at Tyndale House Publishers. And as always, they have shown incredible excellence in publishing the book you are holding in your hands. This book in many ways is a circling of the wagons of all our other books to serve as the foundational book to equip you with what we have learned from our work with marriages for almost three decades about the nonnegotiables of building a lasting marriage. We have listened in the counseling room, to our radio audience on our daily call-in radio program, and to our own hearts as God has ministered to us. In this book we bring you into our own marriage—the celebrations as well as the trials.

As with each of our resources, this book is a team project. We thank Kevin Johnson, David Bellis, and Ed Stewart for their early work in helping to establish this message. We honor Lynn Vanderzalm for her editorial finesse and touch that always brings our books up several notches. Ron Beers, Ken Petersen, and Carol Traver from Tyndale House Publishers are the most extraordinary group of people to work with in the publishing field. We commend you for your consistent commitment to publishing biblical books that help change lives. And our partnership with you is outmatched only by our commitment to our friendship with you. Thank you for allowing us to partner with your excellent team at Tyndale House.

And we thank our parents. We lost my mom to leukemia and Alzheimer's disease during the writing of this book. Audrey Marie Halm Rosberg finished the race on February 21, 2006, and joined my dad, John Rosberg, in heaven to meet again after their fifty-four-year love affair and spend eternity together with Jesus. I thank my mom for finishing strong and building into the first part of my life (as Barb has the second half) much of who I am today. I also honor my dad, whose impact and influence is all over this book as well. I am just writing down what you taught me, Pop. We also honor and love Barb's parents, Jack and Colleen Bedford, married sixty-six years and going strong.

And finally, thanks to our family: Sarah and Scott, Missy and Cooper, as well as our grandchildren, Mason, Kaden, Lilly Anne, and Kia Marie. Thanks for being the safest place on earth in a place called home. This book is part of our legacy, and you each bring credence and heart to the legacy we are passing on to you. Live well and finish strong. We love you.

$\mathcal{G}$ary and $\mathcal{B}$arbara $\mathcal{R}$osberg

# 1

## When Our Dream Marriage Began to Fade

Seven years into our marriage, my life was a blur. I was working hard at being a good provider for my wife, Barb, and our two young daughters, Sarah and Missy. I had a full-time job as the director of a correctional facility. At the same time, I was working toward a doctoral degree in counseling, spending many evenings each week studying at the university library.

Most of the time I felt stretched beyond my limits. As I juggled family, work, studies, and church activities, I prayed daily for strength and wisdom, longing for the day I could focus full-time on counseling families. Even more important, I wanted to free up more time to be with Barb, Sarah, and Missy—my family, the love of my life. The job and doctoral dissertation filled my schedule completely. I tried to eke out a little time here and there to help Barb, but I was at best only a part-time husband and father.

I honestly thought I was doing rather well in my role at that time. Then one day I was sitting in my favorite chair, studying during the final stages of my doctoral degree, when my five-year-old daughter, Sarah, announced herself in my presence with a question: "Daddy, do you want to see my family picture?"

I really felt stressed and pressed for time, with a week's worth of work to squeeze into a weekend. "Sarah, Daddy's busy. Come back in a little while, honey." Sarah obediently left me to my work.

Ten minutes later she swept back into the living room, "Daddy, let me show you my picture."

The heat went up around my collar. "Sarah, I said come back later. This is important."

Three minutes later she stormed into the living room, got three inches from my nose, and barked with all the power a five-year-old can muster, *"Do you want to see it, or don't you?"*

*"No,"* I told her emphatically, *"I do not!"*

With that she zoomed out of the room and left me alone. And somehow, being alone at that moment wasn't as satisfying as I thought it would be. I felt like a jerk. So I got up and went to the front door. "Sarah," I called, "could you come back inside a minute, please? I would like to see your picture."

She obliged with no recriminations and hopped up onto my lap.

It was a great picture. She'd even given it a title. Across the top, in her best printing, she had inscribed: Our Family Best.

"Tell me about it," I said.

"Here is Mommy [a stick figure with long yellow, curly hair]. Here is me standing by Mommy [with a smiley face]. Here is Katie [our dog]. And here is Missy [her little sister was a stick figure lying in the street in front of the house, about three times bigger than anyone else]." It was a pretty good insight into how she saw our family.

"I love your picture, honey," I told her. "I'll hang it on the dining-room wall, and each night when I come home from work and from class [which was usually around ten o'clock at night], I'm going to look at it."

She took me at my word, beamed from ear to ear, and went outside to play. I went back to my books. But for some reason I kept reading the same paragraph over and over. Something made me uneasy, something about Sarah's picture. Something was missing.

I went to the front door again. "Sarah," I called, "could you come back inside a minute, please? I want to look at your picture again."

Sarah crawled back onto my lap. I can close my eyes right now and see the way she looked. Cheeks rosy from playing outside. Pigtails. Strawberry Shortcake tennis shoes. A Cabbage Patch doll named Nellie tucked limply under her arm.

I asked my little girl a question, but I wasn't sure I wanted to hear the answer. "Honey, I see Mommy and Sarah and Missy. Katie the dog is in the picture, and the sun and the house and squirrels and birdies. But Sarah, where is Daddy?"

"You're at the library," she said.

With that simple statement my little princess stopped time for me. Lifting her gently off my lap, I sent her back to play in the spring sunshine. I slumped back in my chair, dazed. Even as I type these words, I can feel those sensations all over again. She had nailed me, right between the eyes. I wasn't in her family picture because I was at the library studying. I was too busy to be her daddy at home.

Although I didn't remember Barb's having expressed those thoughts, she had probably been trying to get through to me for months. All of the cautions I had received from sermons, books, and friends to keep a "balanced lifestyle"—God first, family second, work third—had not penetrated my career-bent brain. But Sarah's simple pronouncement got my attention big-time.

# A MARRIAGE FADING WITH TIME

Not long ago, I had an experience that helped me more fully understand what Sarah's picture really meant at that point in my life. I had pulled out some other pictures: my childhood family album. I flipped through old photos chronicling my life growing up. I stopped to examine a black-and-white photo of my mom and dad when they were newly married. I couldn't help smiling with pride at the images. Dad was one sharp-looking guy, reminding me of a movie idol from the 1940s. And Mom, I must say, was beautiful. I could see the sparkle in my parents' eyes, the look of love, their hope for a bright future.

Yet the photo itself wasn't as clear and sharp as it had been years ago. The crisp sheen that once caused this handsome couple to stand out on the page was now dull. Time had taken its toll on the old family album.

Decay is normal. In the natural process of aging, machinery wears out, buildings fall into disrepair, pictures fade, and our bodies lose their tone and strength. Scientists say, in fact, that everything in the universe is perpetually moving to greater and greater disorder—a state of entropy. You don't have to be a quantum physicist to know that even the most beautifully designed and well-built house will eventually crumble if left unattended. To keep anything fresh, alive, and in good order requires care, maintenance, and at times, repair.

A marriage is no different. No marriage can last unless it is kept fresh and nurtured. Marriage is a dynamic love relationship between a man and a woman, and at every moment that relationship is either growing deeper and richer, or stagnating and decaying. Maintaining a lasting love means guarding a marriage against deterioration.

When Sarah showed me the family picture with her daddy missing, I realized (or at least admitted to myself for the first time) that I wasn't tuned in to the warning signs that my marriage and family life were deteriorating, moving toward a state of entropy.

## I WANT TO COME HOME

I mounted Sarah's drawing on the dining-room wall, just as I promised. And through those long, intense weeks preceding the oral defense of my dissertation, I stared at that revealing portrait. It happened late every night as I consumed my warmed-over dinners while my family slept. I didn't have the guts to broach the issue with Barb. And she had the incredible insight to let it rest until I was ready to deal with it.

I finally finished my degree program. I was "Dr. Rosberg," and I guess it should have been a big deal for me. But frankly, there wasn't much joy. It felt a little hollow.

One night after graduation, Barb and I were lying in bed together, and I found myself working up the nerve to ask her a question. Actually there were three questions. It was late, it was dark, and as I murmured my first question, I was praying Barb had already fallen asleep. "Barb, are you sleeping?"

"No."

*Rats!* I thought to myself. Now I'm committed.

Question number two: "Barb, you've obviously seen Sarah's picture taped on the dining-room wall. Why haven't you said anything?"

"Because I know how much it has wounded you, Gary."

Words from a wise woman, wise beyond her twenty-something years.

Next I asked the toughest question I've ever asked anyone in my entire life. "Barb, I want to come home. May I come home?"

Twenty seconds of silence followed. It seemed as if I held my breath for an hour. "Gary," Barb said, "the girls and I love you very much. We want you home. But you haven't been here. We don't know you anymore."

The words look cold in print, but she said them with restraint and tenderness. It was just the plain, unvarnished truth. My little girl had drawn the picture, and now her mom was speaking the words. I lay there in the dark, pretending to sleep. But I couldn't. Events raced through my mind. I remembered when Missy was two and refused to sit on my lap for more than a few seconds. Why? Because she didn't know her daddy. I recalled missed dinners with friends, evenings Barb waited for me to come home but I had to study just a little longer. I thought about the vacations we had canceled so I could finish a class. My life had been out of control, and the people in my family were on automatic pilot. I had a long road ahead of me if I wanted to win them back.

I didn't know at that time how God would heal the pain in our hearts. I just knew that I was at the end of myself and needed him like never before.

Maybe you have looked into the eyes of your spouse or your kids and known you were not connecting. Maybe you realized that your failure to connect heart-to-heart was mainly your fault. That's where I was that night. I was scared. It felt as if I were slipping down a mountainside, unable to grab onto something to stop the slide. I desperately hoped to regain my balance, but near terror was rising inside me. I was afraid I could never recapture the dream Barb and I had for our marriage and family.

After Barb's chilling words, I slipped out of bed and went downstairs to our living room. I pled with God that night for wisdom, perseverance, and faith. I begged him to restore my family. I was at-risk of losing the security, joy, and direction I had dreamed of and expected from our marriage. Publicly, I appeared fine to our friends, coworkers, and even extended family. But privately, I could not fool the three people closest to me. I was a man "missing in action" in our family. And Barb, Sarah, and Missy knew it.

Deep down inside, I knew that God is a God of second chances. He was capable of leading me through the restoration process with my family. But that night, as I poured out my heart to God in our living room, my hope for the future seemed buried under the avalanche of pain and discouragement in my heart.

And what about Barb? Would she offer me a second chance? I'll let her tell her side of the story in her own words.

## FULL-TIME MOM, FULL-TIME PAIN

Gary wasn't the only one feeling terribly hurt over our marriage relationship and family life. I also was hurting. I was aware, though, that it takes two in every marriage to bear the fault. We were partners in the disconnected lifestyle we were living. We entered Gary's doctoral program in full agreement. We had decided that he would be a full-time wage earner and doctoral student, and I would be a full-time, stay-at-home mom for our two little girls. We charged into this phase of our life together as most couples do, with optimism and our eyes wide open.

At the outset I worked hard at being my husband's greatest advocate and cheerleader. I was very proud of him and his desire to accomplish his goals and dreams. But over time, the stress, separation, and loneliness began to wear me down. Gary was constantly submerged in work and academic demands, distracting him from me and the girls. And I felt left out of his picture. In just a couple of years I went from being an optimistic wife to a woman who felt less and less understood. My resentment began to grow. I wanted to have family time together. At times I felt a bit like a single mom because Gary was absent so much. I cried a lot. I felt isolated. I looked longingly at other young families who were doing so many fun things together, and I wanted that for our family as well.

Our marriage had been my dream come true. But during

those stressful years it was hard to stay optimistic. Our marriage wasn't what I had expected it to be. Gary was my best friend, and I missed him. Most days he left home before seven o'clock in the morning, and many nights he didn't return until after ten o'clock. The girls hardly saw their daddy.

I loved my husband and was devoted to our marriage. The Lord comforted me, but it was still difficult. I was determined to keep my marriage vows to this man and to God, but I lived day in, day out needing more connection with Gary. I didn't understand at the time that God had created me with legitimate needs he intended to meet through my husband. And since Gary was so absorbed outside the home, many of these needs went unmet.

I came to the point where I quit talking to Gary about my thoughts and feelings of isolation. It seemed useless. And in some ways I stopped trying. I stopped expecting Gary to fight this enemy of workaholism that was undermining our marriage. I had made suggestions, tried new approaches, even pleaded. But nothing ever changed. I didn't know how to stop it.

One day a switch flipped on the inside, and I made the decision to give up my dream for our marriage. I never told Gary or anyone else, but I remember the moment I stood in the middle of our living room on the green shag carpet and made the decision to quit trying. I was protecting my heart from feeling the hurt, or so I thought. But by building a wall of protection around myself, I was not only locking up my heart but unfortunately also locking Gary out. On the outside I continued to be respectful, even pleasant—but on the inside I knew the difference. There was less transparency and sharing between us and more formality and distance. We were committed to each other, and I never would have consciously thought about walking away from him. But I had emotionally disconnected from my husband.

I know now that we were in a very vulnerable position at that point. I know now that if our disconnection had lasted for six months or more, I could have become a statistic, a "walk-away" wife.

But God in his mercy intervened before that could happen. He began to answer my prayers once I got out of the way. Then he began to work in my husband's life.

God used our daughter's crayon drawing to break through to Gary. A child's simple picture was the tool. It became a non-threatening voice to help a distracted man get refocused. When Gary asked that night if he could "come home," I had no doubts that he loved me. And my love was so deep and nonnegotiable that all I wanted was for him to come home. But would he? Could he really change? His doctorate was something we both wanted and worked for, but our marriage was suffering because of it. We didn't know how to nurture and tend to our marriage. I had become brittle and demanding. The distance had taken its toll, and we both knew it.

I sensed an emotional distance between Gary and me. When we were together, I didn't feel the same closeness and connection we once had. I desperately wanted Gary to come home, but in order for that to happen, something would have to change. Gary is going to share with you what that change would mean to him.

## THE MISTRESS IN THE LIBRARY

In the weeks and months after I asked Barb if I could "come home," God showed me how I had been neglecting my family emotionally. At first I didn't want to admit that my affections had wandered from home. I had no intention of being lured away from my family, and I certainly had never contemplated divorcing my wife. Barb and our two girls were my treasures.

At the same time, I prided myself in pursuing a career in

marriage and family counseling. And I was doing so for the sake of God's kingdom. Yet even though my goal of becoming a counselor was legitimate, I allowed books and study to lure me away as a temptress. My scholastic pursuits captured my heart and became my treasure. The love of my life—my family—was slowly and insidiously being replaced with coursework and learning: a mistress in the university library, a mistress dressed in pages of black and white.

I never thought it could happen. I never intended for it to happen. And I was unable to see or admit that it had happened until God used my innocent five-year-old daughter as a wake-up call. God showed me through my child's drawing that I had emotionally left my wife and family for the mistress in the library.

## THE JOURNEY BACK HOME

Barb and I both wanted a love that would last, but we didn't know how to turn our relationship around. As I finished my doctoral work, we agreed that something had to change. We committed ourselves to recapturing our dream marriage and to reducing the emotional distance between us. Little did we know that our search would initiate a journey that has become the foundation for our current ministry to married couples and families. In the pages that follow we will share that journey with you.

Can you identify with the distance and deterioration Barb and I felt? How close are you to your wife or husband today? Have the stresses, demands, and disappointments of life created an emotional distance between you and your spouse? Do you know what to do to close the gap? If you are not growing closer together, you are drifting farther apart. Although you may never consider divorce, the road of a deteriorating marriage is always heading in that direction.

Have you lost your dream marriage? Do you need to recapture that dream?

We are not offering you a magic formula or a three-easy-steps program to marital bliss. Rather, we will describe a road traveled by thousands of couples we have encountered in the counseling office, in our conferences, or through our radio broadcasts. It is a road that leads back to your dream. And it is a road Barb and I have traveled personally, though we have not always navigated it perfectly. It is a road rich with purpose, God's purpose. It is a biblical design that is guaranteed to deepen and enrich your relationship beyond your fondest dreams.

We cannot guarantee that walking this road will be easy. But we can guarantee that following God's design will lead you to a lasting love.

## 2

## *Where Are You Headed?*

Just for a moment, think back to your wedding day. Was the ceremony short and sweet or rich with detail and meaning? Did you speak your vows in a cathedral? a chapel? a cruise ship? a backyard gazebo? Were the tables at the reception spread with finger food or a sumptuous feast? Did you zoom away to your honeymoon in a sparkling limousine or putt-putt away in a four-door Rambler as Barb and I did?

One thing is certain: You and your spouse-to-be were drawn to that moment of marriage by the dream of spending the rest of your days with the love of your life. The mysterious and powerful force of love so swept you away that you willingly pledged—before God, your family, and your friends—to stay together for better or for worse, for richer or for poorer, in sickness and in health, as long as you both shall live. Your hearts were filled with a hope, an expectation, a promise, and a dream that your marriage would be great and that your love would last forever.

When you uttered the words "I do," you no doubt believed firmly in that dream—the beauty and mystery and ecstasy of lifelong love. Your heart probably soared knowing that your special someone longed to know you intimately and promised to accept you unconditionally. Perhaps your soul was stirred at the realization that the two of you together could become what you could never be on your own. You anticipated the experience of wholeness, completion, security, and companionship that had eluded you before. You were never happier or more hopeful than on your wedding day.

And then, just like Barb and me, you entered the real world.

## SHATTERED DREAMS, BROKEN MARRIAGES

As a married couple, you may still be living on the mountaintop of perpetual bliss. But more than likely, you and your spouse have lost your footing on that lofty peak and taken a tumble or two. Be honest now: It hasn't been as easy or magical as you expected, has it?

Regardless of where your marriage is, I think you will agree with Barb and me that, for most people today, living out the marital dream in the real world has become increasingly difficult. And all too often, a marriage relationship in difficulty ends in divorce.

We need to remember that divorce is more than statistics. It involves real people with real hopes and dreams—and real pain. Maybe some people in your immediate family—parents, children, siblings—have been divorced. Maybe you have. If that is the case, you are among the 70 percent of all Americans with firsthand knowledge of the tragedy of divorce.

Divorce is far more than population statistics and a social trend. Divorce represents the disconnected hearts of two human beings whose dream of happiness has been shattered. Divorce is the death of a relationship between two people who had hoped to enjoy the safety, security, and happiness of emotional oneness—for a lifetime.

Most couples accept the fact that there is more to a marriage relationship than the exhilaration and excitement they felt on their honeymoon. Most realize that being married in the real world includes plenty of relational ups and downs. If you and your spouse are not intentionally working to make your marriage last, you are in danger of losing your dream marriage.

Disintegration in a relationship usually begins gradually, almost without notice. You may say, "Our relationship is far from a dream marriage, but we're committed to each other. Divorce isn't even an option for us."

True, *physical* divorce may not enter your thinking. Yet if you and your spouse are not taking specific steps to build a lasting love, you are in fact sliding toward *emotional* divorce. You may not move out of the house physically, but you are in the process of leaving each other emotionally and relationally. You become strangers to each other and to your children.

## THE MARRIAGE MAP

One of the first steps in recapturing your dream marriage is identifying where you are in your relationship. We've created a marriage map (see next page) that can help you take the pulse of your marriage and discover whether you are sliding toward deterioration or moving toward your dream.

It's important that both you and your spouse read this section and evaluate your marriage. We suspect that the two of you will not always agree about where you are on the marriage map; most couples won't. But those differences of perspective are important as you try to understand each other. We've provided two blanks for every statement in the evaluative self-tests so that each of you can check the statements that apply to you: Husbands, put your responses in the *H* column; wives, use the *W* column. If it makes you feel too vulnerable to put your responses in the book, make two photocopies of the self-tests (see appendix A for copies of all the self-tests), and record your responses separately. Be sure to discuss them later.

### 1. Living the Dream

The "dream" is a real place on the marriage map, the place where Barb and I want to live with each other, the place where you want to live with your spouse. The dream is the kind of marriage we all hope for and have tasted in our better moments together. It's the scintillating, fulfilling relationship that brought us to the altar in the first place and motivated us to pledge our lives to each other. It's the ultimate relationship between a husband and wife.

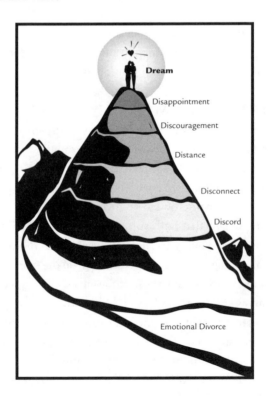

## THE DREAM STOP

*Compare yourself to these indicators, and check any that describe the current state of your marriage:*

**H     W**

☐ ☐  I communicate freely with my spouse, and we keep no inappropriate secrets.

☐ ☐  I forgive my spouse when I am wronged and seek forgiveness when I offend. I am loved without strings.

☐ ☐  My spouse and I eagerly seek to discover and meet each other's needs.

☐ ☐  We have faced and conquered difficult circumstances that have undone other marriages.

☐ ☐  I consciously guard myself against threats and temptations that could pull our marriage apart.

☐ ☐  We enjoy ongoing emotional, physical, and spiritual closeness.

☐ ☐  We are committed to keeping our relationship fresh and alive "till death do us part."

We hope you don't think that living the dream is the same as marital perfection. Now *that* place simply doesn't exist in real-world marriages. Look again at our list. The dream marriage doesn't imply that we don't wound each other. It doesn't assume that we already know everything there is to know about each other. It doesn't pretend that difficult circumstances won't strike our marriage. And it certainly doesn't mean that closeness and communication happen automatically. You can be living the dream while still working diligently to improve your marriage. In fact, that's the normal state of a healthy marriage relationship!

We are painfully naïve if we assume that a dream marriage doesn't need constant work. Perhaps that's why so many couples are shocked to learn that their marriage is sometimes less than they dreamed it would be. They say things like, "I can't believe he did that" or "I can't believe she said that" or "I can't believe we let our marriage get to this point."

Friction and failing are normal in a marriage of two imperfect people. Unwillingness to accept that fact and work on resolving marital tremors will eventually lead you to the next stop on the marriage map, which Barb will describe.

## 2. From Dream to Disappointment

Perhaps like you, I fell in love with and married my dream man. My love largely blinded me to his faults and shortcomings, just as Gary's love blinded him to mine. But it didn't take us long to realize that neither of us got a perfect person. Can you relate to our experience?

If you are like Gary and me, your marriage dream has also been tainted by relational disappointment. Disappointment happens when you or your spouse fail to meet the other's expectations in some way.

Here is how disappointment played out early in our marriage. I fully supported and encouraged Gary's educational goals. I never questioned that he still loved me, even though he was absent from me so much of the time. But knowing that Gary loved me did not keep me from feeling disappointed in our relationship. The problem was that neither of us could bring resolution and closure to those ongoing disappointments.

Gary and I now understand that disappointments happen

in every marriage relationship. We also know that if we had understood how to deal with our early disappointments, our relationship would not have deteriorated as it did. We were not alone in our ignorance. Many couples we talk to haven't learned how to quickly and effectively deal with the relational disappointments in marriage.

Whether you are the "disappointer" or the "disappointee," every disappointment needs a relational resolution. King Solomon understood the importance of acting quickly to resolve the little things. He urged, "Quick! Catch all the little foxes before they ruin the vineyard of your love" (Song of Songs 2:15).

## THE DISAPPOINTMENT STOP

*Compare yourself to these indicators, and check any that describe the current state of your marriage:*

**H    W**

☐    ☐    I have difficulty expressing affirmation to or about my spouse.

☐    ☐    My spouse isn't the flawless person I thought I married.

☐    ☐    I feel surprised and let down when I notice an imperfection in my spouse.

☐    ☐    My spouse and I have caused each other to feel hurt and angry.

☐    ☐    My spouse and I have experienced conflict over personality differences, male-female wiring, or ways of doing things we learned from our families.

☐    ☐    I compare my spouse to other people.

☐     ☐     I have a mental list of things I wish I could change about my spouse.

If you can see yourself in one or more of these descriptions, we want to assure you that you are normal. The key is knowing how to respond to and resolve your disappointment.

Unresolved disappointments that arise early in marriage often set the stage for further, deeper troubles. Gary sees this over and over in the struggling couples who come into his office for counseling. When the honeymoon ends and the glow of the first year of marriage fades, husbands and wives begin to rub each other the wrong way. They offend each other. They hurt each other. These offenses blindside them; they are not prepared for the conflict that inevitably enters every marriage.

Marital disappointments are unavoidable because marriage is the collision of two different perspectives and two ways of living. Each partner brings into the union his or her own family background and traditions; a unique personality; somewhat different values, philosophies, and lifestyles; as well as a truckload of differing expectations. Add to this the fundamental differences between men and women, and you have all the makings for a lifetime of potential disappointments.

Is this where you are living on the marriage map? Can you see how your relationship has been hindered by disappointment? If you fail to address your disappointments as they occur, you may find yourself descending to an even more painful stop on the marriage map.

### 3. From Disappointment to Discouragement
Gary and I have learned from experience that disappointment is not only unavoidable, it is also indispensable to enriching and deepening our love life. In the process we have learned how to make our disappointments a positive relationship builder in

our marriage. Unfortunately we didn't learn this soon enough to keep us from the discouragement that results when marital disappointment goes unresolved.

A teachable couple seeks out the skills to resolve these normal conflicts. Others allow disappointments to pile up, ushering in discouragement. This is the place where I began to settle in when I didn't deal with the letdown I felt in our marriage. I became discouraged from Gary's lack of time spent with me, occasional lack of loving responses to me, and lack of emotional investment in our marriage. As understanding as Gary tried to be, he still didn't comprehend what I needed. And I didn't know how to explain my needs to him. The situation was zapping my courage.

It's difficult to keep your relationship growing when the focus is primarily on the negative. You allow unhealed hurts to cloud your thinking. Your hopes for a better relationship begin to dim, your energy to work hard on behalf of your spouse gets depleted, and you lose heart. You find yourself shrinking back from time together, intimacy, and resolution of conflicts.

Couples living in discouragement find that their basic love needs are not met in the marriage. They may not be ready to file for divorce because of it, but they are living far from their marriage dream and what God has planned for them.

## THE DISCOURAGEMENT STOP

*Compare yourself to these indicators, and check any that describe the current state of your marriage:*

**H   W**

☐   ☐   I often wonder if I am missing out on something in my marriage.

☐ ☐    I have a mental list of reasons why I am dissatisfied with my marriage.

☐ ☐    My spouse implies—or says—that I don't understand him or her or know how to meet his or her needs.

☐ ☐    My own needs are not being met in my marriage. I feel as if my spouse's friends, work, church involvement, and/or the kids are more important than I am.

☐ ☐    Even when I recognize my spouse's needs, I am not successful at meeting them.

☐ ☐    I have a difficult time expressing my needs in a way my spouse can understand and act on.

☐ ☐    I wonder if my choice of a spouse was a mistake.

That's the stuff of discouragement. You can be sure that the cracks in your marriage relationship have widened when you wonder if there isn't more to marriage than you have experienced or if other people are as unfulfilled in their marriages as you are in yours. You can also spot discouragement when you are preoccupied with a me-focused view of your marriage. Sure, we all desire to have our needs met. But a constant me-first attitude can lead you to complain. Self-centeredness can tempt you to think that things will never get better, even when you know your spouse is trying to change.

You may be like many couples who are not tuned in to the warning signs of discouragement. And when either spouse doesn't adequately deal with discouragement in marriage, he or

she can easily slide to a place of relational distance. Gary will describe this stop on the marriage map.

## 4. From Discouragement to Distance

Barb and I can easily spot couples who have reached a point of
emotional distance in their marriage. You have probably noticed
them too. You see them in restaurants—husbands and wives
who come in together, order and eat their meals, pay the bill
and leave, yet don't speak a word to each other the whole time.
If you followed these couples home, you would find that they
are little more than two strangers living under the same roof.
They no longer find each other exciting or even interesting.
They are bored with each other, even in bed.

A husband might fill his time with building his career, going on outings with the guys, or participating in sports or other
hobbies. A wife might busy herself with the children, a career,
volunteering, or investing all of her emotional energy in female
friendships. Both partners use activities, possessions, and
busyness to fill the gap that has grown between them. Partners
become so preoccupied with their own "stuff" that they lose track
of each other and have no emotional energy left for each other.

God knew we needed togetherness as husband and wife.
After God created the world and looked at what he had done, he
said, "It is not good for the man to be alone. I will make a companion who will help him" (Genesis 2:18). God's primary solution to human aloneness is the oneness, companionship, and
togetherness of having a spouse. When husbands and wives distance themselves from each other, they are fighting against
God's plan for their marriage and missing out on the blessing of
oneness that God designed for them.

Barb and I found in our own marriage that we slid easily
into relational distancing. It was a natural by-product of two
people who were very much in love with each other yet

struggled with how to connect deeply in the midst of disappointment and discouragement. We were not purposely cool toward each other, but since we did not spend time on our relationship, we undermined the oneness we both wanted and needed.

## THE DISTANCE STOP

*Compare yourself to these indicators, and check any that describe the current state of your marriage:*

**H    W**

☐    ☐    I could describe our relationship as "fair to partly cloudy, with no clearing in sight."

☐    ☐    I often fill my free time with activities that don't include my spouse.

☐    ☐    I have given up most of my expectations of my spouse.

☐    ☐    I wonder if my spouse ever feels excited about being married to me.

☐    ☐    My spouse sometimes seems like a stranger to me.

☐    ☐    I keep many of my thoughts and feelings from my spouse.

☐    ☐    I worry that we might someday face a problem bigger than our resolve to stay together.

Many couples accept a stale and distant relationship as all that can be expected. They acknowledge that the honeymoon ended long ago and that a mediocre marriage relationship is typical. Interestingly, a majority of the couples Barb and I talk to actually *expect* to drift apart as their marriages age. It's not that people like the feeling of distance in their relationships. But most couples have resigned themselves to emotional distance without understanding how they got there or without believing that their dream for marriage can be recaptured. When disappointment and discouragement in the relationship are not addressed, you will find yourselves drifting apart and your dreams for marriage fading. And you will miss God's best for you.

If you find yourselves at a point of relational distance in your marriage, it is vital that you reverse course. Don't be satisfied with less than the intimacy and oneness God has designed for you. If relational distance is allowed to persist, you may find yourselves descending to the next stop on the marriage map: relational disconnect.

## 5. From Distance to Disconnect

God created us to be relational beings, and he wired into us a need to connect with other people on a deep emotional and spiritual level. The deepest human connection is reserved for the marriage relationship. In the intimacy and security of the marriage commitment, a couple is free to share—and care about—each other's deepest hopes, desires, fears, struggles, and pain. God's plan is for Barb and me to enjoy this deep, fulfilling relational connection—and it's the same for you and your spouse. As this connection grows, we feel less and less alone, and we experience the rich intimacy and oneness God designed for marriage.

But when a husband and wife feel distant from each other, they no longer trust the other with their deepest longings and needs. So they stop sharing at this level altogether. They disconnect relationally. The walls of self-protection are erected, and intimacy is rare.

In a disconnected marriage, a husband and wife may live together, but they are living virtually alone. The problem is, their wiring has not changed. They still have a need to connect with another person at a deep, intimate level. If that God-given need is not met legitimately through a spouse, it may find expression in another relationship. This is often how affairs get started.

A lonely husband receives the attention, sympathy, and caring he craves from a female coworker. A lonely wife pours out her pain to a compassionate male friend. These extramarital connections may not always result in adulterous affairs, but the vulnerability and temptation to sexual intimacy are very great. At the very least, inappropriate connections with a person other than your spouse may create an unhealthy emotional bond. As I learned during those long days in the library, we can be captured and drawn away from a vital connection with our spouses by something other than a person: from work to hobbies to overcommitment in good activities—even church activities.

## THE DISCONNECT STOP

*Compare yourself to these indicators, and check any that describe the current state of your marriage:*

**H    W**

☐    ☐    I sometimes feel lonely even when I'm with my spouse.

☐    ☐    It is difficult for me to "feel" that my spouse loves me. I may know it intellectually, but I don't sense an emotional connection.

☐  ☐    When we are together, we seldom have much to say to each other.

☐  ☐    When we do talk to each other, we often misunderstand and misinterpret each other.

☐  ☐    I prefer to devote my time, energy, and money to something or someone other than my spouse.

☐  ☐    I doubt that my marriage can grow or change for the better.

☐  ☐    I don't think my spouse is very interested in who I am or what I want to do.

Have you ever sensed that you and your spouse were no longer connecting relationally? If your marriage has suffered through unresolved disappointment, discouragement, and distance, you may be in the process of a painful disconnect. You may feel as if you and your spouse are no longer on the same team. And when you are no longer teammates, you can easily become adversaries, allowing your marriage to deteriorate into a state of discord.

## 6. From Disconnect to Discord

Couples who are relationally disconnected are easy prey for conflict and discord. Conflicts that were once suppressed now surface as open contention. Differing opinions escalate to defensive quarrels or arguments. Criticism and anger rule most verbal exchanges. Instead of simply hurting each other's feelings, you deeply wound each other's hearts.

Marriages in a state of discord can run hot. Almost all married couples experience arguments, some of them loud and emotional. But couples in discord are at war most of the time.

Their contempt for one another erupts like a volcano from a smoldering history of disappointment, discouragement, distance, and disconnect.

Relationships in discord can also run cold. Physical intimacy vanishes. The interest in cuddling and sex are gone.

Couples can reach a state of discord early in marriage, as evidenced by marriages that explode within weeks or months of the wedding day. But these "early exploders" are almost always living out problems established in their dating relationship.

## THE DISCORD STOP

*Compare yourself to these indicators, and check any that describe the current state of your marriage:*

**H    W**

☐    ☐    Most of my thoughts about my spouse are negative.

☐    ☐    My spouse and I verbally lash out at each other, saying things that are hurtful.

☐    ☐    I often wonder what it would be like not to be married—or to be married to a different person.

☐    ☐    I daydream or fantasize about another person who would make a better spouse.

☐    ☐    I feel as if my spouse and I are at war.

☐    ☐    True tenderness with my spouse is a faded memory. We avoid sexual intimacy.

☐    ☐    Family and close friends notice that our marriage is severely strained.

Couples living in marital discord seriously wonder if their lives would be better without their spouses. This looking-for-a-way-out attitude can undo a marriage quickly. William Doherty, director of the marriage-and-family-therapy program at the University of Minnesota, says, "The idea of a split slowly gains momentum over time. And a good marriage can be brought down in two years, by focusing on what you are not getting out of the relationship and how your partner fails to live up to your expectations."[1]

If a good marriage can be brought down in two years, how much nearer the precipice is a marriage that is in discord?

Although discord in a marriage is not impossible to reverse, it is intensely dangerous. Unless the situation is defused and the combatants are disarmed, the dream of true love eventually dies, and emotional divorce is the result.

## 7. From Discord to Emotional Divorce

It is possible for a couple to be legally married and yet totally separated in heart. They live under a dark cloud of unresolved disappointment and discouragement. Their daily behavior is characterized by relational distance and discord. They may occupy the same house, but emotionally they live miles apart. Barb and I call this stop emotional divorce.

When a couple reaches the point of emotional divorce, the relationship has died. If the couple file for divorce, the court's paperwork simply serves as the death certificate for the marriage. But the relationship and the dream that gave it birth are already dead and buried. Still, some couples in a dead relationship refuse to file for divorce. They stay together for a number of reasons: the kids, finances, career image, or to avoid the "sin" of divorce. Trying to sustain a dead relationship because of guilt or to maintain appearances is pure torture.

## THE EMOTIONAL DIVORCE STOP

*Compare yourself to these indicators, and check any that describe
the current state of your marriage:*

**H    W**

☐ ☐ I am staying married for some reason other
than love for my spouse.

☐ ☐ I have given up hope that my marriage
could be better.

☐ ☐ I pretend I'm okay with my marriage to
keep up appearances.

☐ ☐ My first goal in my marriage is to protect
myself from further pain.

☐ ☐ My spouse and I have separated or considered separating.

☐ ☐ My heart is deeply attached to someone
other than my spouse, even if I am not
acting on that feeling.

☐ ☐ I know I have already walked away from
my marriage emotionally.

So what's the difference between emotional divorce and legal divorce? In God's eyes, very little. Scripture teaches us that
God is as interested in the attitudes of our hearts as in our out-
ward actions. We can see this principle in Christ's sermon about
adultery. In Matthew 5:27-28, Jesus points out that adultery
isn't just the physical act of sleeping with someone other than
your spouse. Adultery starts with an attitude of lust in the heart.
Jesus tells us, "Anyone who even looks at a woman with lust in
his eye has already committed adultery with her in his heart"

(v. 28). Similarly, does God not view divorce in the heart—emotional divorce—the same as divorce that has been finalized by the court? Many Christians in dying marriages refuse to use the "*d* word." They know God hates divorce (see Malachi 2:16). They remember the line from the marriage ceremony: "Therefore what God has joined together, let man not separate" (Mark 10:9, NIV). So they shun any thought of filing for divorce. Since divorce is as much an attitude of the heart as a legal action, should they not just as ardently seek to reverse the pattern that has led to emotional divorce?

Is there still hope when a marriage has declined to the point of emotional divorce? Barb and I believe in a resurrected Christ, and we also believe that God can resurrect a dead marriage. We have seen numerous dead relationships brought back to life. But that isn't the first place God wants to intervene in a marriage. It is, in fact, the last place he wants to get involved. God is willing and able to rescue a marriage and reestablish a loving relationship wherever couples may be on the marriage map. He wants to see us get back to living the dream of oneness and relational intimacy.

## GETTING BACK TO THE DREAM

Everyone reading this book is somewhere on the road between dream and divorce. And if you are not purposefully moving in the direction of the dream, you are moving—if ever so slowly—in the direction that ends in divorce.

So where are you on the marriage map? Do you see your marriage in any of the indicators we listed in this chapter? And which way are you headed? Are you moving toward the dream or toward emotional divorce? As you evaluate where you are, we trust that you have been challenged and encouraged to join us in the journey back to the dream.

As Barb and I have shared this marriage map in conferences across the country, we have yet to have a couple jump up and yell,

"*Woo-hoo!* We have it all together! We're living the dream every day!" And that's not a claim Barb and I can make either. We are still on the daily journey of recapturing our dream marriage. Marriage takes work if it is going to grow. As difficult as it may be for you to admit that your marriage falls short of the dream, we hope you have been captivated by the reality that there is a path that leads back to the marriage you have always wanted.

## SIX SECRETS TO RECAPTURING YOUR DREAM MARRIAGE

Barb and I believe that the path back to the dream marriage is paved in love, but not just a generalized kind of love. We have identified six kinds of love—six secrets—that will help you recapture your dream and build a love that will last. The remaining chapters of this book will unpack those six loves, which are rooted in God's Word.

- forgiving love
- serving love
- persevering love
- guarding love
- celebrating love
- renewing love

These six loves are the secret to a lasting love. As you begin to practice loving in the ways that God instructs, you will shield your marriage from the ravages of disappointment, discouragement, distance, disconnect, discord, and emotional divorce.

FORGIVING LOVE HEALS HURTS
AND HELPS SPOUSES FEEL ACCEPTED
AND CONNECTED.

*Forgiving love offers a fresh start after you have offended and hurt each other.* When you were first married, you felt important to your spouse, and you let your spouse know how important he or she was to you. But somewhere along the journey, that feeling waned because of offenses ranging from minor disagreements to major blows of betrayal. Forgiving love equips you to communicate such a deep level of acceptance for each other that you can recover from the pain you occasionally inflict on each other and work through your offenses. Forgiving love helps you reconnect after you have hurt each other. It's the kind of love the apostle Paul described when he wrote, "Do your part to live in peace with everyone, as much as possible" (Romans 12:18).

SERVING LOVE DISCOVERS AND MEETS NEEDS AND HELPS SPOUSES FEEL HONORED AND UNDERSTOOD.

*Serving love helps you discover and meet each other's deepest needs.* God created you and your spouse with physical, emotional, and spiritual needs, and he wants you to be involved in meeting those needs for each other. You may feel reluctant to express your needs to your spouse, thinking you shouldn't be needy or you should somehow be able to meet your own needs. Serving love is the process of identifying needs and taking steps to meet them in each other. The apostle Paul wrote, "Honor one another above yourselves" (Romans 12:10, NIV). You honor one another when you serve each other, putting your spouse's needs above your own. When we serve each other, we humble ourselves just as Jesus did when he washed the disciples' feet (see John 13).

PERSEVERING LOVE STAYS STRONG IN TOUGH TIMES AND HELPS SPOUSES FEEL BONDED—BEST FRIENDS FOR LIFE.

*Persevering love sustains you through the trials of life.* Daily life is often hazardous. Accidents happen. Tragedies strike. Losses occur. You need to love in ways that keep your marriage firmly grounded through the stormy trials and pains of life. As you implement persevering love in your marriage, you will bond with your spouse and enjoy a love that will last through thick and thin. Enduring love is described in the New Testament: "We can rejoice, too, when we run into problems and trials, for we know that they are good for us—they help us learn to endure. And endurance develops strength of character in us" (Romans 5:3-4).

GUARDING LOVE PROTECTS FROM THREATS AND HELPS SPOUSES FEEL SAFE AND SECURE.

*Guarding love protects your hearts from threats to your marriage.* Marriages are threatened by many forces today: outside forces such as busyness, job stresses, sexual temptations, and worldly distractions, as well as internal forces such as competitiveness, worry, and high expectations fueled by the media and comparing ourselves to others. If you are not aware of the threats to your marriage or the potential havoc these forces can wreak on your relationship, then you are vulnerable. Maybe you have had some of these questions: Will I wake up someday to find that my spouse doesn't love me anymore? Am I playing second fiddle in my spouse's heart to a career, a hobby, a friend, or other distractions? Will I or my spouse fall prey to an extramarital affair? Guarding love is alert to the threats and does all it can to protect against destructive forces. The Bible reminds us, "Above all else, guard your heart, for it is the wellspring of life" (Proverbs 4:23, NIV).

CELEBRATING LOVE REJOICES IN THE
MARRIAGE RELATIONSHIP AND HELPS
SPOUSES FEEL CHERISHED AND CAPTIVATED.

*Celebrating love equips you to maintain a satisfying emotional, physical, and spiritual connection.* Remember the spark and magic that characterized your first months of marriage? It may have been something like the excitement Solomon experienced when his wife enticed him: "Take me with you. Come, let's run! Bring me into your bedroom" (Song of Songs 1:4). Solomon returned her love by saying, "[I am] held captive in your queenly tresses. Oh, how delightful you are, my beloved; how pleasant for utter delight!" (7:5-6). King Solomon and his wife celebrated their love. They felt cherished and captivated by each other long after the honeymoon. Celebrating love keeps that spark alive, not only in the bedroom but also in all areas of the relationship. As you learn to celebrate your oneness, you will fall in love all over again.

RENEWING LOVE REFRESHES AND SUPPORTS
THE MARRIAGE BOND AND HELPS SPOUSES
FEEL CONFIDENT AND ROOTED.

*Renewing love regards the marriage covenant as unbreakable.* God's opinion of divorce is very clear in Scripture:

You cry out, "Why has the Lord abandoned us?" I'll tell you why! Because the Lord witnessed the vows you and your wife made to each other on your wedding day when you were young. But you have been disloyal to her, though she remained your faithful companion, the wife of your marriage vows. Didn't the Lord make you one with your wife? In body and spirit you are his. And what does he want? Godly children from your union. So guard yourself; remain loyal to the wife of your youth. "For I hate divorce!" says the Lord, the God of Israel. (Malachi 2:14-16)

God hates divorce, yet marriages are dissolving around us every day, even the marriages of Christians. What guarantee do you have that your marriage will make it? Renewing love protects you from insecurity and provides you with assurance as you face the future with your spouse.

## WALK THE PATH TO YOUR DREAM

As you commit yourself and your marriage to these six key kinds of love, God will equip and empower you to reclaim your dream marriage. Don't settle for merely gutting it out in a relationship that is a constant source of unhappiness. That's no dream for marriage; it's a relational nightmare! Pursue God's best for your marriage. Pray for God to help you love your spouse in ways that are beyond imagining.

Practicing the six loves will offer you a hedge of protection around your marriage and family. You will develop a relationship in which you are known, understood, honored, protected, and esteemed to the point that your deepest love needs are fulfilled. It will enable you to love in ways that will protect you from the fears, dangers, and threats that plague so many marriages. The six secrets will lead the way to loving your spouse in a biblical way. They provide the path to the marriage of your dreams.

Barb and I know that path because we eventually reclaimed our dream after sliding carelessly toward marital entropy. Two years after Sarah showed me her picture of the family with the missing father, our daughter Missy drew another picture. Only this time I showed up in the crayon drawing. That picture hangs in my office today as a testimony to God's faithfulness to Barb and me. Even though our marriage never reached the brink of

legal divorce, it was headed in the wrong direction. But God in his mercy rescued us from the heartache and pain of ignoring his plan for us as a couple.

As we have followed God's path for building a lasting love, God has fulfilled his promises to keep our relationship intimate and fresh. He has done the same for countless other couples. And he will do the same for you. He promises.

So let's begin the journey.

# Forgiving Love

*Forgiving love heals hurts and helps spouses*
*feel accepted and connected*

# 3

## *The Rocky Road of Hurt and Anger*

"I knew something was wrong with Mark, but I didn't know what it was," says his wife, Shannon. "He was distant from me and the kids, quite preoccupied. Most nights after dinner, he would hide out in the study, hunched over the computer, working on spreadsheets until after I went to bed. I called him 'The Zombie' because he just wasn't there for us. He was also detached from the rest of our family and friends."

Things were not going well at work for Mark either. The top salesperson in his division for years, Mark still moved products well enough to keep his bosses at bay. But his commission-based income had inexplicably plummeted, putting his family under severe financial strain.

The reason for Mark's distraction was revealed when he was fired for logging on to pornographic sites on his company computer. With his dark secret exposed, Mark also admitted to Shannon that he wasn't working on spreadsheets during his late-night sessions on the home computer. He tearfully confessed to her that he was addicted to Internet pornography.

Even after Mark sought help through counseling and a biblically based sexual-addiction support group, Shannon had difficulty dealing with the impact of her husband's activities on her own life. "Mark was out of work, so I had to take a job I hated in order to pay our bills. Even worse, I felt as if I had lost Mark's heart to a bunch of women on the Internet, women who didn't really exist. I was furious. I wanted to rant at someone. I wanted to confront a live person, someone whose head I could rip off. Instead, I just stayed angry at Mark."

Eventually this hurting couple began a transformation, starting with Shannon. "I gradually realized that in order to move ahead, I had to forgive Mark for the hurt he had caused me. At the time I thought forgiveness meant brushing aside what he had done, acting as if it didn't matter or that he didn't need to change. But as Mark and I began to study the topic of forgiveness in the Bible, I learned that forgiveness isn't just a matter of saying 'I forgive you' and trying to forget about it. We went through a long, tough process of understanding and practicing forgiveness. Our relationship still isn't perfect, but we both came through the process feeling relieved and knowing God was restoring our hearts. Our marriage has recaptured some of the freshness of the dream we lost a long time ago."

Four years after Mark's dark secret was exposed, Mark and Shannon stood in front of their church and shared their story to a hushed congregation. Within a few weeks, half a dozen men contacted Mark to say they wanted to join the biblically based sexual-addiction support group he was helping to lead. And Shannon has grown through the ordeal to the point that she is ready to work with wives and girlfriends who have suffered as she has.

## HOW DO YOU DEAL WITH THE HURT?

Have you ever been hurt by your spouse, burned in some way by the husband or wife you trusted? If you can't answer yes to that question, you either haven't been married long or you married the proverbial angel!

How has your spouse offended you? Have you been insulted? criticized? lied to? violated? mistreated? avoided? betrayed? How many of these offenses have you suffered in your marriage? How have you and your spouse failed to measure up to each other's expectations?

Couples won't get far in their marriage before tripping over at least a few relational transgressions. You already know about some of the pain Barb and I have caused each other. You have almost certainly felt let down by your spouse. You may have even been downright bewildered by his or her hurtful behavior. Or perhaps you suffer more in silence with a spouse who doesn't talk or doesn't seem to care.

We have all been on the offending side of conflict, and we have all been on the receiving end, feeling the pain of hurt and disappointment. Whether you were hurt or caused the hurt, every offense in a marriage needs a resolution.

How do you and your spouse handle offenses? How do you deal with hurt and anger? Can you pinpoint the causes of friction between you? Can you think of a conflict you are facing right now, an issue that is bringing hurt to one or both of you?

Tragically most couples are without a clue about how to deal with offenses and regain the health of their relationships. Why? Because few have learned how to move past their disappointments. So rather than heal the hurt, they allow their hearts to harden. Frustrations and conflicts go unresolved.

Unresolved conflict was exactly what Barb and I were experiencing early in our marriage. Had we known how to deal with the disappointments we caused each other, our relationship would not have deteriorated as it did. But neither of us knew how to close the loop on our hurt, to bring resolution to our ongoing disappointments. So unconfessed and unforgiven offenses became an increasingly heavy burden to our struggling relationship.

We needed a love that would allow us to begin our relationship afresh after we hurt one another, a love that would enable us to move past offenses both large and small. We learned that the first secret to a lasting love is forgiving love, a love that heals hurts and helps spouses feel accepted and connected again.

## A PATTERN THAT PRODUCES PAIN

As we have worked with couples over the years, we have noticed a painful pattern for dealing with offenses in marriage. You have likely lived out this scenario many times, just as we have. Barb will explain.

### The Offense

It all starts when one spouse offends the other in some way. Offenses may be major, such as Shannon's being hurt by Mark's "affairs" with women he saw on a computer screen. Or they may be as minor as hanging the roll of toilet tissue the "wrong" way. Gary and I could supply a long list of ways we have offended each other over the years, but we are sure you have a list of your own.

It would be nice if all conflicts were as small as which way the toilet tissue is supposed to hang. But many offenses in marriage are far from trivial. Few couples escape the conflicts that result from differences in family backgrounds, personalities, or values. Couples squabble over where to spend the holidays, how to budget the money, and how to discipline the kids. Conflicts start with down and dirty personal sniping, such as cruel comments that set off a string of painful slights and slams. No matter how our marriages grow in maturity, we always seem to find ways of hurting one another, either intentionally or unintentionally. And with every offense comes pain.

## The Hurt

Just as a physical wound brings pain and injury to tissue or bone, so relational offenses traumatize our emotions. And they hurt. Some offenses seem to sting no more than a pinprick. Some of them pack a wallop that sends us reeling. At times we feel blindsided by an offense we never suffered before. Or we feel pain from the constant bludgeoning when the same offense is repeated over a period of weeks, months, or years.

Regardless of the severity of the painful incident, if it is dealt with quickly, it will have minimal consequences on the relationship. But many times the offender is unaware of the pain he or she has inflicted or is in no hurry to correct the situation. This leaves the offended spouse vulnerable to more hurt, just as a cut or abrasion in the skin may become infected if it is not cleansed. And the hurt only lingers or becomes worse until the offense is resolved.

Hurt leaves us wide open, feeling as if our hearts have been torn out, our tenderness brutalized, and our equilibrium upset. Sometimes we don't recognize the inner pain right away. And when we do, many of us try to hide it. We don't tell our spouses when they have wounded us. We don't want to appear vulnerable, so we suppress the hurt and act as if nothing happened.

Early in our marriage, I developed a pattern of hiding my hurt whenever Gary offended me in some way. We honeymooned in San Francisco because Gary was in the final stages of securing a great job there. Yet I felt the inner pain of being uprooted from my home in Iowa, and I imagined being left alone in a strange new city as he jetted around the country as a consultant. But I said nothing to Gary, while quietly nursing my inner wound.

When the job fell through, we came home to Iowa to get our old jobs back. But in that first year of marriage, Gary started to work on his master's degree while we both worked full-time. Again I felt hurt, and again I said nothing. Gary was ready to conquer the world, and I just wanted to establish a home and a marriage. We didn't stop to work through our basic differences—how his calling and type A ambition clashed with my longing for security.

I stuffed all those things. I didn't know how to express my needs and my hurt, so I gave up and stopped talking about it. Gary will now tell you how unexpressed needs and pain lead to the next step of the pattern.

### The Anger

When we feel hurt, our emotions sound an alarm. The warning tells us that we should stop immediately and resolve the situation. But, like most people, Barb and I didn't heed that alarm and deal with the pain in our marriage. As a result, the hurt turned to anger. When hurt is not addressed, anger develops, and anger often prevents conflicts from being resolved peacefully.

Anger is taboo in many Christian circles. We often deny that we feel angry, and we keep our anger in check. But in the privacy of our homes, we often feel free to let it explode—with grim consequences.

One of the things Barb and I discovered when we went to God's Word is that God never said, "Don't be angry." He said, "In your anger do not sin" (Ephesians 4:26, NIV). Anger itself is not sin, but handling anger inappropriately may lead to sin—hurtful words, bitterness, or violence.

Just as it can be difficult for us to recognize hurt, it can also be difficult to spot anger. As long as you deny that you feel angry over your unresolved disappointments and hurts, you won't deal with the problem. Barb and I guarantee it: Where there is an offense, there is hurt. And where there is unresolved hurt, there is anger.

Hurt may not cause you to become red-in-the-face scream-ers. But everyone, Christian or not, *does* experience anger. It is a

God-given emotion. In his book *Good 'n' Angry,* psychologist Les Carter explains: "Anger per se is neither good nor bad. It is how people use their anger that makes it positive or negative. Ideally, anger was given to humans by God as a tool to help build relationships. In its pure form, anger is an emotional signal that tells a person something needs to be changed. It was intended to be a positive motivator to be used in giving one another feedback about how life can be lived more productively."[1]

It is crucial to admit that our anger exists. We need to be open to what God can teach us whenever our emotions are stirred so strongly. You may find it difficult to admit and work through the hurt and anger caused by your spouse. But the process is often necessary to restore the acceptance and connection that results when you practice forgiving love in your marriage.

In the normal process of the offense-hurt-anger pattern, hurt comes before anger. But when you have weathered a series of offenses, your mind can learn to skip the hurt and go straight to the anger stage. For example, your spouse has so often criticized the way you dress that you explode at the first disparaging comment he or she makes about your clothes.

The cause of anger can also be confusing. Although most anger is triggered by specific situations or events, anger can also be *displaced*—sparked by one person or event but taken out on someone else. For example, your spouse calls to say he or she will be late for dinner—again. You hang up the phone, and all through dinner you take out your anger on the kids, even though they are not the cause of your hurt.

Anger can also be *leftover*—stemming from the past. Sometimes the offense happened so long ago that you've even forgotten the cause. For example, your spouse fires off a volley of angry words at you for no apparent reason. When you sit down to talk about it, you discover that he or she was hurt by something you did a month ago, something you barely remember.

Wherever the anger comes from, God has provided a biblical way to address it and disarm the offense-hurt-anger pattern that robs your relationship of intimacy and connection.

## RESPONDING TO THE PATTERN: YOU HAVE TWO CHOICES

Whenever you experience the downward spiral of unresolved offenses, hurt, and anger, you have two options. First, you can simply ignore the offense and the hurt while allowing the anger to fester. But beware: This will take your marriage to a sad place you never dreamed you would go. You may continue to stuff your unresolved feelings deep inside, resulting in bitterness, resentment, and depression. You may explode, venting pent-up anger without regard for how it wounds and alienates your spouse. Either way, by failing to break the negative pattern, you continue to wear each other down. You continue to slide away from your dream marriage. The end result may be a relational earthquake that rattles your relationship to its foundation.

But you have a second option. It's called forgiving love. When you face hurt and anger, you can decide to resolve the conflict. That's the biblical way to deal with the offense-hurt-anger pattern. What we want to work toward—as individuals and as couples—is a commitment to address the pain and anger, to resolve the conflicts, to forgive the offender, and to renew the relationship. The goal is to bring the relationship to a place of healing, wholeness, and openness, helping you feel accepted and connected again.

In the next chapter we will introduce a process that will enable you to move past offenses, discover healing for your hurts, and find relief for your anger. What is important to understand first, however, is the power that makes this resolution possible: forgiving love.

## WHAT IS FORGIVING LOVE?

Forgiving love safeguards your marriage by healing hurts and helping you feel accepted and connected. It's the love that brings you and your spouse back together when the inevitable offenses of a married relationship have pushed you apart. It's the first love every marriage needs if it's going to last. And it's a love that is securely rooted in God's love for us.

The New Testament uses several words for *forgive*. The root of the most common word means to "send away" or "dismiss." Another word sometimes translated as *forgive* means to "let loose" or "release." Yet another means to "bestow favor unconditionally." Practically speaking, biblical forgiveness means that we actively choose to give up our grudge despite the severity of the injustice done to us. It doesn't mean that we say or feel, "It didn't hurt me" or "It didn't really matter." Many disappointments wound us deeply. But after we recognize the hurt, we should choose to let it go. And when we cause the hurt, we seek that same release from those we offend.

The Bible says that our wrong behaviors alienate us from God and make us his enemies (see Colossians 1:21). But God's forgiveness, provided through our response of faith to Christ's sacrifice on the cross, opens the door to incalculable benefits. When God forgives, he removes our transgressions "as far away from us as the east is from the west" (Psalm 103:12). But that's not all that happens. Along with forgiveness, Christ also

- rescues us from darkness (see Colossians 1:13)
- redeems us (see Colossians 1:14)
- reconciles us to God (see Colossians 1:22)
- makes us able to stand before God without blemish (see Colossians 1:22)
- clears us of all accusations (see Colossians 1:22)
- cleanses us from every wrong (see 1 John 1:9)

When you and your spouse extend forgiving love to each other, you enjoy the same relationship-restoring experience. By offering forgiveness, you offer the grace—the unmerited favor—that God has given us. You follow the Bible's wise command to "make allowance for each other's faults and forgive the person who offends you. Remember, the Lord forgave you, so you must forgive others" (Colossians 3:13).

When you exhibit the grace of forgiving love toward your spouse, you change the entire tone of your marriage. No longer are you like referees counting each other's fouls, ready to toss each other out of the game. Marriage becomes a safe place where you don't have to hide your foibles and your failings. Instead of feeling scrutinized and condemned for your shortcomings, you feel accepted and forgiven.

Think of a recent conflict between you and your spouse. Imagine what forgiving love can accomplish in this conflict and others. Forgiving love

- brings your relationship into the light
- sets free the offended—and the offender
- reconciles you to each other
- allows you to stand before your spouse without blemish
- clears you of guilt—and grudges
- cleanses you from every wrong

Forgiving love dispels the wrongs done against you—and done by you. It allows you to see your spouse as if he or she has done nothing wrong. Can you imagine picking up your relationship as if the offensive behavior never happened? It's a divine makeover, a fresh chance to make the right choices. You are free to accept and connect with each other again.

Forgiving love restores a wounded relationship. It turns you back in the direction of your dream marriage. When you practice forgiving love consistently, you build a lasting love.

## THE COSTS AND BENEFITS OF FORGIVING LOVE

Forgiving love is often the most rewarding step in breaking through our relational disappointments. But it can also be the most difficult.

Gwen has an eye for antiques. She can list from memory the inventory of every antique store within fifty miles of her home near Des Moines. So when she has a free afternoon, she likes nothing better than discovering new shops, strolling aisle after aisle, store after store, digging for some fantastic find. Her favorite antiques are old ceramic dolls. Her collection isn't large, but it's beautiful. Occasionally she comes across a doll so unique and beautiful that she aches to add it to her collection. But as often as not, the price for such exquisite handiwork is far too high. So she walks away disappointed and empty-handed.

Forgiveness is like one of those china dolls. You may appreciate the value of forgiveness. You may discern the beauty of a marriage overflowing with forgiving love. You may wish you could bring this kind of godly grace home, enjoying the uninhibited connection with your spouse that only forgiving love provides. But you fear that you will have to give up too much to get it.

Yes, forgiveness can be costly. A major step in the process of forgiveness is releasing your offending spouse, giving up control of revenge and retribution and allowing God to work in his or her heart. It means letting your spouse off the hook, giving up your right to hold an offense over his or her head. And if you are the one who caused the offense, forgiveness means surrendering your pride, admitting guilt, and seeking restoration. That's tough stuff.

But the benefits found in a renewed relationship are well worth the cost of forgiveness. In fact, the benefits of forgiveness are so overwhelming that if you cannot forgive for the sake of your spouse, you will want to forgive for how it will benefit you alone. Christian ethicist Lewis Smedes writes, "When you release the wrongdoer from the wrong, you cut a malignant tumor out of your inner life. You set a prisoner free, but you discover that the real prisoner was yourself."[2] Your choice is to let go of the wrongs done against you or to pay a heavy personal price.

When we forgive, we reap one-of-a-kind benefits. We are able to cast off the bondage of carrying an offense only God can bear. That's the supernatural power of forgiveness. Through it, God allows us to start over. In fact, forgiving love allows a relationship to grow deeper and become more meaningful.

Both Mark and Shannon realized that the benefits of God's forgiving love were worth the high cost. Shannon says, "I grew up in an abusive home and knew well how to hide my feelings. But one day I cracked. Everything inside me came rushing out. I was able to tell Mark as a woman and as his wife how I felt about pornography. I told him about the fear he had caused in me by taking us to the brink of financial ruin. I confronted him with what I thought about his neglect of me and the kids.

"There's a verse that says that if we expect God to forgive us, we have to forgive others.[3] I realized I had become bitter over Mark's betrayal. Not only that, but I was taking my anger about my painful childhood out on him. Honestly, once Mark confessed his problem, he made rapid progress in breaking with his past habits. I was the one who took many months to make the slightest movement back toward Mark. I had to find God's way. And I discovered that God's grace toward me gave me the ability to forgive Mark."

Forgiveness allows us to bring our relationship into the light. Forgiveness sets free the offended and the offender, reconciles us after a conflict, cuts loose the guilt and grudges, and cleanses us from every wrong.

# DO YOU HAVE WHAT IT TAKES TO FORGIVE?

Can you remember your jitters when you stood at the cash register of your favorite toy store when you were a child? You had studied every possible toy before carrying your choice to the register. Trembling, you put your toy on the counter and handed the clerk your change. You had counted your dimes and nickels a dozen times. You were sure you had enough money—well, not totally sure. And sometimes you came up short. Not to worry. Standing behind you in the checkout line was your dad or your mom, with a wallet or purse in hand.

At times you may be so deeply hurt by someone that when you reach into your heart to forgive, you don't know if you will find what it takes. In reality, you will never find enough in yourself.

On our own, we lack the limitless grace that can release the offender completely and forgive the offense. The good news is that God hasn't left us alone, fidgeting at the counter. He knows all about the cost of forgiveness. The Bible tells us that an innocent man, God's own Son, came to earth to fulfill the plans foretold in Scripture—to fulfill his Father's will. Jesus brought no one harm. He did not sin; he was perfect. He cared not for himself but for others. He taught about love, forgiveness, faith, hope. He did nothing wrong. Yet they crucified him. He didn't fight it. He turned the other cheek. God's Son was beaten, mocked, spit on. Then they nailed him to a tree. Pain. Agony. He went willingly. Why? Even though he was guiltless, he loved us enough to die the death of the guilty. He was our sacrifice for sin, the Perfect Lamb. And in the final moments, he cried out: "Father, forgive these people" (Luke 23:34). Then he died.

That's what Jesus did for us. God chose the one way—a very costly way—to forgive sinful human beings. He gave us *grace,* favor we don't deserve.

God not only knows all about the cost of forgiveness but also is the Great Forgiver who wants to fill our hearts with what it takes to forgive our spouses. He has lavished on us this gift of forgiveness, amply supplying us with exactly what he wants us to give to others. God's command is that we forgive as he has forgiven us (see Colossians 3:13). The power to forgive in a marriage ultimately comes from God. All he asks is that we pass along his gift.

Forgiving love comes from God, and when God's forgiveness fills us, we have more than enough forgiving love to share with others, including our spouses.

## DISPELLING THE MYTHS OF FORGIVENESS

Forgiving love is difficult and costly. But we often attach to forgiveness some costs that aren't even valid. These are the myths of forgiveness, false requirements many of us assume are true but are nothing more than obstacles to expressing God's forgiving love. These myths are popular in our society. We tend to believe them because we hear them so often. If you are to exercise forgiving love when you have been offended or hurt by your spouse, you need to make sure you don't believe these myths.

*Myth #1: "When I forgive, I must also forget."* The Bible says that God forgives and forgets: "I will forgive their wickedness and will never again remember their sins" (Jeremiah 31:34). But you are not God. He has the power to forget, but you don't. Actually Barb and I don't believe God intends for us to forget the pain we suffer. To the contrary, we are to remember it so we can value the lessons we learned. Remembering also helps to keep us from repeating the mistakes or needlessly placing ourselves back in a position where hurt happens.

*Myth #2: "The hurt is too great. It is impossible for me to forgive."* We have all endured situations so painful that we wonder if we can let go of the offense and forgive the offender. But forgiveness is always possible. God would never command us to do something that is impossible. Barb and I know husbands and wives who have forgiven each other for adultery. We have heard heartbreaking stories in which a spouse forgave and endured the pain of betrayal because of his or her commitment to restoring the marriage. We have seen spouses forgive each other for

- secret spending that took the couple to bankruptcy
- wounds inflicted when a husband continually took his mother's side against his wife
- scars when a stepmother sided with her child against her new husband
- betrayal through addiction to pornography

Forgiveness can overcome the greatest of offenses, even offenses that threaten to drive couples to divorce. We have seen incredible peace come to people who have endured the most traumatic sins against them—victims of violence, men and women abused as children, husbands and wives betrayed by their spouses. They didn't dodge forgiveness. They walked through the eye of the storm to experience the pain necessary to later experience the healing they hoped for.

In our pain we experience God and his faithfulness. Author C. S. Lewis understood this when he wrote, "God whispers to us in our pleasures, speaks in our conscience, and shouts in our pains; it is His megaphone to rouse a deaf world."[4] Countless hurting, offended couples have walked through the process of acknowledging their feelings of hurt and anger and then choosing to begin the process of forgiving the offending spouses. It is a peace-imparting, real-world process we will share with you in the next chapter.

*Myth #3: "I don't feel like forgiving, so my forgiveness can't be genuine."* When your spouse has offended you, you often don't feel like forgiving him or her. But forgiveness really isn't about feelings. It's a choice, an act of the will. If you wait until you feel like forgiving, you are choosing to feed the monster of resentment and bitterness.

Although the choice to forgive supersedes our feelings, it doesn't deny them. It embraces them and allows us to express them through effective communication, then resolve the conflict by entering the process of forgiveness. Even when we don't feel like forgiving, we need to ask God for strength to enter the process. He will direct us if we honestly seek him.

*Myth #4: "I can't forgive until the other person asks for it."* We may fantasize about receiving a groveling apology from an offender: "I was so wrong, and I'm so sorry I hurt you. Can you find it in your heart to forgive me?" But if you wait for that kind of response when your spouse hurts you, you may have to wait a long time. Besides, forgiveness is an act of grace. It's unmerited love. Your spouse doesn't have to jump through all the right hoops to earn it.

Our forgiveness of others must be patterned after God's forgiveness of us. When we forgive with no strings attached, we put into action the Bible's command, "Be kind to each other, tenderhearted, forgiving one another, just as God through Christ has forgiven you" (Ephesians 4:32). Did we earn God's forgiveness? Did Jesus die on the cross because we did something to merit such a sacrifice? No. God forgives us out of his grace. Forgiveness cannot be earned. So we must not offer forgiveness with any conditions, such as an apology or confession of wrong. Simply forgive as God does.

*Myth #5: "In order to forgive, I must pretend that nothing bad happened."* Forgiveness doesn't pretend that nothing happened or that the offense didn't cause hurt. Rather, true forgiveness acknowledges the truth then chooses to let go of the offense. Forgiveness says, "I know what you did, and it really hurt. But in full view of this reality, I choose to forgive you. I do this because of the example and power of Christ, and because I want our relationship to be healed." Forgiveness never says that a hurt didn't happen, because if it didn't happen, there would be nothing to forgive.

*Myth #6: "I must forgive right away, or it doesn't count."* Often this myth is based on the apostle Paul's admonition, "Don't let the sun go down while you are still angry" (Ephesians 4:26). Barb and I have heard about couples who have stayed up all night trying to resolve a conflict because they honestly thought the Bible commanded them to do so. Often they ended up too tired to deal with the problem effectively, and the conflict worsened. If you want to apply this verse literally, you need to solve all your problems by sunset—not bedtime.

This verse isn't a formula for the amount of time it should take to grant forgiveness. It is a command that we should not let anger fester in our hearts. Since forgiveness is an act of the will, it may take you some time to come to the point where you are ready to forgive. If the offense was minor, the forgiving process may take less time. But if the offense was major, you may need to prepare for a longer healing process. The only mistake we make is in refusing to enter the process.

## A BETTER WAY TO FORGIVE

Think about how our Christian culture deals with forgiveness. We know that the Bible commands us to forgive those we offend. So in our task-oriented efficiency, we occasionally make a list of people we have offended and either visit them, call them, or write them to ask for forgiveness. Or we make a list of those who have offended us, confront them, and await their apology. Having done our Christian duty, we check these people off our list.

This process can result in what Barb and I call "cheap forgiveness." For some of us, this is the only kind of forgiveness we know. We apply the formula, but we never come to a genuine resolution of the conflict. It's like painting over a crumbling wall instead of fixing it first. Cheap forgiveness gives rise to the myths of forgiveness we have just discussed. Cheap forgiveness does not reckon with the genuine costs of real forgiveness.

We think there's a better, more biblical way, a process we will share with you in the next chapter.

# 4

## Closing the Loop

Ryan and Jackie started out like two lovebirds settling nicely into their cozy little marriage nest. Just past their one-year anniversary, however, the couple began finding their nest to be a little uncomfortable.

One day Ryan pulled up the footrest on his recliner and flipped on the TV—while Jackie was talking to him. This had happened a number of times in their first year together, and it made Jackie furious. This time she turned, grabbed her purse, and stormed toward the door. "I'm going shopping," she said.

"Don't spend any money," Ryan called over his shoulder, his eyes glued to the TV screen.

On the way to the mall, Jackie dialed three friends on her cell phone without finding one who could meet her there. Then she called her mother.

Jackie had a couple of female friends who would listen while she vented. Yet when she was really desperate, she called her mom. Jackie was surprised to find herself asking for relationship advice from her mom. Not that her mother ever solved anything, but she didn't like Ryan much and was happy to hear Jackie's complaints.

What Jackie shared with her mom that day was nothing

new. "I can't figure out where the man I married has gone," she said. "Ryan used to be so fun. He was the one who taught *me* how to lighten up. And now it's as if his brain is somewhere out in space. He's always lying around. If I try to talk about bills or how work is going, he blows up. Then he stomps out to the garage to fuss with that stupid car of his. It's the only time he ever moves his sorry backside."

Back at the house, Ryan leaned back in the recliner and closed his eyes. He knew Jackie was bothered by something, but he couldn't figure her out at the moment. *I feel smothered,* he thought. *We never do anything I want to do. Jackie used to be interested in watching games and playing softball and hanging out with me in the garage. Now she acts like she's my mother.* Then he added something he would never say to anyone out loud: *And sex isn't all that I expected either.*

Both Ryan and Jackie buried their disappointment and hurt. Ryan withdrew. He went straight from work to hanging out with friends. When he did spend time around the house, he often lashed out at Jackie with unkind words. Jackie formed a habit of sneaking off to spend money on things she knew Ryan wouldn't approve of. She continued to complain about him to anyone who would listen.

Several years passed before something forced Ryan and Jackie to change the focus of their relationship. When Jackie was five months pregnant, they learned that complications might prevent the unborn baby from surviving to term. During the difficult weeks that followed, they were forced to be honest with each other. Jackie told Ryan that she needed to know he was there for her. He couldn't be wandering off to who-knows-where at any time. As Ryan gazed into her pleading eyes, he realized again why he had married her. They both knew they had let the dream slip away.

Ryan and Jackie discovered that offenses and hurt are inevitable in a marriage relationship. Even before their first anniversary, Jackie had felt the sting of Ryan's sharp tongue, and Ryan had been burned by his young wife's temper. As the years passed, things had gotten worse instead of better. Their close relationship before marriage—talks and long walks, nights out with friends, spontaneous fun—had deteriorated into a series of unresolved conflicts and unhealed hurts.

But their threatened pregnancy brought them to a crossroads. Ryan and Jackie needed to clear the air between them. They needed to resolve the offenses and hurts, forgive each other, and find acceptance and connection once again. They knew they had to join together as a team to battle the problems they faced.

They finally have begun the process of facing their conflicts and differences. But like other marriages riddled with offenses, hurt, and anger, they will recapture their dream marriage and forge a lasting love only if they put forgiving love into action. Only forgiving love heals the hurts, resolves the conflict, and allows husbands and wives to feel accepted and connected again.

## WHERE ARE YOU IN THE LOOP?

Barb and I often meet people like Ryan and Jackie through our radio program and marriage conferences. Couples trapped in the pattern of unresolved offense-hurt-anger with no idea of how to resolve their differences are caught in what we call an "open loop." The loop is a concept I developed while dealing with thousands of couples in my counseling practice. As I worked to understand the couples' struggles, I saw that the pattern of offense-hurt-anger is just the beginning of a cycle of conflict that has two possible endings. The first outcome—an open loop—happens when conflict goes unaddressed and unresolved. See figure 1 (on the next page) for what this pattern looks like.

Some marriages have dozens of open loops. For example, couples may live in ongoing conflict over how to discipline their

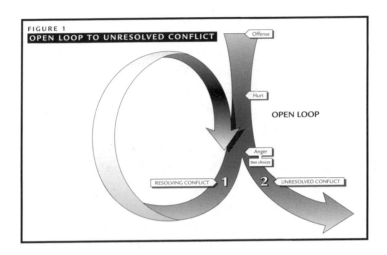

children, over who is responsible for taking out the garbage or who balances the checkbook or how often they have sex. Some unresolved issues may be even more personal, such as wounds from criticism, insults, apathy, or lack of love. When couples do not resolve their conflicts, the pain accumulates and anger burns. Bitterness hardens hearts. And two people who were once very close and connected grow more and more isolated from each other.

But this bleak condition isn't a couple's only option. They

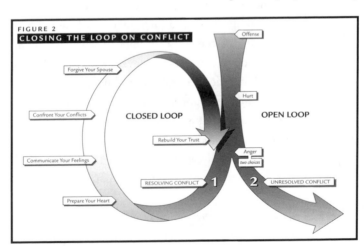

can choose to work through the process of "closing the loop" through forgiveness. Only forgiveness enables couples to rebuild trust and enjoy a fully restored relationship. This is the outcome we are aiming for in our ministry to couples. Examine this outcome and the steps to closing the loop in figure 2.

Suppose an offense happened just this morning between you and your spouse. Not just any offense, but one that happens so often that you are both weary of dealing with it. You hate the flash of anger it ignites within you. For the first hour after you went your separate ways for the day, you replayed the conflict in your mind, thinking of all the nasty comments you could have shot back. By midmorning your fury has started to cool, but you dread the next round when you meet at the end of the day.

You have a choice. Every conflict with your spouse brings you to a fork in the road. What will you do? After the offense has led to hurt and the hurt has turned to anger, you are faced with the choice of how to handle the situation: Will you work to resolve the conflict and close the loop? Or will you let it pass and leave the loop open to collect the debris of more hurtful conflicts? Figure 3 shows what that choice looks like.

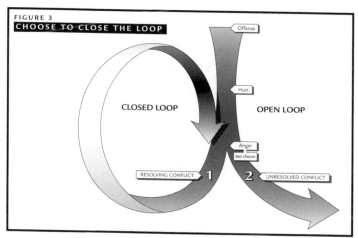

**FIGURE 3**
**CHOOSE TO CLOSE THE LOOP**

Offense

Hurt

CLOSED LOOP        OPEN LOOP

Anger
two choices

RESOLVING CONFLICT   1      2   UNRESOLVED CONFLICT

One path—closing the loop—leads to restoration. The other path—failing to resolve your hurt and leaving the loop open—allows your disappointments to deepen.

Have you ever been at that fork in the road? Do you recognize what we're talking about? Can you identify some current situations where you stand at that point of choosing whether or not to work toward closing the loop?

At first thought, it sure seems easier to ignore the problem, to shove aside the wrong you suffered—or the wrong you inflicted. But that quick fix won't last. It takes courage to restore and rebuild a relationship, regardless of which side of the offense you're on. It takes time, patience, trust, and maybe even some tears. But if Barb and I could sit down with you and your spouse, we would look you in the eye and assure you that whatever conflicts you face right now, the benefits of a restored relationship far outweigh the effort of closing the loop.

Closing the loop is forgiving love in action. This is the biblical pathway to confronting offenses, resolving conflicts, and healing hurts. This is God's way to restore mutual acceptance and intimacy in the wake of misunderstanding and pain. Closing the loop through forgiving love is a vital component in building a lasting love.

## CLOSING THE LOOP STEP-BY-STEP

Couples often ask Barb and me how long it will take for their relationship to "get better." In other words, how long does it take to close all the loops? We wish we could tell you the process is easy. We wish we could offer you a few platitudes that might make you feel better. But good feelings don't lead to lasting change. Many people approach us with hurts that take time to sort out and heal. We encourage you to take a head-on approach to dealing with conflicts and hurts in your relationship. Don't bury them. Don't beat around the bush. Just face them, and close the loop, no matter how long it takes.

We want to coach you on five biblical steps for sharing forgiving love with your spouse and closing the loop of offense and hurt. We know the process works because it is God's way of healing hurts and restoring relationships.

## Step 1: Prepare Your Heart

Ryan and Jackie's hearts were broken the day they learned about the complications with their unborn child. Confusion overtook them as they were asked to make decisions regarding medical procedures they had never heard of. Worse yet, they both realized that this new stress was piling up on top of all the hurts they had caused each other, making it doubly difficult to focus on closing the loop.

The couple wisely sought their pastor's help in working through the necessary medical decisions. As their unborn child's condition stabilized, Ryan and Jackie began dealing with the backlog of unresolved offenses.

Like Ryan and Jackie, some couples are forced to deal with their differences because they are in crisis. Other couples take much longer to deal with the clutter of unhealed offenses, hurts, and anger. Either way, healing begins only when one or both partners choose to engage in the necessary heart work that clears the way for closing the loop. Here are several elements in the process of heart preparation:

*Humble yourself and pray.* Step back, go to God, confess your sin, and pray! "God, give me the humility to resolve this issue in a way that honors you. Help me to be gracious to my spouse and sensitive to his [or her] perspective. Help us talk things through. Help us to close the loop and rekindle our love for each other." You can also pray the words of one of the psalms of David, a man who created deep hurt through his offenses.

"Search me, O God, and know my heart; test me and know my thoughts. Point out anything in me that offends you" (Psalm 139:23-24).

Prayer softens our hearts. Prayer helps us reprioritize. While you're talking to God, tell him that you are committed to loving your spouse, to humility, and to obedience. You can pray through Philippians 2:3-5, which describes how to close the loop in a Christlike manner: "Don't be selfish; don't live to make a good impression on others. Be humble, thinking of others as better than yourself. Don't think only about your own affairs, but be interested in others, too, and what they are doing. Your attitude should be the same that Christ Jesus had."

*Look for the underlying cause of the conflict.* Sort through the surface stuff, and look for the *real* source of the hurt. Is your anger really about the offense, or did something else set you off? Try some of these ideas to help you dig deeper:

- Look for external forces—such as pressure at work or finances—that cause stress in the relationship.
- Decide what really matters. Is the basic issue of your conflict a nonnegotiable, or is it a matter of personal preference, like the proverbial difference of opinion about how to squeeze the toothpaste tube? Is the issue a "hill to die on" or a minor irritation?
- Brainstorm about ways to set aside stresses on your marriage, even temporarily, so you can focus on the relationship. Consider going away for a day or enjoying a night out or a quiet evening at home without the kids.
- Try to understand and accept how your spouse deals with conflict.
- Be realistic. Don't expect everything to be done the way your mother—or your spouse's mother, for that matter—did it.

*Commit to making your relationship the top priority.* One of the greatest saboteurs of healthy relationships is the tendency to put them on the back burner. When we're stretched and stressed and living in the fast lane, sometimes the people closest to us are the ones who get hurt the most.

In their book *Fit to Be Tied,* Pastor Bill Hybels and his wife, Lynne, write about "crisis mode living," which they define as "spending every moment of every day trying to figure out how to keep all your balls in the air and all your plates spinning." The implication of crisis mode living is that relationships suffer. As Bill and Lynne Hybels write, "Your bond with your spouse that used to be strong and intimate becomes increasingly weak and distant. You hope he or she doesn't have a serious need because you don't have the energy to deal with it."[1]

God wants your marriage to be a safe place to resolve conflicts. Your relationship will become a haven as you commit to God and to each other to keep the relationship alive no matter what.

*Involve a trusted accountability partner.* The more deeply rooted the conflict and hurt, the more important it is to involve a trustworthy third party who will hold you accountable for closing the loop. It should be someone who loves and respects both you and your spouse equally—instead of "my friend" or "your friend"—and who will guard your relationship with the utmost confidentiality. Find a pastor, Christian counselor, accountability group, or mature mentoring couple to keep you focused on forgiving love. Invite this person(s) to hold you accountable by periodically asking you questions like these:

- Are you maintaining a high value on your relationship?
- Are you valuing and respecting both yourself and your spouse?
- Are you facing your conflict head-on?

    ❧ Are you shrinking back or avoiding conflict?

    ❧ Are you resisting tendencies to control or manipulate?

    ❧ Are you working hard at reconciliation?

These are tough questions to answer, but they will help keep the process of forgiving love on track.

## Step 2: Communicate Your Feelings

Communication is often called the number one problem in marriages. Why? Maybe it's because communication breakdowns lead to breakdowns in so many other areas. When we stop communicating, conflicts flare up, tension builds, and intimacy cools.

Communication in the context of closing the loop involves honestly describing your thoughts and feelings about the offense you suffered. This is where you become transparent and vulnerable with your spouse by sharing the impact the conflict has had on you.

By the time Ryan and Jackie could take a breather and constructively talk together about their disappointments, they each had compiled a long list of grievances. Their complaints were filled with language such as, "I expected . . ." and "I thought . . ." Jackie felt abandoned. Ryan felt manipulated. Jackie couldn't tell if Ryan even liked her anymore. Ryan was frustrated at having to answer to Jackie for "every minute of every day" with no time to let down. Jackie felt controlled by Ryan for every penny she spent, even though they both earned good salaries.

It was a painful, tearful exchange, but Ryan and Jackie opened their hearts to each other and aired their hurts. In the process, they gained new insights into each other's feelings. Accusations of "You're never . . ." and "You're so . . ." turned to "I didn't realize I hurt you when I . . ." and "I had no idea you thought that . . ." Their honest communication helped them reach a better understanding of their conflicts; they began to see the issues through the other's eyes.

We recommend a number of crucial strategies for effectively communicating your feelings to your spouse:

*Think ahead about what you want to say.* Make a list or write a paragraph on each issue so you will be able to state your grievances simply and clearly.

*Recognize gender differences in communication.* Men sometimes zoom straight to the point, omitting details. That's not the warmest approach for a woman. Women sometimes meander through every detail, clouding the bottom line. Men want to hear the bottom line; women want to have a context for the bottom line.

*Get a referee.* When the issues are too big or too painful to deal with on your own, find an objective, trustworthy third party to help you talk them out.

*Deliver your whole message.* Speak kindly and calmly, but say all that you have come to say. A whole message consists of thoughts, feelings, and needs. Share your thoughts, which include your perception, values, and attitudes about the conflict. Then share how you feel about it. Do you feel fearful? anxious? disappointed? hopeful? optimistic? Then move to completing the whole message by sharing what you need from your spouse. Do you need an answer? a hug? space for a few hours? another viewpoint?

*Commit to listening.* As you listen to your spouse describe the offense and hurt, resist the urge to defend yourself or prove him or her wrong. Instead, listen first and then ask questions that lead to clarification and understanding. The Bible reminds us, "My dear brothers and sisters, be quick to listen, slow to speak, and slow to get angry" (James 1:19).

*Focus on the positive.* Affirm positive traits or habits. Say things such as, "I appreciate . . ." or "I am so grateful that . . ." or "You are so good at . . ."

*Avoid the silent treatment.* Sometimes—especially when spouses are angry—they clam up and give each other the silent treatment, thinking that the silence will communicate their perspective. Don't mistake silence for communication. In fact, silence is often only manipulative. The goal is to open active communication, not to play games.

*Say what you mean.* Don't say, "I hate football" if what you really mean is, "I wish we could spend some quality time together on Saturday afternoons." Before you speak, think carefully about what really upsets you.

*Don't use generalizations.* Avoid statements such as "You *never* take out the garbage like you're supposed to" or "You are *always* talking to your mother on the phone." They are usually exaggerations, and they are certainly not helpful.

*Use I-messages.* "I sometimes feel ignored and lonely" goes down a lot easier than, "You never pay any attention to me." Focus on your thoughts and feelings rather than harp on your spouse's failures. Invariably, generalizations will lead to a defensive response from your spouse because he or she will feel the need to set the record straight.

*Agree on a plan for handling conflicts.* Answer this question with your spouse: How do we want to talk to each other when a conflict arises?

When you are in a conflict, it is imperative that you communicate openly and honestly. Failure to share your feelings and talk through your differences will stifle any efforts to clear the air and restore intimacy.

## Step 3: Confront Your Conflicts

Barb and I teach regularly at FamilyLife conferences around the country. At one point during each of these "Weekend to Remember" conferences, we instruct husbands and wives to look each other in the eye and repeat a statement that we hope will burn into their memories: "My spouse is not my enemy." Don't you love that thought? So often in the midst of a conflict, husbands and wives view each other as adversaries to be defeated. Instead of working toward resolution, we aim darts at each other's heart. But the essential truth is that we are on the same team. We should be working together to find a solution.

However, even in the atmosphere of team spirit and honest communication, certain hot-button issues must be confronted and resolved. For example: Are we going to hang the toilet tissue your way, my way, or alternate with each roll? Or more seriously: Will we spend Christmas morning with your parents, my parents, or at home with our kids? How many nights a week shall we commit to being home together? Who will pay the bills? Will it be you, me, or both of us together? If you don't make the needed decisions on how to proceed, the conflict won't go away.

We would like to offer you a starting point that virtually guarantees success. It's a four-word phrase that may surprise your spouse, but it will also help disarm the conflict and set the stage for the decision-making discussion. The starting point is this: "Let's pray together first."

Prayer makes a positive impact on the resolution of conflict. Prayer takes two people on opposite sides of an issue and welcomes into the debate a third person—Jesus. Bringing Jesus into your debate means deciding together to play by his rules.

Once you have prayed, the most practical way to make Jesus part of this decision-making step is by going to the Bible to find solutions. What does the Bible say about your situation? What clear commands do you need to obey? What biblical principles apply to this issue? When you look to God's Word, you level the playing field by welcoming God's solution.

During Ryan and Jackie's difficult heart-to-heart talk, they expressed some honest hurts and disappointments. They vented their anger. It felt better to have the issues out in the open, but they still needed to come to some conclusions: Just how much time should Ryan spend with friends? How could Jackie make Ryan feel more relaxed at home? How was Jackie going to put a stop to her backbiting? What was going to change about how the couple handled money? And how were they going to stop the war of words?

The first thing Ryan and Jackie agreed on was making time to connect after work. Ryan, who arrived home first, got a few minutes in his recliner to settle his brain after a long day. But as soon as Jackie got home, it was talk time.

On the financial side, they agreed to discuss any purchases that would be above a certain amount—fifty dollars felt reasonable to them as long as they were both working. They decided the best way to put a lid on Jackie's complaining—especially to her mother—was to get together as a couple with Jackie's parents. No one-on-one time with her mom until Jackie felt that she had some nice things to say about Ryan. And they decided that doing these things and keeping open lines of healthy communication would be the fastest way to keep their conversations from degenerating into shouting matches.

Can you see how Ryan and Jackie found middle ground that respected both of their needs? That's a prime goal of confrontation. Here are some other ideas for loving confrontation:

*Choose an appropriate time and setting.* Do you and your spouse really need to solve an issue moments before two dozen guests arrive for a dinner party? Select a time and place that minimize distractions and guarantee privacy from the children.

*Ask permission to address the conflict.* For example: "Are you ready to talk about our disagreement over how to discipline the children?" or "I'm ready to confront our money problems. Are you okay with that?" Make sure your spouse is ready to face the issue before you bring it up.

*Avoid statements that assign blame.* I-statements encourage discussion; you-statements shut it down. Start your sentences with "I feel . . ." or "I think . . ." rather than "You are . . ." or "You should . . ."

## Step 4: Forgive Your Spouse

After Ryan and Jackie agreed on the issues that had been undermining their marriage, they experienced an even more significant breakthrough in their relationship. "The biggest thing we've learned is to forgive," Jackie says. "We know now how to say, 'I was wrong,' and we are learning to ask for and grant forgiveness. We can't think of a more important skill for our marriage."

The core of forgiving love is the act of forgiveness. This stage is very difficult for many people, yet it brings the greatest amount of healing for hurts and conflict. Barb and I believe that forgiveness brings us closer to God than anything else we can do. Relationships demand it. Jesus modeled it. Our hearts need it. It all begins in your marriage when you and your spouse agree to let each other off the hook.

Have you made the decision to forgive? Are you ready to experience "whole forgiveness" together? As you will see, whole forgiveness takes two people—one seeking forgiveness and one granting it—and the heartfelt statements described below.

### Requesting Forgiveness

Think of a conflict you have experienced recently with your spouse, and imagine how it could be resolved by making the following statements:

*"I was wrong."* When you need forgiveness, it's not enough to say, "Okay, if you think I did something wrong, let's talk about it." It's also not appropriate to say, "I don't think what I did was such a big deal, but if you think it was, let's talk." We need to

confront the wrong for what it is. Here are some ways to say it: "I was wrong"; "What I did/said to you was wrong"; "I did something wrong, and I need to talk to you about what I did to offend you."

*"I'm sorry."* How often have you sought forgiveness and said "I was wrong," thinking that would take care of the problem? Perhaps the offended person appeared confused, leading you to think, *Well, I said I was wrong. Shouldn't that be enough?*

Admitting wrong behavior is vitally important, but it's not enough. You need to express your sorrow over the hurt your wrong behavior caused: "I was wrong, and I'm so sorry that I hurt you." It takes both elements for your offended spouse to sense your sincerity. By expressing your sorrow, you demonstrate empathy for the other person. "I'm sorry" helps restore the relationship by diminishing the resistance between two hurting people, allowing communication to open up and self-protection to be put aside.

*"I don't ever want to hurt you like this again."* This is a statement of repentance and is different from the first two statements. "I was wrong" is a statement of confession. "I'm sorry" is a statement of contrition or sorrow. They should be followed by a statement of repentance, your desire to change and to turn from your hurtful ways. Confession and contrition without repentance leave forgiveness incomplete. "I don't want to hurt you again" is a way of saying the hurt you caused—and may cause in the future—is unintentional and distressing to you. Repentance swings wide open the door to deep healing.

*"Will you forgive me?"* At this point you demonstrate the ultimate humility in the process of seeking forgiveness. When you sincerely ask, "Will you forgive me?" you place yourself at the feet of your spouse, taking the servant's position. This question brings the process of forgiveness to a resolution. It is forgiving love at its best.

Let's review these four critical steps again:

1. Confession—"I was wrong."
2. Sorrow—"I'm sorry."
3. Repentance—"I don't ever want to hurt you like this again."
4. Request—"Will you forgive me?"

If you leave out any of the four elements of your request for forgiveness, you risk leaving the conflict unresolved. Too often we leap to the request for forgiveness without acknowledging our wrong, expressing our remorse, or offering repentance. This is cheap forgiveness, leaving the offended person with the pain of the wrong suffered.

### Granting Forgiveness

The spouse from whom forgiveness has been requested must respond in two ways: grant forgiveness *graciously* and grant it *specifically*.

"*I forgive you, and close the loop on this issue.*" Forgiving graciously means letting go of the offense and welcoming your spouse back into your heart. This is the way God forgives us when we confess in sorrow and repent. God's forgiveness is free. It's undeserved. It can't be earned or bargained for. He won't ever rescind it. Forgiveness is a no-strings-attached gift in response to our humble confession of sin. You must graciously forgive your spouse because God has graciously forgiven you.

"*I forgive you for . . .*" Forgiving *specifically* means stating the wrong for which your spouse has asked you to forgive him or her. You fill in the blank: critical words, insincerity, lying, wasteful spending, not meeting your needs, infidelity, insensitivity, ignoring you, belittling you, etc. By naming the issue, you assure your spouse how complete and inclusive your forgiveness is. It doesn't leave the offense hanging in the air. Rather, it dispels any questions in your spouse's mind: *Did he or she understand what I was asking forgiveness for? Did he or she really forgive me for what I did?*

Forgiveness—the ability to let go of past hurts—is perhaps the single most important relationship skill you can develop in marriage. Keeping your spouse on the hook for past offenses may give you a gratifying sense of power, but it is always gained at the expense of the relationship. Power may feel good at the time because of the momentary relief it provides you from the resentment and hurt still seething within you. But the *only* way to restore harmony in the relationship is to permanently remove those negative feelings. No relationship can recover from serious disappointments and grow in intimacy if one or both partners cannot let go of the bitterness. You cannot enjoy trust, acceptance, or connectedness at the same time that you are secretly—or openly—resentful of your spouse.

Once forgiveness happens, you can move toward reconciliation. Family counselor David Stoop writes, "Forgiveness is unilateral. It is something we can do all by ourselves. Reconciliation requires the participation of another person. We cannot 'make it happen,' no matter how hard we try."[2] Reconciliation—the true healing and coming together of two people who had been in conflict—can occur only when both spouses want it and are willing to work for it: to confront the offense, the hurt, and the anger, and choose to communicate.

True reconciliation cannot occur unless both spouses are willing to participate. It may *look* like reconciliation as two people reopen the lines of communication, but something will be missing: genuine forgiveness. And that lack will be a gaping hole in the foundation of the relationship.

So, are you stuck forever if one of you refuses to complete the reconciliation? Not fully. You can forgive your spouse even if he or she will not complete the process. Although one-sided forgiveness is not the ideal, it is the only way some people can close the loop with spouses who are either unwilling to confess wrong or who are no longer living. In such cases, you can grant unrequested forgiveness and feel released and free of resentment.

### Step 5: Rebuild Your Trust

What would it take for Ryan and Jackie to feel that they have finally moved past their conflicts and pain? They have exercised forgiving love by communicating feelings, confronting issues, and forgiving each other. Wouldn't it be great if all the worries and fears that went along with those hurts would disappear? Wouldn't it be freeing for Ryan to know that Jackie is no longer criticizing him and for Jackie to come home each night to a husband who is ready and willing to talk to her? Don't you think such a change of heart and behavior would propel their marriage back toward the dream?

This is what happens during the last step in closing the loop: rebuilding trust. In some conflicts and hurts, trust may not need much repair. But when the wounds are deep and trust has been eroded, it is essential.

If you have hurt your spouse deeply or repeatedly, he or she may be willing to forgive you. But that doesn't mean that the relationship is completely healed, that you can go on as if nothing happened. For true restoration to occur, you must be willing to work at rebuilding your spouse's trust over a period of time. You need to prove to your spouse over the long haul that your confession, contrition, and repentance are genuine.

Trust isn't rebuilt overnight. If you have been unfaithful to your spouse, it may take long months of single-minded devotion before a foundation of trust is reestablished. If your spouse has endured years of unjust criticism from you, you have a long road of affirmation and appreciation ahead of you. The sanctity and peace of your relationship may be in ruins at your feet. But through the power of Christ's redeeming love, your marriage can be transformed from rubble to restoration. Begin that healing process today. Begin to rebuild trust today. Be faithful and patient, and you will experience the restoration you seek.

Throughout your marriage, you will frequently find yourself at the familiar fork in the road, the choice between ignoring hurt and deciding to close the loop. No marriage completely escapes the pattern of offense-hurt-anger. But every time you choose the healing process of closing the loop, you will experience the healing power of forgiving love. And you will be one step closer to recapturing the dream you left at the altar. If you need more help with handling conflict areas in your marriage, read our book *Healing the Hurt in Your Marriage: Beyond Conflict to Forgiveness.*

# SECRET TWO

## *Serving Love*

*Serving love discovers and meets needs
and helps spouses feel honored and understood*

# 5

## *In Honor of Your Spouse*

The first time Gary spoke at a Promise Keepers stadium event, I went along to support him and pray for him. Gary stood before a vast sea of men—about sixty thousand of them—and preached with fire and passion about the importance of godly marriages. I sat behind the stage, watching the monitor, praying, and beaming with pride.

Toward the end of Gary's message, I was stunned to hear him mention my name. "I'm going to ask my wife, Barbara, to join me on the platform," he said. "She doesn't know I am going to ask her to do this."

As his surprising invitation swirled inside my head, someone led me up the metal steps to the massive stage. Just when I thought my knees would give way from fear, a man guided me to a chair. I didn't dare look at the crowd, thinking I would surely faint at the overwhelming sight of sixty thousand men.

So I focused my attention on Gary, waiting for some hint of what he was about to say or do. In mild panic, I flashed him a silent question with my eyes: *What now?* His return glance communicated all I needed to know: *Trust me.*

Gary stood before me with Bible in hand. As he began to

read from Scripture, I realized he had turned to the Gospel of John: "'No,' Peter protested, 'you will never wash my feet!'" (John 13:8).

Fear engulfed me. Feet? Whose feet? Oh no, nobody's washing my feet—not in front of sixty thousand men!

All I could do was trust Gary, my soul mate, my best friend. So I watched and waited. Gary had a bottle of water and his handkerchief in his hands. He knelt in front of me, removed my shoes, and began washing my feet. Tears rolled down his cheeks as he demonstrated the depth of his love for me, serving me as Christ had humbly served his disciples. My tears flowed too. In those solemn moments, I felt as if Gary and I were the only two people in the stadium.

When he finished, Gary stood again before the awestruck crowd of men. Forcefully and compassionately, he challenged them to go to the next level of love for their wives. He invited them to kneel while he prayed. Across the stadium, men dropped to their knees, committing publicly to return home and love their wives with servants' hearts.

Do you have any idea how I feel living with a man like Gary? No, I don't mean the kind of man who calls me up in front of sixty thousand men without warning. I mean a man who unashamedly kneels to serve me in front of sixty thousand men. A man who is the same man in public that he is in private, inside the walls of our home. I'm talking about a husband who strives to discover my needs and meet them, who showers me with a love that causes me to feel understood and honored.

I value what Gary did on the platform that day because it matches how he lives with me day in, day out. Don't get me wrong; Gary's not perfect. I'm not blind to his mistakes and tendencies to get distracted. But over the long haul of our three decades together, Gary has been a consistent model of serving love. There's no need too small for him to notice, such as bringing me a cup of coffee in the morning, tossing in a load of laundry, or washing the dishes. He prays for and with me, and he's been known to e-mail three hundred strangers to pray for me. When I had surgery, Gary slept at the hospital and suffered through the same bland food I had to eat. His heart is totally wired into my needs.

Gary's willingness to serve me—as he demonstrated not only in that dramatic moment at a Promise Keepers rally but also in the everyday moments of our marriage—convinces me on the deepest level that no matter what comes our way, no matter what flaws I have, no matter what I might do to disappoint him, he cares for me and is committed to meeting my needs. Gary and I call this *serving love*.

The second secret to a lasting love is serving love, which discovers and meets needs and helps spouses feel honored and understood. Are you connecting with your spouse at this level? Serving love means honoring your spouse to the degree that you purposefully seek to discover and meet his or her needs, even placing those needs before your own. Serving your spouse in this way helps him or her feel honored and understood.

## SERVING LOVE: JESUS' KIND OF LOVE

When you said "I do," a large part of your marriage dream, whether conscious or subconscious, was probably that your new soul mate would meet your needs. You wanted a spouse who understood your basic human needs—physical, emotional, relational, and spiritual. You wanted someone who was sensitive to your needs as a woman or man and to your needs as an individual with a unique personality. And you probably expected that your understanding spouse would devote his or her life to meeting those needs.

Have those expectations been realized? Are you experiencing serving, need-meeting love? If your answer is "no" or "not very often," you may wonder if it is really possible for spouses to serve each other with such deep understanding and willingness. You may even wonder if such serving love really exists.

Yes, it does exist. It is an expression of biblical love that is clearly seen in Jesus. That day in the stadium when Gary washed my feet, he was reenacting an amazing biblical scene that illustrated Jesus' serving love for his disciples.

The Bible tells us that on the night before he was crucified, Jesus devised a way to demonstrate to his disciples "the full extent of his love" (John 13:1). At supper, Jesus "got up from the table, took off his robe, wrapped a towel around his waist, and poured water into a basin. Then he began to wash the disciples' feet and to wipe them with the towel he had around him" (John 13:4-5).

Now, you have to understand the customs in biblical times to grasp the significance of this picture. You had a dozen men who had been trudging the dusty roads all day in leather sandals. It was common courtesy for a host—more likely, the host's servants—to wash the feet of his guests. So Jesus wasn't acting out of sentimentality. He wasn't merely creating a symbol or coming up with what would be a touching Bible story. He was actually performing a customary act of service for his disciples. Consider what was happening when Jesus took off his robe, grabbed a towel, and washed his followers' feet:

First, Jesus met a genuine need through an act of servanthood. Jesus took the job that usually fell to the lowest servant in a household. Foot washing soothed and cleansed the guests' dirty, tired feet.

Second, at least one disciple felt uncomfortable being on the receiving end of Jesus' serving act. Peter pulled away when Jesus approached him to wash his feet. Why? It could have been Peter's pride or self-sufficiency. Perhaps it was his discomfort at the thought of Jesus' taking on a dirty task that Peter himself would not have dared to do. Or maybe Peter feared that if he accepted the Lord's serving ministry, he might have to do the same for someone else.

Third, Jesus demonstrated that even the greatest among us is called to be a servant of all. Jesus, the teacher who took a lowly servant's role, would soon elevate serving love to infinite heights by dying for the sins of humanity.

We dare not miss Jesus' words that tell us the value and importance of serving love:

> You call me "Teacher" and "Lord," and you are right, because it is true. And since I, the Lord and Teacher, have washed your feet, you ought to wash each other's feet. I have given you an example to follow. Do as I have done to you. How true it is that a servant is not greater than the master. Nor are messengers more important than the one who sends them. You know these things—now do them! That is the path of blessing. (John 13:13-17)

None of us is greater than our master, Jesus. None of us is above serving. None of us can shirk his example. Furthermore, none of us can afford to miss out on the blessing Jesus promised to those who minister to others through serving love. And couples who desire to build a lasting love must practice serving love.

Gary and I realize that serving love is countercultural. It's not human nature to be other-centered, to purposely take a lower place to honor another, to willingly get dirty so someone else can be clean. Wives, you may think that serving love puts you at the mercy of spouses who holler, "Where's my supper?" Who wants to be barked at and bossed around? Husbands, you may fear that serving love means signing up to be nagged and henpecked.

We need to be clear that servanthood doesn't mean the

bondage of slavery. As Jesus picked up the towel and served his disciples, he conclusively proved that God's kind of serving love flows from choice not coercion, from strength not weakness, from gladness not guilt. Serving love is positively liberating.

## THE MYTH OF THE 50/50 MARRIAGE

A common problem Gary and I see is couples who measure out their need-meeting service for each other in reciprocal portions. The best that many marriages ever do is operate according to the popular "50/50 plan," the I'll-meet-your-needs-if-you-meet-mine philosophy. In this plan, marriage becomes an issue of trade-offs and compromises, with spouses keeping score so one person never gets or gives more than the other. The goal is to meet each other halfway.

To be fair, some couples who live by this rule are generous to each other and even moderately happy. But apportioning love usually doesn't result in the spouses' feeling honored and understood. The problem, writes Dennis Rainey in his book *Staying Close,* is that "it is impossible to determine if your spouse has met you halfway. Because neither of you can agree on where 'halfway' is, each is left to scrutinize the other's performance from his or her own jaded perspective."[1]

Ben and Carrie both grew up watching their mothers get trampled by demanding husbands. So when Ben and Carrie married, they vowed that they would evenly divide all tasks and responsibilities between them. Household work would be split down the middle. They insisted that their 50/50 relationship would be 100 percent fair.

Instead of creating a fair and stable environment, Ben and Carrie have created a monster. They argue about who last washed the dishes—or did the laundry or cooked. Carrie's weekend with her college roommates is matched minute-for-minute and dollar-for-dollar by Ben's hunting trip with his buddies. They track their child-care duties as if they have a stopwatch ticking in their heads. When Ben comes home from work, Carrie knows she is off duty. They also keep track of the money they each earn, the running totals clearly distinguished in separate bank accounts. A friend of ours calls people like Ben and Carrie "ledger people."

Since the highest goal of Ben and Carrie's marriage is keeping everything even, their marriage is more about grabbing for self than giving to the other. Even in things as simple as pouring sodas to enjoy in front of the TV, they wait for the other to give in and serve first. By striving to be fair, Ben and Carrie cultivate a me-first attitude. And they miss out on the blessings Jesus promised to those who follow his example to serve one another selflessly.

In a 50/50 marriage, serving and submitting to one another is often replaced by a strong emphasis on getting what is rightfully yours. However, in this kind of marriage, a key person is missing—the person who desires to live right in the middle of a marriage, the one who makes the rules and mediates between your needs and your spouse's needs. That person is Jesus Christ, who provides not only the example but also the power of serving love through the Word of God and the Holy Spirit.

## THE JOY OF A 100/100 MARRIAGE

Let's face it: We all love to have our needs met. We all desire the understanding and honor that result when someone cares enough to serve us without expecting anything in return. That's why I felt so special the day Gary washed my feet and why I continue to feel that way because of his continual desire to love me with a serving love.

The problems come when we focus on being served—even in a 50/50 arrangement—instead of serving. A me-first attitude can lead to complaining, for example, that our spouses never spend time with us, even though we are constantly busy with the kids, volunteering at church, or spending time with our friends.

There's a better way. It's the 100/100 marriage, as illustrated by Robert and Nancy's story. Robert says, "Nancy and I dated for four years before finishing school, settling into our first jobs, and getting married. We were both professionals, driven to do well in our careers. We had it all, as they say, but we were restless in our relationship."

But this couple was not about to settle for second best in their marriage. Robert continues, "It took us a while to grasp the problem. As assertive as Nancy was in her work, I realized that in our marriage she hadn't been up-front with me about her needs. She was so eager to please me that when it came to any decision—like picking a restaurant or choosing where to spend a holiday or even where to live—she almost always responded with, 'Whatever you want, honey.' Or she parroted back what she knew I wanted. But Nancy was feeling trampled. I was frustrated because I truly wanted to honor her desires, but she wouldn't let me know what they were."

Nancy admits that when her unmet needs and desires started coming to the surface, they boiled over as anger. "For a couple of years I trampled on whatever Robert wanted," she says. "Everything had to go *my* way. He was the one saying, 'Whatever you want, honey.' I didn't like the imbalance in that way of doing marriage, and it certainly left Robert unsatisfied. When we stopped and looked at what was happening to our marriage, we admitted that we were not only dealing with a desire to control one another but also missing out on God's design for a husband and a wife. A friend encouraged us to study what the Bible had to say about the roles of husbands and wives in marriage. Over time we discovered that we were missing what God intended for us. As we studied the apostle Paul's words in

Ephesians 5, we learned that a husband's love for his wife is to be like Christ's love for the church, a sacrificial kind of love. Listen to what Paul said: 'Husbands, love your wives, just as Christ loved the church and gave himself up for her to make her holy' (Ephesians 5:25-26, NIV).

"When a husband 'gives himself up for his wife,' he chooses to serve her because of his desire to be obedient to God's design for him. He is stirred not only by pleasing her but also by pleasing God."

As Robert began to understand this biblical truth, he realized that by loving Nancy sacrificially, she would in turn respond to him with serving love. As they began to live this out, the issue of control diminished. Nancy began to trust Robert in a way she never would have imagined in the past. And as she trusted him, she realized that her ultimate trust was in the work God was doing in her life as well as in her husband's.

Nancy and Robert now say, "Our goal is to outdo the other. Our marriage is a 100 percent commitment to serving God and each other."

Deep inside each of us is a longing to understand and be understood, to honor and be honored. When a marriage lacks that kind of need-discovering, need-meeting love, feelings of disappointment give way to frustration and conflict. Perhaps you have experienced these bitter verbal clashes in your own marriage—the ones that spill out when your spouse says you don't meet his or her needs. Or instead of an open fight, you may have each launched into guerrilla warfare, quietly undermining each other or avoiding each other. A lack of serving love leaves needs unmet and keeps you far from the dream God has planned for you.

Serving love is the alternative. Gary will now share how serving love will make a good marriage into a great marriage, a marriage that will last forever.

# THE BENEFITS OF SERVING LOVE

Barb and I have a good marriage. In fact we have a *really* good marriage. There are times when we think we have the best marriage on the planet. We'll look each other in the eye and say, "What we have couldn't get any better." Then there are other times when we know we haven't arrived yet. But armed with our love for each other and the necessary tools, we keep working to make our marriage the best it can be. We want a *great* marriage, and that's our desire for you too.

We have already admitted our marriage isn't perfect. When I allowed my heart to be drawn away by my doctoral program, Barb was past disappointed. She was discouraged by my lack of attention. I was too busy to discover her needs and lovingly meet them. She didn't feel honored and understood because I was distracted in my career and schooling. The result was a distance and discord that we never expected and never want to experience again. And, of course, that was not the only time we have done things that headed us in the wrong direction.

We have both found that when we forget that our marriage is a marriage of three, with Jesus Christ in his rightful place, we act out of our natural selfishness. God's sanctification and his moving us toward maturity continually cause us to have to confront our own tendency to go our own way. We still have a lot of growing to do, but we know we are on the right path.

Does this sound painfully familiar? Is the sense of mutual honor and understanding infrequent in your marriage or missing altogether? Serving love, the love that selflessly gives to meet needs, is the answer. Here's why.

*Serving love allows you both to feel honored and understood.* If you want to feel understood, if you want to feel satisfied, if you want to feel honored, then build a marriage overflowing with serving love. If each of you is committed 100 percent to understanding and meeting the other's needs, then both of you will enjoy 100 percent honor and 100 percent understanding that result from that mutual commitment.

For Barb and me, our individual lives and our source of fulfillment originate in our relationship with Christ. He meets our deepest needs, and we each enjoy the overflow of God's blessing in our individual lives. I benefit from the overflow of Barb's relationship with Jesus on a daily basis, and Barb tells me that she enjoys the same benefit from my relationship with Christ. Through each other we have gained completeness that otherwise wouldn't be there. When you become what your spouse needs, you are God's instrument of serving love. You complete your spouse. In the world's eyes that's codependency; in God's eyes it is a true interdependence—a marriage of three: Jesus, husband, and wife. It is God's design. If you serve each other without meeting needs, your serving means little and leaves you both frustrated. But when you genuinely meet each other's needs out of the abundance of Christ's love in you, you become fulfilled persons.

Barb and I are not ashamed to admit that we have a deep desire in us to push our lives and influence for the Kingdom of God to the uttermost. But, next to serving Christ, our greatest desire is to be the best husband and wife that we can be. That means doing everything possible to discover and meet each other's deepest needs, thus lavishing each other with honor and understanding. And since we share the same goal, our dream is becoming a reality. Our marriage doesn't hold us back from our dreams; it has been the *reason* for our dreams.

*Serving love allows you to live out your vows to each other.* When you got married, you promised to love and cherish each other, to face good times and bad, hand in hand. Those wedding vows were all about meeting each other's needs. When you serve each other in love, you meet the needs of your spouse and fulfill your marriage vows.

When you focus on discovering and meeting your spouse's

needs, you are doing what God has called you to do in marriage. As a husband sets the pace by initiating serving love, he often finds that his wife becomes increasingly secure in responding to his serving heart. And when husband and wife do this mutually and wholeheartedly, the relationship is doubly strengthened. The results are a fulfilling, lasting marriage that only gets better with time.

Some of the New Testament's most powerful verses call us to sacrificial, serving love. Jesus said, "The greatest love is shown when people lay down their lives for their friends" (John 15:13). And the apostle Paul admonished, "Don't just pretend that you love others. Really love them. Hate what is wrong. Stand on the side of the good. Love each other with genuine affection, and take delight in honoring each other" (Romans 12:9-10).

God wants us to consider the needs of our spouses as more important than our own. When you meet your spouse's needs sacrificially, you are being "God with skin on," a phrase we use to describe the privilege we have of reflecting Christ's love to each other.

*Serving love protects your marriage from deterioration.* Failing to meet your spouse's deepest needs could ultimately cost you your marriage. How many times have you heard a divorced person lament, "He didn't meet my needs," or, "I needed more from her"? Perhaps the bottom-line reason for meeting your spouse's needs is that if you don't, you could lose him or her to someone—or something—who will meet those needs.

You would never think of ignoring your husband's or wife's need for food and water. He or she would die without these essentials. Yet your spouse's emotional, relational, and spiritual needs are just as vital. If they go unmet, your marriage will begin to die. It's that simple. When you generously minister serving love to your husband or wife, you guard your marriage against temptation and decay.

Tim and Grace enjoyed most of the trappings of material success. As a young, dual-income, childless couple, they devoted most of their time and attention to their careers—to the detriment of their marriage. But as Tim became more and more successful in his business, the person he longed to impress—Grace—seemed totally involved in her own world. Neither of them guarded the boundaries of their relationship, and Tim eventually found himself opening his heart to a coworker at the office. Kathy was always there, friendly, helpful, praising his accomplishments and listening sympathetically to his needs. Months later in my counseling office, Tim confessed to Grace that his heart was being drawn to another woman.

When asked how and why this happened, Tim said, "Grace was rarely there for me. She was so caught up in her own things that I got tired of trying to get her attention. Kathy seemed interested in what I did. She would ask me how my projects were going. She affirmed me a lot. She seemed to value who I am. Kathy encouraged me when I was struggling."

Grace sat there stunned at first, pain etched on her face. Then the questions came fast and furiously. "Tim, did it get physical? Did she kiss you? Did you touch her?"

"Grace, nothing physical ever happened," Tim assured. "We just talked. Remember how we used to do that? I just needed affirmation from someone. I am sorry I have hurt you this way. I let down my guard and let her in. I know it wasn't right. And I want you, not Kathy. But I really need you to support me, to encourage me, and to let me know that you think I'm a good guy."

Both Tim and Grace heeded this clear wake-up call and made it safely through the depths of betrayal and pain.

Your situation as husband and wife is probably different from that of Tim and Grace, and we hope you haven't experienced the pain they did. Yet your spouse has needs, and you are wise if you seek to discover those needs and meet them. As you do, you will be exercising serving love and taking a major step toward protecting your marriage.

## A DECISION TO HONOR YOUR SPOUSE

How important is serving love in our relationships, including our marriages? The Bible calls us to the same serving love Jesus has shown for others:

> Is there any encouragement from belonging to Christ? Any comfort from his love? Any fellowship together in the Spirit? Are your hearts tender and sympathetic? Then make me truly happy by agreeing wholeheartedly with each other, loving one another, and working together with one heart and purpose.
>
> Don't be selfish; don't live to make a good impression on others. Be humble, thinking of others as better than yourself. Don't think only about your own affairs, but be interested in others, too, and what they are doing.
>
> Your attitude should be the same that Christ Jesus had. Though he was God, he did not demand and cling to his rights as God. He made himself nothing; he took the humble position of a slave and appeared in human form. (Philippians 2:1-7)

After reading these verses, you may feel that you could never manage the level of serving love Jesus demonstrated. If so, you're right! Serving love starts with the strength of Jesus— in the encouragement, comfort, and fellowship of a personal relationship with him. And if you are growing in these qualities, you are beginning to imitate his servant heart.

Do you want a marriage that lasts? Do you want a relationship characterized by intimate understanding and mutual honor? When you meet the needs of your spouse, you build the foundation for a lasting love. And without serving love, you won't experience honor or understanding.

How can it happen in your relationship? It all begins with honoring your spouse. Barb will kick off this section.

# IDEAS FOR HONORING YOUR SPOUSE

One of the most valuable gifts Gary gives to me is honor. If you were to eavesdrop on our conversation most mornings, you would hear him affirm who I am and what I do. He generously voices his appreciation for me with an attitude of honor. Once he gets focused for work, he doesn't say as much. The work mode has a way of changing the whole focus of a man. Then hours later we can be seated in a team meeting, and Gary will begin talking about his "wonderful wife" and something she said that was strong, wise, and relevant. Sometimes when he does this, he catches me so off guard that I lean forward at the board-room table thinking, *I wish I could meet this woman.* Gary makes me sound far better than I am, and I'm honored by it.

Your spouse is your best teacher in how to meet his or her needs. In the next chapter we will talk about how you as a couple can begin to discover and communicate those needs. The goal of this section is to help you lift up and honor your spouse. We suggest that you select two or three things to do or new habits you want to put into action in your relationship. Don't announce them. Don't make a big deal about your intention of honoring your spouse. Just quietly start doing it.

## For Husbands Only

It's easy for men to get caught up in work and providing for the family. Sure, they appreciate all their wives do, but sometimes they forget to communicate appreciation in a way that conveys honor. Men often assume that their wives already know how they feel. All we women really want is to see those feelings demonstrated.

A lot of women talk to me about how they wish their husbands would treat them. So, men, let me share with you what I hear. Gary will share a similar list of suggestions with wives in the next section.

1. Ask her how you can help her, or dive in and help without being asked. It sounds like this: "Where do you need more of my help?" In a word: initiate!

2. When you disagree, immediately acknowledge her position. You don't have to understand or agree. Just acknowledge that she has the right to her thoughts and feelings. It may sound like this: "I respect the fact that you feel strongly about this issue, and I always want to listen to your feedback. I need you to listen to my perspective as well."

3. Never humiliate her. If she does something embarrassing in front of others, don't make it worse. Regardless of the details or even if she's at fault, don't criticize her.

4. Share with others how important she is to you. Keep pictures of her in your wallet and on your desk. Talk about her to your friends and coworkers. Let her overhear you bragging about her—it does wonders for the relationship!

5. Support her in front of the children. Whether or not you agree with a decision she makes, back her up, then discuss your differences later in private. Tell the kids how much you love their mom and how much you appreciate all her gifts.

6. Never remind her of her mistakes, especially in front of others. Learn to forgive and work through concerns privately with her. This builds confidence in the marriage.

7. Remember special dates! Obviously, her birthday and your anniversary are key. But you should also commemorate dates such as the anniversary of the death of a parent or

another loved one. Send her a note, and comfort her on those days.

8. Never compare her to other women. This includes your mother, previous girlfriends, women friends, or coworkers. Don't even compare her to other women in a positive way.

9. Eat together. Don't start eating the meal until she sits down, and don't leave the table until she's finished. And don't leave her to eat in front of the TV!

10. Talk over decisions with her *before* they are made—even the minor ones.

11. Set family goals so your wife doesn't feel as if she is bearing the whole load. Be specific about what each family member must do to get the work done.

12. Share with her what you're reading. Tell her what you're learning from the book. Discuss current events together.

13. Ask her about her childhood. Work to understand her heritage and why she is the way she is. (Just steer clear of mother-in-law jokes!)

14. Compliment her cooking. Make special requests!

## For Wives Only

Just as Barb can speak with authority on how a wife likes to be honored by her husband, I think I can share several helpful tips about how men would like to be treated. I know it's easy for you to get caught up in the busyness of everyday life, whether it's working outside or inside the home, keeping up with household responsibilities, caring for children, or spending time with your family and friends. You see your husband as your partner in getting things done, but he is also your partner in marriage. It's important to keep your husband's wants and needs in front of you. How can you honor him and communicate that you really appreciate him?

Here are some simple acts of serving love that will make a huge difference:

1. Make time alone with him a priority. In this busy world, other things become more important than husband-and-wife time. Learn to say no to other activities in order to love, honor, and cherish your husband above all else.

2. Honor his favorite things. Make a list of his favorites (favorite dinner, dessert, date activity, TV program, etc.), and make sure he gets to enjoy those things occasionally.

3. Celebrate his birthday. Make his birthday a big deal even if he says he doesn't want you to.

4. Say please and thank you.

5. Tell him what you need. He can't read your mind—at least not always!

6. Lift a burden. Ask him, "If I could take something off your to-do list today, what could I do for you?"

7. Allow him to be himself. Don't assume that your husband is going to think, feel, or behave as you do or as "the ideal husband" does. He will make mistakes. Allow him that freedom.

8. Affirm your husband's maleness by showing interest in his hobbies. Attend a sporting event or watch a ball game with him occasionally. If he participates in sports, be there to cheer him on.

9. Be more curious than critical of your husband. What interesting things does he do? Don't judge him. Investigate and ask questions about why he does the things he does.

10. Appreciate his hard work. Thank him for working hard for you and your family. Let him know that you notice and admire his work.

11. Praise him to your children. Tell the kids how hard he

works and what a good man he is. Tell them how much you love him and how important he is to you.

12. Compliment his efforts to be sensitive. If he makes special attempts to understand, listen, or comfort you, let him know how meaningful they are to you. Be specific about what you particularly like.

The suggestions we have offered in this chapter will help you demonstrate serving love in a general way. Even though your spouse shares many similarities with others of the same gender, he or she is also unique. Your spouse has a number of specific needs, and your efforts to discover those needs and lovingly meet them is an even higher expression of serving love than the ideas just presented. In the next chapter, we will equip you to identify and communicate your deepest needs so that mutual understanding and honor will grow even deeper.

# 6

## Communicating Your Needs

When Robertson McQuilkin's wife of forty years was diagnosed with Alzheimer's disease, he was president of Columbia Bible College and Seminary (now Columbia International University) in Columbia, South Carolina. Because he was committed to care for his wife full-time, he resigned his prestigious position. At that moment his world of widespread Christian leadership and global ministry shrank to a life of meeting Muriel's every need, including feeding her, bathing her, grooming her, and taking her to the bathroom.

A friend wrote to Dr. McQuilkin and suggested that he place Muriel in a care facility. "Muriel doesn't know you anymore," the man said, "doesn't know anything, really, so it's time to put her in a nursing home and get on with life."

But Muriel needed him, McQuilkin protested, and he needed her. "Do you realize," he wrote to his friend, "how lonely I would be without her?"

When McQuilkin left his job to care for Muriel, he was living out a choice he had made four decades earlier. In his book *A Promise Kept,* Dr. McQuilkin writes, "The decision was made, in a way, 42 years ago when I promised to care for Muriel 'in sickness and in health . . . till death do us part.' . . . I love Muriel. She is a delight to me—her childlike dependence and confidence in me. . . . I don't *have* to care for her. I *get* to! It is a high honor to care for so wonderful a person."[1] McQuilkin regards meeting Muriel's needs as just a small return on the care she gave him for more than forty years.

Muriel died in 2003, but for twenty-five years after the onset of Muriel's illness, Robertson McQuilkin entered into her world to understand and meet her most basic needs. He saw himself not as a co-victim of Alzheimer's but as the recipient of Muriel's love. "In her silent world Muriel is so content, so lovable, I sometimes pray, 'Please, Lord, could you let me keep her a little longer?' If Jesus took her home, how I would miss her gentle, sweet presence. Oh yes, there are times I get irritated, but not often. It doesn't make sense. And besides, I love to care for her. She's my precious."[2]

One of the most poignant insights from McQuilkin's story is how he continued to grow in understanding Muriel's needs even though she was unable to communicate with him. She lost both her ability to speak and her ability to communicate altogether when first one hand, then the other went limp. "That right hand was the last way she had to communicate," McQuilkin writes. "She would reach out to hold hands, pat me on the back when I hugged her, push me away when she didn't like what I was doing. I missed her hand."[3] Even after those losses, without a word or gesture from Muriel, Robertson McQuilkin keenly discerned and met his wife's every need on a daily basis.

The ministry of serving love involves discovering and meeting needs. Being *committed* to serving love is one thing; *knowing how to discover and meet those needs* is quite another thing. Robertson McQuilkin is a shining example of both deep commitment to serving love and dogged persistence in meeting his wife's needs, even though she could not communicate in normal ways.

# COMMUNICATION: KEY TO DISCOVERING AND MEETING NEEDS

Barb and I believe that communication is indispensable to the ministry of serving love in marriage. Let's face it: None of us is a mind reader. If Barb doesn't communicate her needs to me, my chances of meeting those needs are mighty slim. And if I don't communicate my needs to her, she's flying blind when it comes to serving me. In a marriage relationship, discovering and meeting needs in an atmosphere of serving love presupposes that husband and wife are willing to talk. It is in the process of communication that needs are shared or discovered.

When I was growing up, I witnessed firsthand a couple's commitment to enter each other's world and to discover and meet each other's needs through serving love. Those people were my parents. Every evening when we kids heard Dad drive into the garage after work, we yelled, "Dad's home!" We rushed to meet him at the back door, and he greeted us by ruffling our hair or hugging us. But then, for the next sixty minutes, the four Rosberg kids disappeared (most of the time) while Dad and Mom sat and talked. Sixty minutes!

Barb and I have carried that tradition into our own home. Within minutes of greeting each other at the end of the day, we are sitting in two overstuffed chairs and talking—just the two of us. We talk about the kids, we review Barb's day and mine, we celebrate each other's highs, and we mourn each other's lows. We talk about everything! Sometimes our discussions are deep and serious; other times they are just newsy, connecting chats.

During this time, as we listen intently to each other's heart, we notice what brings joy or tears. And we discern needs. Most significantly, we walk away from our chat with a better idea of the struggles we face individually and as a couple. We know better how we can meet each other's needs in the midst of our trials. In our talking, we discover exactly where to apply serving love. Barb learns how to help me; I learn how to help her.

Barb and I hate to imagine what would happen if we didn't have this daily connecting time. Actually, we don't have to imagine it, because we encounter the grim results in our ministry all the time. Nearly every day during our call-in radio broadcast, a love-starved husband or wife laments to us the pain of a marriage lacking in communication. When couples do not share their lives and hearts with each other consistently, the atmosphere in the home can get colder than an arctic winter. Without communication, we fall out of sync and disconnect, leaving plenty of room for chilly distance and selfishness to grow.

Communication is the process of sharing yourself verbally and nonverbally in ways that your spouse both understands and accepts—though not necessarily agrees with—what you are sharing. Studies show that couples who communicate frequently have a more satisfying relationship. And couples who achieve deep levels of communication enjoy the most satisfaction of all.

So what does deep communication look like? Here are five levels of communication, each one deeper and more enriching than the previous one:[4]

1. *Sharing general information.* We speak largely in clichés: "How are you today?" or "I'm fine, how are you?" or "Lovely weather we're having" or "How about that team of ours!"

2. *Sharing facts.* We discuss people and events, but nothing personal: "What did you do today?" or "I took Susie to the dentist and Brett to soccer practice" or "I had lunch with the sales manager" or "There was a terrible wreck on the expressway."

3. *Sharing opinions and beliefs.* We share personal information, but nothing too risky: "Brett is turning into a very good soccer player" or "I think the coach is a jerk!" or "I really want that job in the sales department" or "Wrecks like that wouldn't happen if the speed limit were lower."

*4. Sharing feelings and emotions.* We begin to open our hearts: "I'm worried that Susie is going to need braces" or "If they promote Frank over me, I'm going to quit!" or "I'm so glad it wasn't you who was hurt in the accident. I would feel so sad."

*5. Sharing needs, intimate concerns, hopes, and fears.* We vulnerably share our heart of hearts: "If you lose your job, what are we going to do? We have bills to pay" or "If I can't make it in sales, I'm washed up, finished!" or "I love you and need you. I don't know what I would do without you."

Can you guess what kinds of communication promote serving love? Of course, those further down the list: sharing opinions and beliefs, sharing feelings and emotions, and especially sharing needs, intimate concerns, hopes, and fears. The more we share our hearts with one another, the better prepared we will be to discern and meet each other's deepest needs.

## GOING DEEP: GETTING INSIDE YOUR SPOUSE'S HEART

When we urge you to communicate your needs to one another as husbands and wives, we know we are pressing you to go deep, to unveil the deepest parts of your souls. But it is the only way to gain this crucial insight: "By wisdom a house is built, and through understanding it is established" (Proverbs 24:3, NIV). If you want to build a lasting love, you must understand each other. And to understand each other, you must share your hearts with each other.

Hardly a husband and wife on earth would say they have no need for further growth in deep communication. If Barb and I walked into your church on Sunday morning and asked all the married people to raise a hand if they needed to work on communication, we would expect to see a room full of flailing arms. Some people would have both hands raised. Some wives would be raising their husbands' hands—and vice versa! Everyone has room for improvement in the area of communication.

Understanding and meeting your spouse's needs through communication is kind of like exploring a cave. We don't mean a little hole in the side of a hill like the one you may have played in as a kid. We're talking about a *real* cave—one with a vast labyrinth of underground caverns someone could spend a lifetime exploring.

When you were first married and just learning about each other, you felt your way through the dark, unexplored cave of your relationship hand in hand. In the dim light, you could make out features common in many caves—the stalactites and stalagmites of the human soul, the kind of stuff you already knew about some of your best friends.

The deeper you go into a cave, the more you are surprised and awed by what you find: rushing underground rivers, rare rock formations that glisten like buttered popcorn, precious gems and minerals you never expected. You may squeeze through a small crack in the rock wall to find a cavern as breathtakingly beautiful as any cathedral. At times you may stumble on a pile of rock debris you must clear away before you can go any farther. But every step, every turn in the labyrinth, every new day of exploration yields surprises and challenges too good to miss.

Similarly, the further you venture into your marriage relationship together, the more you will appreciate its uniqueness. The more you explore the heart of your spouse through honest, vulnerable sharing, the more fulfilling your marital journey becomes. Your discoveries will take your breath away—sometimes in fear, sometimes in excitement. Surprises await around every corner. You will discover new wonders daily—if you dare to enter in and keep exploring.

# OVERCOMING OBSTACLES TO DEEP SHARING AND MEETING NEEDS

Barb and I want to coach you in the skill of exploring your hearts and communicating your needs. Unfortunately, it won't be easy. Remember: We're comparing this journey to the rigors and dangers of cave exploration, not a ride on a merry-go-round. Communication isn't automatic, but it is a skill every couple can learn. Communication is a cornerstone of serving love.

The first step to communicating needs is getting rid of those inner barriers that keep us from talking about our needs. Some of these obstacles are rooted in our attitudes about serving and being served, our reluctance to reveal our neediness, and past hurts that block us from sharing. Are any of the following obstacles keeping you and your spouse from sharing your deep heart and meeting each other's needs?

*"My spouse doesn't care about my needs."* We have heard countless husbands say something such as, "She devotes all her time and attention to the kids. Don't get me wrong, I love my kids. But what about me?" This isn't the poor-me tune of a self-centered whiner. Wives, you need to know this is the heart cry of men who feel neglected and in need of their wives' attention.

We have also heard wives complain, "I feel as if I am last on my husband's list. All I want is a night away from the kids occasionally, a time when we talk about something other than bills." Husbands, these are women who want to connect with their husbands. Our experience has shown that when you step out and take care of your spouses' needs, your own needs will be met as well.

*"After what my spouse did, I'm not interested in meeting his [or her] needs."* This spouse is saying, "You hurt me, so I'm not sure I want to open my heart to you again." This is deep stuff that must be worked through with forgiving love. Have you ignored your

mate's needs in the past? How have you hurt your spouse? Start by going through the process of closing the loop on your own offenses. As you do, you will find opportunities to communicate ways your spouse has let *you* down.

"If I admit I have needs, I'll feel as if I'm begging." We know wives who are reluctant to ask their husbands to take a walk with them just to talk. We know of husbands who rein in their sexual urges, thinking that they are asking too much of their wives. We also know that God has put your spouse in your life to meet your legitimate needs, whatever they are. If your spouse has somehow caused you to feel that your needs are unimportant, make that a point to talk about. But start with "I feel like . . ." rather than "You never . . ."

*"If I share my needs, I'll be mocked for being weak."* This spouse is saying, "I'm not supposed to have needs." That's a myth, a lie. Yet many husbands fail to share their needs with their wives because they see it as a sign of weakness on par with reading the instructions, stopping for directions, or admitting they need help in any form. And many women don't share their needs because, after all, who wants to be known as a clinging, needy wife? Both of these attitudes ignore the truth that God has created us with needs.

*"If I give an inch, my spouse will take a mile."* One husband remarked, "When you talk about serving love, all I can hear is the sucking sound as my wife drains all my energy!" The goal of serving love is not to enable controlling or demanding behavior in your spouse. Rather, you are striving to be God with skin on, serving your spouse selflessly as Christ has served us. In our experience, when one spouse begins to consciously apply God-powered serving love, it is usually reciprocated.

But it rarely starts with a cognitive decision to serve each other. It typically comes through pain. It may be loss or fear of loss, but it likely is rooted in a family's response to difficulty and pain. We have repeatedly found that as God works through the brokenness of our lives, serving love becomes increasingly apparent. And invariably it starts with the brokenness of the husband. When a husband and dad reaches the end of himself and trusts God deeply, he sets a pace for the entire family. When a husband and father is sold out to Christ, his wife and children will feel the security and protection of his servant leadership.

*"Why bother? My spouse won't notice if I do something nice."* It will be difficult for your spouse to ignore your efforts to discover and meet his or her genuine needs. It will be even harder for your spouse to resist being asked about personal needs. If you think your spouse is reluctant to be served, assert your desire to love him or her with a servant love. Show kindness the way your spouse wants it shown, not how you think it should be shown.

Some of you may be saying, "Every one of these obstacles exists in our marriage." These misunderstandings, conflicts, and hurts must be addressed by closing the loop through forgiving love. Barb and I encourage you to make that a priority. As you do, you will be clearing the path for the rich and exciting experience of deeper heart exploration.

For most couples, serving love is lacking simply because of inattention. Or perhaps the two of you have fallen into a pattern of petty selfishness: "I won't meet your need until you meet mine first." Someone needs to take the initiative and start serving, regardless of the obstacles. Even better, why don't you both agree to serve the other in spite of your fears and reservations.

Serving is the fastest way to break into new behaviors. We are asking you to put your selfish attitudes aside and serve your imperfect spouse. Ask God to open your heart so you can serve freely with the attitude of Jesus.

## DISCOVERING EACH OTHER'S NEEDS

In order to serve each other meaningfully, you must have an idea of what the other needs. One of the most fruitless and potentially damaging assumptions Barb and I have heard relates to needs. It goes something like this: "If I treat my spouse the way I would like him or her to treat me, I will be meeting his or her needs." This statement is rarely true. When it comes to needs, the Golden Rule *does not* always apply.

Why? Because a man's needs often differ from a woman's needs. Take intimacy, for example. Typically, a woman's need for intimacy is met with deep, intimate conversations. Because these chats fulfill a woman's needs, she assumes they meet her husband's needs as well. However, a man's need for intimacy is often met through sexual intercourse. But his need is often greater than his wife's. If he thinks having sex with her several times a week fully meets her needs simply because it meets his needs, he is mistaken. A couple practicing serving love will ensure that each partner's unique needs are being met.

Your spouse is your best coach and resource in helping you meet his or her needs. That's where communicating about your needs comes in. But what do you communicate *about?* We may be able to coach you and give you something concrete to talk about as you explore each other's love needs.

Barb and I surveyed more than seven hundred couples (fourteen hundred people) to discover the top needs for men and women. We presented each person with a list of twenty basic love needs. Then we asked people to rank in order of importance (1) what they needed most from their spouses, and (2) what they thought their spouses needed from them.

Before reading our findings, you may want to complete this exercise yourself. Turn to appendix B and read through the list of needs. Then rank your top five needs.

The chart below summarizes the results of our extensive survey. Here is how the husbands and wives ranked their needs.

| Husbands' Top Five Love Needs | Wives' Top Five Love Needs |
|---|---|
| 1. Unconditional Love and Acceptance | 1. Unconditional Love and Acceptance |
| 2. Sexual Intimacy | 2. Emotional Intimacy and Communication |
| 3. Companionship | 3. Spiritual Intimacy |
| 4. Encouragement and Affirmation | 4. Encouragement and Affirmation |
| 5. Spiritual Intimacy | 5. Companionship |

Because each of these is so important, we have devoted an entire book, *The Five Love Needs of Men and Women,* to discussing what the needs look like in husbands and wives and how these needs can be met. Here we include only a brief snapshot of each.

## Husbands' Needs

Most husbands' top five needs included the following:

*1. Unconditional love and acceptance.* This reflects the deep desire to be accepted and loved just the way we are, no matter what.

*2. Sexual intimacy.* Much of a man's masculinity is rooted in his sexuality, a part of his maleness he cannot erase. As most couples discover, men spell intimacy S-E-X.

*3. Companionship.* Husbands need a place to let down and be themselves, a place where they do not have to perform. This is a need for friendship.

*4. Encouragement and affirmation.* Husbands need to hear two primary voices cheering them on: their wives' and God's. The more encouragement and affirmation husbands receive from their wives, the easier it will be for them to discern God's voice.

*5. Spiritual intimacy.* Husbands need a spiritual connection—with God, with their wife, and with other believers. Wise wives will help their husbands discover pathways to spiritual growth.

## Wives' Needs

Most wives' top five needs included the following:

*1. Unconditional love and acceptance.* In a world where women often compare themselves to one another and come up short, wives need husbands who are totally accepting.

*2. Emotional intimacy and communication.* Wives spell intimacy T-A-L-K. For many women, conversation is the primary way they process thoughts, feelings, ideas, and problems.

*3. Spiritual intimacy.* Wives find no greater comfort or security than in knowing that their husbands walk closely with God and support the family's spiritual growth. They need their husbands to pray for them and with them.

*4. Encouragement and affirmation.* Wives need daily doses of support. When they have a problem, they value their husbands' comfort and understanding more than any advice on how to fix the problem.

*5. Companionship.* Wives need a place to let down, where they don't feel as if they are valued only for what they do, and to be themselves. This is the need for friendship.

How do the top love needs from our survey compare with your own list? In what ways are they similar or dissimilar? Does the ranking of needs in our survey surprise you? You now have something to talk about, something that will start you down the path to understanding and meeting your spouse's top needs. "Talk about needs?" you may object. "Hey, Gary and Barb, we don't have enough time to talk about family finances, the kids' education, and what's for dinner tonight, let alone our top love needs."

We hear you. And if it's any consolation, most couples are in the same boat. One of the biggest enemies to discovering needs is time: time to reflect, time to talk, time to pray together. Yet you are wise to spend your most precious resource—your time—on your most precious possession—your marriage. You can have all the communication skills down pat, but if you don't schedule time to exercise them, what good can be accomplished? To help create the atmosphere in which you can discuss and meet each others' needs, we have written *40 Unforgettable Dates with Your Mate,* a book that gives date ideas—twenty for husbands and twenty for wives—that will help you meet your spouse's top five needs. The book also includes dozens of reflection and discussion questions that will help you discover and understand each other's needs.

Your marriage is a living organism. It thrives with attention. So take some time over the next few days to discuss your top love needs with your spouse. Take the initiative; don't wait for your spouse to do it. Here is a suggestion for working through this discussion. If necessary, consult the list of twenty needs presented in appendix B.

1. Make a list of what you think are your spouse's top five needs.
2. At the same time make a list of your own top five needs.
3. Sit down with your spouse, and say something like, "I want to learn what your needs are so I can meet them more fully. I have made a list of what I think are your top five needs, and I want to discuss the list with you. But even more important to me is what *you* think are your top needs. I am committed to honoring you by meeting your needs." Then begin to discuss your spouse's needs.
4. If your spouse asks you what your love needs are, you will have your list ready.
5. Read the two books we described above to help you grow in your awareness of and ability to meet your spouse's needs.

This is only the beginning. Our hope is that you are motivated to continue the process of healthy, ongoing communication about your needs, desires, and dreams. Barb and I want to help you with this. Let us coach you on a few key skills for good communication.

## CONNECTING THROUGH GOOD COMMUNICATION

What do you think of when we say *communication?* Talking, to be sure. But just because someone's mouth is moving doesn't mean communication is taking place. Communication is sharing yourself verbally and nonverbally in a way that your spouse both accepts and understands. If the message is spoken but not understood, it's not clear communication.

In addition to talking—or what we call *expressing*—there are two other vital elements to communication: *listening* and *responding.* When we communicate, we have a responsibility not merely to unload what is on our minds but also to ensure that our message is understood. Expressing, listening, and responding are all part of the communication process. We want to explain these three components and coach you on how you can use them to improve your communication as husband and wife.

### Expressing

As the youngest child in a family of five verbally aggressive siblings, Marita got the feeling that nobody really cared what she thought. By adulthood she had developed the habit of waiting to be asked before expressing her opinion. To her husband, Rich, it was like playing a frustrating game of twenty questions. Marita rarely expressed her thoughts and feelings voluntarily. And if Rich didn't ask the right question, he was seldom rewarded with the information he sought. Rich longed to explore his wife's heart, but it was locked, and he couldn't find the key.

Some of us express ourselves naturally and easily. But for others, expression is a skill to be learned. If you want to communicate clearly, you must begin with deliberate expression. When you have something to share with your spouse, sort what you want to say into three categories—what you *think,* what you *feel,* and what you *need.* Then start talking. Give details. Don't be put off if your spouse asks you clarifying questions. And don't expect the other person to read your mind or fill in blanks.

Expressing openly and in detail doesn't mean expressing carelessly. Your words can be dangerous: "The tongue can kill or nourish life" (Proverbs 18:21). Be careful about what you say.

Try these three rules for effective expressing.

*1. Take one issue at a time.* A full day's worth of news and experiences and troubles can be overwhelming. Pouring everything out at once seldom gives your spouse much information about anything. It's one way we tend to skim over our issues and never get to the core of them.

You can help your spouse stay on track with a few helpful phrases: "Tell me more about . . ." or "What were you saying about . . . ?" or "That sounds like another issue. Let's talk about the other one first and come back to this one later." If your spouse needs reassurance that the issue won't be brushed aside, write it down in front of him or her.

*2. Allow one person to speak at a time.* When you are communicating with your spouse, keep him or her in the spotlight. When your spouse is expressing, give him or her room for full expression—no interruptions, no feedback. If you both fight to be heard at the same time, communication is bound to break down.

*3. Be specific and to the point.* Barb and I communicate kind of like we trim a Christmas tree. Our styles are reflective of basic male-female differences. I like to start at the top. The most important thing—the star—goes up first, then I work my way down from there. When Barb trims the tree, she takes out each ornament, rotates it slowly in her hand, and recites the ornament's history to anyone within earshot. Eventually all the ornaments make it on the tree.

Similarly, when I express, I start at the top—the main point—and go from there. To Barb, this approach sometimes feels rushed and even a little rough. She would rather talk around the topic and eventually arrive at the main point. To me, that's like filling in the background before you draw attention to what you really want to say.

Wives, you will likely be more successful at expressing if you accommodate your husbands' need to hear the bottom line up front. And husbands, you will make communication more enjoyable for your wives if you include plenty of detail with your main point.

### Listening

If you are like most couples, the biggest single step you can take to improve communication in your marriage is to improve listening in your marriage. My dad always said that we have two ears and one mouth for a reason. Even though he didn't become a Christian until late in life, he had a good handle on James 1:19: "My dear brothers and sisters, be quick to listen, slow to speak, and slow to get angry." Dad knew that one of the secrets to great communication was to listen attentively.

When Natalie didn't have Jerry's attention during their conversations, she was tempted to use the technique her three-year-old daughter used when her daddy wasn't listening—except Natalie knew it was a childish way to express herself. Whenever Tabitha noticed that her daddy wasn't totally focused on her, she grabbed his chin and put her face nose-to-nose with his.

So as Natalie worked at communicating her needs to Jerry, one of the first things she said was, "Sometimes I feel as if I don't have your attention when we talk." But instead of citing the hard evidence of his frequent attention lapses, she shared a personal confession. "When you are excited to tell me something, I know I have a habit of cutting you off. When I am focused on doing something, I don't exactly encourage you to talk."

Then Natalie asked Jerry what *he* thought got in the way of their communication. At first he hesitated. Then he said sheepishly, "We talk a lot less since I bought a TV for the bedroom." Natalie nodded in agreement.

By the time Natalie and Jerry finished talking, they had closed the loop on this issue—and reinvigorated their listening habits.

If you want your spouse to freely share his or her heart with you, you must convey with absolute certainty that he or she has your undivided attention. Listening attentively isn't easy. Maintaining eye contact may be unnerving to you. Jumping in with a solution may be hard to resist. But listening is the key to understanding your spouse's needs.

## Responding

At some point in a discussion, it is appropriate to move beyond listening to join the conversation. The point is not to introduce your own agenda but to clarify and fully understand what your spouse is expressing. This communication skill is called responding. We can get into trouble at this point if we fail to look out for our spouses' best interest: "What a shame, what folly, to give advice before listening to the facts!" (Proverbs 18:13).

Typically, men and women have different ways of responding. Men tend either to try to fix the situation, get defensive, get angry, or withdraw. Even though they are listening to their wives state the problem, husbands are often already working on a solution: something to fix, a wrong to right, an error to correct.

Women tend to seek security, reassurance, a sympathetic ear, and validation in response from their husbands. Wives don't always want a solution right off the bat. First they need empathy and understanding. Once a wife feels emotionally connected to her patiently listening husband, she may be ready for suggestions on what to do.

Once again Monique awaited Jim's arrival from work with dread. For the third time this year she had crunched their late-model SUV. She knew the consequences well: a traffic fine (it was her fault—again), another insurance deductible to pay, an increase in their already sky-high rates. And this time her traffic citation came with an embarrassing bonus: a requirement to attend what the police officer at the scene referred to as "driving school for dummies." Jim's recounting of all these facts only made Monique feel more inept.

Husbands, if you were Jim, how would you respond? You know the practical implications of damaging a vehicle. You have likely dented a car or two in your time. But that probably isn't what you want to say to Monique. If you're like many men, you want to rehearse the details and lovingly but firmly make sure it doesn't happen again.

But right now Monique isn't looking for a lecture. She needs a response that makes her feel as if you understand her reaction to the accident. Try these: "Are you okay?" or "Was the other driver hurt?" or "Were you okay driving home?" or "Did the officer make you feel stupid?" or "Did the other driver yell at you?"

When your spouse has laid bare his or her soul, a wise response has three elements. Just remember the acrostic A-S-K:

**A**sk—"What do you need most from me right now?" or "How can I help you?"

**S**uggest—Offer to assist by saying, "Would it help if I . . . ?"

**K**neel—Assume an inner posture of servanthood. Reassure your spouse that you will do whatever he or she needs you to do.

Maybe your spouse already knows exactly what he or she needs in a situation. But how much better to ask proactively, "What can I do to help you?" These are the caring words of serving love.

As we have shared with you about communication skills, maybe you can't imagine expressing your deepest needs to your spouse. Or you may wonder if you're ready to hear what your spouse needs from you. What makes deep sharing possible? Barb has an important insight on this topic.

## HOW CAN WE COMMUNICATE SO DEEPLY?

Earlier in the chapter, Gary explained from our national survey that both men and women identified unconditional love and acceptance as their number one need from their marriage partner. Unconditional acceptance simply means loving and receiving your spouse no matter what. It's a commitment that says, "I will always stay with you. I will always love you. I will always affirm you and support you." Robertson McQuilkin is one of our heroes, a shining example of someone who shows unconditional love.

Now let's be real: Admitting our needs to our spouses isn't very flattering. It's rather humbling. I would prefer to have it all together, to need nothing from Gary or anyone. I want to be an omnicompetent wife, the total Proverbs 31 woman. But God in his wisdom didn't wire me that way. Instead, he designed Gary to love and accept me unconditionally despite my obvious (and not so obvious) needs, weaknesses, and failures. And God designed me to accept my dear but needy and imperfect husband the same way.

This is the beauty of unconditional love and acceptance. I am able to be honest about my needs with Gary because I know he won't pounce on me—put me down with either condemnation or an immediate solution. He will love me, affirm me, and support me because we are committed to each other unconditionally.

Communication of needs flows freely in an atmosphere of complete acceptance. Therefore, it is imperative that husbands and wives continually grow in meeting this critical top need in each other. We need to extend open arms to our spouses, assuring them, "You can tell me anything. You are safe with me."

Let me share something special with you wives. Your husbands may be like many men in our culture today, a culture that is far more concerned about image than authenticity. Men are more reticent to admit their weaknesses and pain. Remember: They grew up with the sad and inaccurate mantra, "Big boys don't cry." Even the smallest hurt in your husbands' past may have prompted them to cover up with a mask. Like Phantom in the popular production *Phantom of the Opera,* they may still wear a portion of that mask to cover old inner wounds that have never fully healed. They may be trying to cover a fear common to many men—the fear of failing you.

One way your unconditional love and acceptance can minister to your husbands is by helping them take off the mask. God has generously gifted you with the ability to be gentle and loving. Demonstrate these qualities by being transparent about your own weaknesses to show your husbands that they no longer need to hide behind an image of strength or perfection. If your husbands act as if nothing bad ever happened to them, they are hiding behind a mask of false bravado. Your own transparency and your acceptance will help free them to trust you with their pain and needs also.

Husbands, let me share a final word with you. Most guys are quick to rush in with answers to their wives' problems. It might be easy for you to love them in practical ways: unstopping a plugged toilet, mowing the lawn, always being the one to top off the gas tank in the family van. But the real servants serve not only where it is *easy* but also where it is *needed*. If you desire to have servant hearts, give yourselves humbly to your wives. Ask them what they need. Listen to them. Study your wives with the intense purpose of a servant who is eager to please.

Husbands and wives, you are launching into the exciting adventure of discovering and meeting your spouses' needs. You are practicing one of the secrets to building a lasting love.

If you need more help to discover and meet your spouses' love needs, read *The Five Love Needs of Men and Women* and use the *Serving Love* workbook to expand your understanding and application of this topic.

# Persevering Love

*Persevering love stays strong in tough times*
*and helps spouses feel bonded—best friends for life*

# 7

## Love That Endures Tough Times

Barb and I became friends with Dan and Jeannie through church. Dan is a hardworking, kindhearted Christian guy who was known around town for cheerfully moving snow for many of his neighbors. He and Jeannie are also actively involved volunteers in many community service projects. And the couple is doing a great job of raising their children.

Dan is a bridge builder by trade. One day he jumped from a half-completed bridge deck to a platform a few feet below—a hop he and his coworkers deftly made a dozen times a day. This time, however, the platform broke beneath his feet, and Dan fell thirty-two feet to the ground below. Even though he survived the fall, the impact severed his spinal cord.

Dan's accident, which happened a few days before Good Friday, plunged them into the greatest time of trial and need in the history of their marriage. After the Easter service at our church, Barb and I stopped by the hospital to see this dear couple. We were blown away by what we found. All they could talk about was their gratitude to God for sparing Dan's life. No complaining, no blaming God, only gratitude. We had gone to minister to them, and instead they ministered to us! It was one of our most memorable Easters ever.

A short time later, when it was clear that Dan's paralysis from the waist down was permanent, I asked one of his sons if I could do anything to help. With a smile—and not a hint of resentment, bitterness, or self-pity—Matt said, "Don't worry about that, Gary. Dad's got me covered."

Since then, the loving partnership Dan and Jeannie built in the years before Dan's accident has only grown stronger through the adjustments to Dan's new life as a paraplegic. He and Jeannie have fallen more deeply in love. It's a love they have passed down to their children. At their daughter's wedding, Dan used his wheelchair to proudly escort his daughter down the aisle. And when the happy couple said "I do," Dan spun his chair in celebration!

## THE POWER TO HANG IN THERE

How would you respond if your world came crashing down as Dan and Jeannie's did? Would a similar tragedy strain your marriage to the breaking point?

Dan and Jeannie discovered a love that thrived in good times and continues to flourish in the worst of times. And they're not the only miracle couple we know. Barb and I have watched in awe as numerous marriages thrived and grew stronger under life's most difficult trials. We are amazed at the faithfulness of couples we know who have stayed connected despite a wide array of problems, such as

- chronic illness
- financial ruin
- a runaway child
- physical handicaps
- job loss and extended unemployment

- the death of a child
- a spouse who doubts God
- conflict with extended family
- sexual addiction
- depression
- infertility
- blended families
- countless other tragedies

Even though unfortunate circumstances, poor choices, and even the devil himself could have driven these couples apart, they stayed together and followed God's plan for their marriages. Sadly, we also know countless other couples whose marriages have blown apart under the same pressures.

Like most couples, you face pressures from life's many inconvenient, tragic, or evil circumstances. Sometimes a variety of pressures pile up on you all at once. Sometimes tragedy hits with the force of a wrecking ball, then goes away. Other times the same nagging pressure can hover like a dark cloud for months or even years. It's not a matter of *if* your marriage will face pressure; it's just a question of *when*.

No couple is immune from the kind of pressure that has the potential to threaten a marriage. After the terrorist attacks of September 11, 2001, Laura Bush described the event as "the biggest crisis" of her marriage. Laura and her husband, President George Bush, were in different parts of the country when the planes hit the Pentagon and the World Trade Center towers. Like most of us, neither of them knew what would happen in the subsequent hours, but they knew their lives were in danger. Laura comments on that day: "When he landed in Washington, I went back to the White House. . . . We just hugged." The president later told friends that "he feared he might lose her that day."[1]

What held the First Couple's marriage together during the weeks and months following the crisis? Two things: their friendship and their faith. The Bushes have a close relationship. "She's his confidante, and he's hers," observes a close friend. They find time for each other every day. Their friends agree that "George and Laura are best friends."[2] An adviser to the president said of the couple, "It's been a strong marriage from the very beginning, and that is principally because they both share the same common purpose in life, which is to serve other people. . . . [They] have unwavering love for one another that's grounded in a deep and abiding faith."[3] The Bushes agree. Laura reflects, "Our faith is very important to our marriage. . . . It's gotten so much stronger and deeper."[4]

How can you make sure your marriage, like the Bushes' and like Dan and Jeannie's, will weather the storm? What will prevent your relationship from crumbling under the weight of pain, problems, and tragedy?

If you want to safeguard your marriage against the storms and struggles of life, if you want a deeper bond and a richer friendship, you need the third secret to a lasting love: persevering love. It's the kind of love that triumphs over trials and grows stronger when you are most vulnerable. Persevering love doesn't just hang on through calamity by its fingernails; it hangs in there and thrives. It's the kind of love described by the apostle Paul: "Love never gives up, never loses faith, is always hopeful, and endures through every circumstance" (1 Corinthians 13:7). Persevering love bonds husbands and wives into lifelong friends.

What does this kind of love look like? We want to share with you what we have observed in couples like Dan and Jeannie, couples whose marriages are fortified by persevering love. In this chapter we will present six qualities of persevering love. And in the next chapter we will coach you on specific ways you can cultivate persevering love in your relationships.

## PERSEVERING LOVE REQUIRES TOTAL COMMITMENT

Paul and Nina were the darlings of their church's high school youth group. Both of their families were influential in the church, so the couple's engagement was big news there. Paul and Nina married after college and returned to their hometown and home church to begin their new life together.

Who could have anticipated that the first major attack on Paul and Nina's marriage would come from within the body of Christ? After an embezzlement scandal involving their senior pastor was discovered, Paul and Nina found themselves torn in opposite directions. Paul's family lined up with those in the church wanting to restore Pastor Evans. But Nina's family sided with those who would settle for nothing short of dismissal and prosecution. Each family exerted pressure on the young couple to conform to their respective viewpoints.

Eventually Nina's family left with dozens of other people to form a new church. Paul's family stayed. The couple's extended families weren't speaking to each other. Both sets of parents implied that disagreeing with the family position was tantamount to disobeying Christ. Furthermore, many of Paul's and Nina's childhood friends were embroiled in the split and exerting pressure on them.

All eyes were on the young couple. How would they respond to the pressure? Naturally, Paul and Nina each felt a tug of allegiance toward their families. And they personally disagreed on how the scandal should be resolved. These loyalties threatened to pull them apart. Both wondered if their marriage had been a mistake.

But their love endured. They agreed that their commitment to each other superseded their important but subordinate commitment to their parents, families, friends, and church. Paul and Nina kept talking through the tense situation and their disagreement. Instead of pulling away, they took refuge in each other. They affirmed that their relationship was stronger than family pressure. They wisely decided to exit the no-win situation and join a church attended by neither of their families.

From what Barb and I have witnessed and experienced, the starting point for persevering love is an all-out commitment to each other. It's the tough stance that says, "Our marriage is bigger than any issue. No matter who or what is arrayed against us, we will stand together. Neither of us will ever go through a trial alone."

Persevering love doesn't say, "I'll stick with you because I have to—because I promised to" but, "I will hang in there with you because I care for you more than anything in the world."

Have you committed yourself 100 percent to endure together whatever life may throw at you? How are you demonstrating that commitment in the face of life's problems and pressures?

## PERSEVERING LOVE REQUIRES UNCONDITIONAL ACCEPTANCE

Right after Travis and Mary celebrated their fifth anniversary, Mary visited her doctor about an incessantly bloody nose. The physician removed a small benign growth from inside her nose, and there was no further treatment.

One morning a year later, after Mary's routine physical exam, the doctor telephoned. He wanted her to come in immediately—that afternoon—for a biopsy. She called Travis at work in a panic and blurted out the news. His response was immediate: "I'll be home within the hour and take you to the doctor. I don't want you to go alone. I will be right there with you, whatever happens."

The morning after the biopsy, Mary underwent surgery to

remove a cancerous growth from her nasal cavity. Despite a painful course of radiation, the cancer returned a year later. Four years and six surgeries later, Mary's determined optimism was fading. Each successive surgery removed additional tissue and bone, until the right side of her face was severely disfigured. Even her eye was removed. Although the procedures ultimately bought her another seven years of life, Mary considered herself grotesque.

In order to conceal Mary's disfigurement, a team of artists and doctors created a lifelike mask for her. Although the mask fooled those who saw her in public, she couldn't wear it around the clock. Except for hospital workers, Travis was the only person who saw Mary without her prosthesis in place. And until the day she died, Travis told Mary that she was the most beautiful woman in the world. He had lived up to his promise: "I will be there with you, whatever happens." Their love endured and became strong against the ravages of terminal cancer.

The unconditional acceptance of persevering love says, "No matter how good or bad you look, no matter how much money you earn or lose, no matter how smart or feebleminded you are, I will still love you." That's the stuff of our wedding vows—for better or for worse, for richer or for poorer, in sickness and in health. Persevering love chooses to continue loving even when life dumps on us a world of reasons to fall out of love.

## PERSEVERING LOVE REQUIRES DEEP TRUST

Ross and Judi responded eagerly to their church's mission to support an orphanage in Southeast Asia. They gave generously to help provide shelter and education for several hundred former street kids. But the couple was moved to do more. Within eighteen months Ross and Judi had adopted three siblings from the orphanage, two girls and a boy. The kids looked nothing like their new parents, and they spoke a language the couple could not understand. Yet Ross and Judi embraced the kids as their own.

All three children struggled to adjust to their new surroundings, but by middle school it was obvious that Megan's problems were the most severe. No matter what Ross and Judi did, Megan kept acting out, disobeying, and rebelling. She was virtually uncontrollable. Then one night, their eighth-grade daughter ran away from home.

Ross and Judi were desperately worried for their daughter, and they were furious at each other. Megan's sudden disappearance released a flood of unspoken questions and accusations: "Why did we want these children?" "Did we make the right decision?" "Who is this person I'm married to—the one who can't fix this situation?" "Why weren't you a better mother to Megan?" "Why weren't you a better dad?" The conflict raged through that first night.

By four o'clock in the morning, Ross and Judi had vented their darkest doubts about themselves, their parenting, and their marriage. Then, as they gazed at each other through tear-rimmed eyes, they realized that they had no one better to trust than each other and God. They had too much good history together to turn on each other now. They had made it this far; they could make it the rest of the way if they continued to trust in each other.

Ultimately Megan returned home, and with the help of long-term biblical counseling, she was able to address the deep pain and hurts of her life. She wasn't the only one who went deep. Ross and Judi learned that this harrowing experience took them to places they didn't know existed. Yet the pain led them to a deeper trust in God and each other, enriching their lives.

Persevering love is the product of deep trust between husband and wife. Trust says, "I will depend on you to guard and protect my heart and my life, to fight beside me always." You may need to trust a lot of people to pull you through a crisis. But more than anyone else on earth, husbands and wives should rely on each other.

King Solomon wrote, "If one person falls, the other can reach out and help. But people who are alone when they fall are in real trouble" (Ecclesiastes 4:10). Another rendering of the same verse describes the crisis even more strongly: "Pity the man who falls and has no one to help him up!" (NIV). The wise king continued, "A person standing alone can be attacked and defeated, but two can stand back-to-back and conquer. Three are even better, for a triple-braided cord is not easily broken" (Ecclesiastes 4:12). Although these verses do not refer specifically to the marriage relationship, they do reveal that a trust-based relationship, especially one that is "triple-braided"—such as husband, wife, and God—is tough to beat. When you face pressures, allow them to bond you together and build your friendship instead of pull you apart.

Facing trials requires a depth of trust that doesn't grow overnight. This is why the trust of persevering love grows richer over time, as you each prove yourselves trustworthy to the other. It may be true that trust begins to build during courtship, and your commitment to trust may be inherent in your wedding vows. But *complete* trust is established over time and under the pressure of daily life.

## PERSEVERING LOVE REQUIRES ENDURANCE

As a boy, Jake was ridiculed constantly by his peers for being small, weak, and homely. As a defense, he developed a biting, sarcastic wit. He never thought he would be attractive to a woman, so he was amazed years later when he and Lori fell in love and married after dating only a few months.

Most of the time Jake kept his sharp tongue under control around Lori. But sometimes when she raised an issue, he launched into a barrage of cutting words. Five years and four children later, both Jake and Lori wondered if their choice to marry was a mistake.

Without any input from Lori, some of Jake's male friends from church sat him down and confronted him about his sharp language with Lori. They didn't know the whole story, but they had seen enough to intervene. Jake resisted their efforts. So these men called in the pastor who, in turn, called in the church's board of elders. Jake felt like a little boy again, surrounded by an army of peers who mocked and humiliated him. His anger deafened him to what these Christian friends and leaders were saying. Within three weeks, Jake felt so alienated that he vowed never again to set foot in church.

Lori is still upset by what she calls "SWAT team tactics" used by the men at church. But she knows their efforts were well-intentioned and that they were not the cause of Jake's problems. She even acknowledges that, in some ways, her marriage is better now. The confrontation by the guys didn't change Jake, but it did change her. When Lori saw how Jake overreacted to the threat he perceived in those men, she finally understood what Jake had endured as a child.

For the past three years Lori has treated Jake with a compassion he has never experienced elsewhere. Lori keeps on loving the husband who is confronting the pain in his heart and beginning to sort out his relationship with God. In tender moments he is opening up to her at levels he never thought he could. She has become a model of quiet endurance. She's faithfully loving Jake, even though he still loses his cool with her. She is determined to do her utmost to bring him back to God and the church, and she knows the only thing that will bring him back to God is firm, steadfast love.

Every kind of trial—emotional burdens, financial difficulties, spiritual questions, physical pain, relational stresses—presents a new opportunity for a husband and wife to persevere. Commitment helps you stay connected to each other through trials; perseverance is the determination to outlast the problems, to help each other get to the other side. Lori is doing most of the persevering in her marriage right now. But think of the intimacy and friendship that can develop in your relationship when *both* of you are committed to persevering through every trial.

## PERSEVERING LOVE REQUIRES ABIDING FAITH

Barb and I know a few couples who have gone through fiery trials without counting on God's strength. How difficult that is! But we also know many couples who have discovered that trusting in God, relying on his strength, and walking in his ways were more than sufficient to take them through the flames.

Karen's greatest fear was that her husband's refusal to take care of himself would leave her without a husband and their children without a father. She had good reason to be afraid. Both Brian's father and grandfather had died in their fifties from heart attacks. At forty-eight, Brian's cholesterol was dangerously high, and his power lunches were loaded with high-fat foods.

Brian knew that Karen's warnings (he sometimes called them nagging) were motivated by her love and concern for him. But he was unwilling to change. After weeks of ignoring chest pains and Karen's pleas to see a doctor, Brian suffered a massive heart attack one morning while climbing the steps to work. He didn't die, but he faced a long recovery. And his health would never be the same.

In an instant, Karen's life changed. She worked day and night providing full care for Brian and trying to bring order and stability to a family in crisis. Because Brian was unable to return to his high-powered job, their lifestyle changed dramatically. Karen was forced to take a job outside the home.

Karen knew she faced a choice. She could resent Brian for his stubbornness and careless behavior, or she could forgive him and shower him with the love he didn't deserve. She knew that as long as she withheld forgiving love from Brian, her own anger and resentment would imprison her. So she made the commitment to follow God's plan and allow Christ's love to flow through her.

As Brian was enfolded in Karen's self-sacrificial, Christlike love for him, he realized the depth of pain he had caused his wife and children. He confessed his stubbornness and sought their forgiveness. He renewed his commitment to Christ. Things that once seemed so important to him—country club membership, exotic vacations, large stock portfolio—were replaced by such simple pleasures as a walk around the block. Brian and Karen discovered the joy of spending time together in prayer. And they began to enjoy a level of intimate understanding and connection that they had never experienced during the "good times."

If marital love is to endure life's pressures, it needs to be grounded in a sincere, abiding faith in the God who designed marriage. Like Brian, any of us can stubbornly pursue a lifestyle that our culture deems important and live independently of God. Sometimes a severe trial moves us to let God have his way with us and to see what truly matters in life. We often don't really appreciate the important role faith plays in our marriage until a crisis forces us to throw ourselves on God's mercy.

Faith is such a vital facet of the marriage relationship and such a source of strength for building a lasting love, that we will spend all of chapter 12 discussing how you can develop greater spiritual intimacy with your spouse.

## PERSEVERING LOVE REQUIRES DILIGENT PREPARATION

Anyone who lives near a hurricane zone knows that the time for action is long before the storm hits. Once the wind is wailing, the surf is boiling, and the rain is coming at you sideways, it's time to head for cover and hunker down. It's too late to board up the windows, buy drinking water and batteries, and add flood coverage to your homeowner's policy.

Extensive hurricane preparation makes a lot of sense, but some people may be lulled into inactivity because killer storms don't strike every day. In fact, years may elapse between serious threats. Yet the time to prepare for a hurricane is during the calm between the storms.

When it comes to marriage, all of us live in a hurricane zone. And since the pressures, crises, and tragedies of life seldom blow in with advance warning, it is during the calm stretches of life that we must get ready for them. Persevering love is founded on the devotion and friendship a husband and wife build before the storm strikes.

Janis peered through the living room curtains and watched Pete drive up from his last day at work. She smiled. Pete walked into the house carrying a few files and a couple of balloons. He said the retirement party was no big deal, low-key just as he had wanted it to be. The real retirement party—a surprise to Pete—would be later that evening. Janis had invited Pete's boss, a dozen of her husband's close associates, and their spouses.

Pete had toyed with the idea of retirement six years earlier. He even took a three-month leave to see how he would like not going to work and doing whatever he wanted to do. During that time, Pete felt as if he was constantly underfoot in Janis's domain, and they were both clearly irritated with the new arrangement. They had not expected the retirement experiment to become a crisis, but it had.

After a month Pete was back at work. "We kept bumping into each other," he told the guys. But even though Pete and Janis were happy to return to a few more years of "normal" life, they both realized that they weren't ready to face each other for twenty-four hours a day. The friendship they had enjoyed as a young couple had waned. If they were to survive Pete's real retirement, they had some work to do on their relationship.

You and your spouse may not be facing the "crisis" of retirement, but one thing is for sure: If you are not presently in a difficult trial, there is one on your horizon—a financial crunch, an injury or illness in the family, a conflict with children, a disagreement between you and your spouse, etc. We're not being fatalistic, just realistic. Hurricane season in family relationships lasts year around. You just don't know when or how soon the next one will hit.

If you and your spouse find yourselves in one of those lulls between storms, rejoice! And while you are rejoicing, take the opportunity to prepare for stormy weather ahead. Now is the time to shore up your marriage. Work on a Bible study together. Take a second honeymoon—or third, or fourth. Read some good books on marriage enrichment and discuss them together. Attend a Christian marriage conference. Seek out a biblically based Christian counselor, and ask him or her for pointers on how to deepen your friendship. The more you invest in your marriage *between* the storms, the better prepared you will be to *endure* the storms together—and even come through them stronger.

After Pete's failed attempt at retirement, he and Janis admitted to each other their disappointment that retirement didn't feel right. But they determined to do something about the distance that had crept into their marriage. They sought out couples who had retired and who looked happier than ever. And they took the next few years to rediscover each other and enter into each other's areas of interest.

When Pete finally came home for good, they had a head start on many retiring couples. Their only regret was that they had missed out on each other's friendship for so long.

For all the planning Pete and Janis did, Pete's retirement didn't turn out as they expected. Six months after Pete retired, their daughter-in-law committed suicide, leaving their son to raise three young children alone. As Pete and Janis wept and prayed about the tragedy, they realized that they were in a unique position to help their son and grandchildren. They stepped in and for several years took care of the two kids who were not in school during the day. And for many more years Pete or Janis, or both, were at their son's house to greet their grandkids when they arrived home from school.

Pete and Janis were ready when the storm hit. Having fortified their friendship, they were prepared to help their son and grandchildren survive the devastation of suicide. They had no idea how their bonding over the previous years would benefit their son and his family. But for the first time in their lives, they faced a trial truly *together*.

Are you nurturing your relationship today so you can face whatever tomorrow brings? Are you building a relationship that will be ready for the tests you can't anticipate? In the next chapter, we will see how these six qualities of persevering love—commitment, acceptance, trust, endurance, faith, and preparedness—can see you through when the next storm hits.

## 8

# *Weathering the Storms*

If your marriage is anything like Gary's and mine, you live in a pressure-cooker world. You have more than your share of daily stress. On top of career demands, you have a spouse to love, kids to tend, and perhaps aging parents to care for. Each of these relationships is a privilege, but each one also clamors for priority status in your complex and busy life.

Like every married couple, Gary and I have had our share of ups and downs: the joy of bringing new lives into the world, the dark uncertainty of illnesses and surgeries, the fulfillment of ministry to others, the pain of being ignored by each other. But through it all we have been committed to facing these ups and downs together as a team—partners and best friends in the whirlwind of life. With the help of God, we have found our way through perilous life passages and withstood many trials. And in each case, we came through with greater determination, devotion, and a deeper love for each other because we took the precarious journey together.

Then the big one hit, a marital storm with the potential to do us in. It rocked our world with the impact of a category-five hurricane. If ever our relationship needed persevering love, this was it.

## BLINDSIDED BY GRIEF

It happened in 1997, a year after Gary's father died. Gary was very close to his father, so he struggled with a tremendous sense of grief and loss. The grieving process takes time, but Gary didn't have any time to grieve. A few days after the funeral, he was back to work speaking, counseling, and writing. Caught up in the responsibilities, pressures, and demands of the ministry, Gary did not allow himself to thoroughly process his grief. And he began to pay the price.

As Gary tried to press on with life, it was soon clear that he was in a depression. This was not just a temporary funk but an extended clinical depression. He couldn't concentrate. Some nights he was unable to sleep. Other times he would sleep fourteen to sixteen hours straight. His appetite left him, and he lost twenty-five pounds. He felt sad, helpless, and hopeless most of the time. Life wasn't fun for him anymore.

Gary and I are a committed team both in marriage and ministry. We live together *and* work together. So I was not a bystander in this trial; I was a full-time active participant in Gary's grief and depression. Although I did not suffer clinical depression, his pain was my pain as well. We both felt overworked and emotionally drained.

Some days Gary and I would go to work together as usual. But some mornings he would wake up so weighed down that he just wanted to stay home. On those days I canceled everything on my calendar just to sit and hold Gary as he processed his grief. Neither of us could fully comprehend what was happening. In our darkest hours, living a day at a time seemed too much. We were reduced to living five minutes at a time!

Now, I'm a woman who likes a semblance of order in daily life. But Gary's debilitating depression threw our family schedule completely out of whack. I felt frightened and absolutely helpless. Needing a sense of control, I increased my public responsibilities in our ministry to compensate for Gary's absence. But in my private moments, I wept over Gary's anguish and inner turmoil. He was retreating more into himself, sometimes coming home from work and going straight to bed without dinner. And I was not handling it well.

Our family had been extremely close, full of love, warmth, and laughter. But Gary was not himself anymore, and his depression was a dark cloud over our daily life. We still had our share of lighthearted moments, but most days were difficult for us all. Gary was sometimes abrupt with our girls, or he would tune them out completely. I tried to assure Sarah and Missy that their dad would be all right, but I was afraid that he would *not* be all right. In my darkest moments I felt like I was sinking down into Gary's private hell alongside of him.

If you had asked me two years before Gary's depression if a storm like this could happen to us, I would have answered, "Absolutely not!" Gary had been a lighthouse of strength for me over the years. But that strong beam was fading. I didn't know if this storm would ever end.

As difficult as this trial was for me, Gary was the one bearing the brunt of it. He now will tell you more of the story.

I must admit that 1997 was the longest, most difficult, most painful year of my life. Some days I simply isolated myself from others and shut down. I would sneak out the back door of my office and drive down the highway looking for a place to be alone, to cry. I didn't think I could provide for my family. I didn't think God could use me. I didn't think I could ever climb out of this deep hole.

During these times I would often walk for hours, hoping the exercise would bring relief. It helped some, but the deep feelings of failure and insecurity were almost more than I could bear.

One day I planted myself on a park bench with my Bible and a bottle of water. I cried out to God, "I am not leaving until you reveal yourself and your promises to me in your Word." I read and read. The hours passed. In the fifth hour I came across this passage: "Moses answered the people, 'Do not be afraid. Stand firm and you will see the deliverance the Lord will bring you today. . . . The Lord will fight for you; you need only to be still' " (Exodus 14:13-14, NIV).

That was the beginning of the turnaround for me. God had spoken. My deliverance was his responsibility. He was going to war for me against the depression that had crippled me. I sensed the burden begin to lift.

I drove home to Barb, my best friend, and told her what had just happened. "I know there's hope, Barb," I said. "I'm going to come through this."

As we talked that day, Barb reminded me of some basic truths that are foundational in our marriage. "Gary, I don't expect you just to get over this. I expect you to walk through it with me by your side. I also want you to remember that God will fight for you, just as he revealed to you on that bench. You need to trust him and be still. Let him carry you in your spirit, and let me carry you as your soul mate."

She reminded me that I could trust her. "I am sticking to you like glue, and nothing can separate me from you. We are one. The wedding vows we exchanged are the real thing. My promise to you is true. For better or worse means that even at the worst of times, we are a team."

How I praise God that his promises are true. He *did* fight for me. By his grace and strength, I recovered from depression. I even gained back the twenty-five pounds I lost. I also praise God that Barb's promises were true. She stuck by me like glue. I couldn't have made it without her persevering love.

# BUILDING A LOVE THAT ENDURES

Maybe you have yet to be hit by a storm as severe as ours. Or maybe you are in the middle of something even worse. No matter what you have faced in the past, you can be sure there will be trials in the future. Barb and I want to coach you on a way not only to survive those trials together but also to grow even stronger in the process.

What we need is a love that provides strength to withstand life's pains. We believe persevering love is the answer. Persevering love stays strong when the storms howl in your marriage. Persevering love bonds you even closer together, strengthening your friendship. How can you make sure that you and your spouse have what it takes to get through these storms? Here are five vital keys to building a fortress of love that will endure in your marriage. Barb will get us started with the first two keys.

## Connect and Stay Connected

Your ability to endure together in the hard times is directly proportional to the depth of your partnership in good times. Two hearts must link up to grow strong together. If you want to stay glued together in difficulties, you have to apply the cement of partnership now.

Gary and I start our day by connecting even before we crawl out of bed. Gary is the morning person in our house, so he's usually awake first. I'm still half-asleep when I hear him whisper, "I love you, Barb. . . . I need you, Barb." But what gets me every time is when he says, "Baby, baby, baby!" Every time I hear it I laugh, bringing joy to my soul.

Before you go your separate ways each day, give each other a heartfelt, "I love you." Stay connected by calling each other during the day. Find ways to be readily available to each other even as you travel or tote the kids around. Taking time to connect and stay connected builds security and intimacy in a relationship. It's part of building a lasting love. And it's essential when trials hit.

Jon was in the middle of a prolonged, stressful period with his company. His division was being phased out, and although he still had a job, he was assigned the task of shutting down his department. This meant handing out pink slips by the dozen and enduring months of ugly, confrontational meetings on and off the job site. Jon was seldom in the same location for more than a few hours.

Heather expressed concern for her husband's emotional well-being, saying it bothered her that he was almost impossible to reach during the day. In order to stay better connected, Jon consistently carried his cell phone so that he and Heather could be in contact with the touch of a finger. Jon and Heather both found that it eased their edgy nerves to know the other was only the push of a button away.

Some colleagues heard about it and joked that Jon's wife had him on a pretty short leash. But instead of unplugging his phone, Jon asked a pointed question: "Why don't you feel a need to be connected during this stressful time? Let's not allow the shutdown of our division to shut down our other relationships too."

These days, people might tell you that even a healthy, God-ordained level of dependence on your spouse is a form of sick codependence. Yet in our disconnected world, you need to do everything you can to strengthen emotional and spiritual ties with your spouse. Whether times are easy or hard, your spouse will deeply appreciate your efforts to stay in touch. Do what it takes to feel connected and present for each other even when you're apart.

## Make Your Relationship a Safe Place

Jay and Kari know what it's like to suffer the winds of monstrous storms—literally. They live in tornado country. When Jay was in high school, the roof of his parents' house was blown off. The son of Kari's close friend was killed in a tornado. And together this couple has felt the sting of thousands of dollars of storm damage to their own home and property. So when the weather sirens wail in their community, Jay, Kari, and their two small children run for cover.

But their dash for safety is anything but helter-skelter. Jay and Kari have everything neatly set up ahead of time. A box stored in the safest corner of their basement contains not only emergency lighting and a weather radio but a lot more—crackers, candy, juice boxes, some sunshiny storybooks, and a stash of blankets and pillows. By day they make their bolt to the basement an impromptu party. And at night it takes them less than a minute to carry their sleeping kids to the basement and tuck them into makeshift beds. Whether a storm strikes by day or by night, they have created a safe place.

Is your relationship a safe place where both of you can run from the troubles and terrors of life? Your spouse needs to know *now* that your loving arms will always be a shelter in the midst of a trial or tragedy. He or she will sense that assurance only if you practice empathy and comfort now.

Chuck's mother was angry when her children suggested it was time for her to sell the family home and move to a senior citizens' apartment complex. She protested, and the kids—all in their fifties themselves—backed off. When a stroke forced Mrs. Olson directly into a nursing home a year later, she spewed bitterness.

Chuck was utterly devoted to his mother and took the lead in sorting through her things, preparing her home for sale, and overseeing her finances. Yet he was deeply wounded by his mother's constant unkind remarks. He was a terrible son, she said, for moving her out of her own place. In reality, the stroke—not Chuck or his siblings—had forced her move.

Melinda, Chuck's wife, could only watch from the sidelines as he took on all the details of caring for his aging mother. Melinda continued to hold down the fort at home, shuttling their three kids to school, lessons, and other commitments. But Melinda wisely made time to let Chuck express his hurt and frustration and to reassure him that he wasn't mistreating his mother. Melinda gave Chuck—the devoted son who would never complain about his mother—a place where he could feel safe.

Some people feel too threatened to confide in anyone, sensing that no one really cares what they think or feel. Many see this kind of bonding in marriage as potential bondage. Some are so worried about losing personal freedom that they never attain the depth of fulfillment that comes from true closeness.

In reality, your marriage can be a fortress of protection where each of you is safe to show your wounds. Safety happens when your spouse is emotionally present—totally with you—and you are present for him or her. Your relationship becomes a safe place when you lower your defenses and share yourself fully with your spouse, knowing that you are accepted and loved for who you are, that you don't have to pretend to be anything else. If you can provide this safe haven for one another, you are well prepared for any trial.

Another key for weathering the storms of life through persevering love is communication. Gary will share some important insights on this vital skill.

## Keep Communicating

Barb and I know from experience that it's tough to communicate during tough times. Even the smallest of trials can drive a wedge between a husband and wife. And if small conflicts can divide you, think how much more some of the devastating blows of life can push you apart. Here are three reasons why trials are a threat to communication.

*Trials isolate us in our own thoughts.* Trials have a way of forcing even the most communicative people inward. Rosa, for example, had always worn her thoughts and feelings on the outside. Her husband, Andy, said he never had to wonder what was going on in Rosa's head because it was always simultaneously coming out her mouth! Yet when two of Rosa's sisters died of breast cancer, she retreated within herself.

Then cancer became a personal issue. When Rosa's doctor recommended that she undergo a radical preemptive mastectomy, she knew she faced a decision only she could make. Her world closed in on her like the long winter in Iowa, where the sun may not be visible for months. Even though the decision was ultimately Rosa's to make, vital information for making this decision came from her husband. He told her that he wanted her around forever and that he would love and treasure her whatever she looked like. Andy asked some key questions to help her start communicating again. We will discuss those questions in a moment.

*Trials invite denial or the belief that you can handle it all alone.* Denial is the handy psychological term for our tendency not to admit a problem exists. It's a refusal to deal with the facts. Asserting that you can handle a problem alone may be a healthy sign of independence, but it may also be an unhealthy attempt to avoid looking bad or asking for help. It can set us to humming the old Simon and Garfunkel tune "I am a rock, I am an island." Both denial and stubborn independence push your spouse to the periphery, saying, "I don't need to talk about it."

When you uncover deep pain, you also will often find issues of privacy and emotional safety. In fact, it's the fear of not having a safe place to sort through our problems that prompts us to keep those hurts under wraps for so long. That's why developing safe patterns of friendship is so vital *before* a trial hits.

*Trials leave us feeling that no one understands.* When Michael and Karley learned that their fourteen-year-old son, Evan, had a rare and deadly disease, they felt that no one in the world knew what they were going through. They struggled with loneliness for a few weeks until their doctor put them in touch with a support group of parents whose children had the same illness and who connected by phone and e-mail.

Michael and Karley received help and comfort from people who knew exactly what they were going through because they had gone through it—or were still going through it—themselves. This couple tapped into what the apostle Paul describes in 2 Corinthians 1:3-4: "All praise to the God and Father of our Lord Jesus Christ. He is the source of every mercy and the God who comforts us. He comforts us in all our troubles so that we can comfort others. When others are troubled, we will be able to give them the same comfort God has given us."

Don't believe the subtle lie that "no one understands." Your spouse understands what you're struggling through, though perhaps not fully. Reverse the roles for a moment. If your spouse was going through a crisis and thinking no one could understand his or her pain, you would hate being locked out. You would be hurt if your help and comfort were unwelcome. Why? Because as someone who has also faced hurt in life, you have genuine comfort to offer even in an unusual trial. If you ever feel tempted to lock your spouse out of your agony, resist that urge. Dare to open up.

When you face times of trial and pain, asking each other three critical questions can help you to keep communication open.

1. *"What's the problem?"* At first glance, the answer is obvious: It's the trial itself—cancer, bankruptcy, rebellious child, layoff, etc. But here's our point. First, the problem isn't us; we're on the same side. The problem is something outside of us, and we are battling it together. Second, the problem is something we can name and tackle together.

Here's how Andy finally got Rosa talking again. When Andy asked her to define the core of her struggle, she said, "You won't like the way I look after breast surgery. You won't love me as much." But Andy quickly disagreed, assuring his wife that his love for her would never change. To him the only issue was her health and survival. Andy's clarification shifted the focus to the main issue—getting rid of her cancer. Assured of Andy's love and acceptance, Rosa was free to elect the surgery.

2. *"What do we need from each other?"* After you have defined the problem, ask yourselves what kind of help you need to solve it. Identify areas where you have the strength and know-how to support each other. Do you need the other to step in with a decision? Do you need some space? How about comfort and encouragement? Perhaps you need your spouse to brainstorm with you or to seek God's truth with you in his Word and through prayer.

3. *"What kind of outside help do we need?"* Resolving a trial or crisis is often beyond your ability and resources. In the case of marriage-threatening trials, in fact, this is *always* the case. God wants to put other people in your life to lift you up. Your task at this stage can be as concrete as making a list of the people you need and what they can do for you.

The greatest resource for meeting your needs, of course, is God. He is the ultimate answer for your every need. God also provided your spouse to comfort and support you. Christians also have the resources of God's church, the body of Christ. And God surrounds you with other people—family, friends, neighbors, physicians, counselors—to help you through trouble. Even if you don't have the skills to meet your spouse's needs, you have a wealth of resources around you. Take advantage of them.

Therese had always led an ordered life. She had everything under control, from precisely monitoring her weight to guarding her emotions to running her home with tidy precision. Ron often feared disrupting her orderliness, even when he felt he was being treated like one of the kids.

One night, after Therese had hosted a birthday party for their twelve-year-old daughter, Megan, and a dozen other girls, Ron watched as his very in-control wife curled up on the couch and began to weep. Within minutes she was crying as he had never seen her cry before. Ron had no idea what was happening, but he knew enough to sit down next to her and wrap her in his arms.

After an hour of uncontrolled sobbing, Therese gathered herself and said, "Ron, I don't know how to tell you this. When I was growing up, I was sexually abused by a teenage boy in our neighborhood. I don't know why this is coming out today. I suppose it's because the abuse started when I was Megan's age. Seeing all those innocent little girls . . ." Another wave of tears choked off her words. She eventually cried herself to sleep in Ron's arms.

In the morning Ron called work and said he wouldn't be in. He took Therese for a walk in their favorite park. As they sat together on a park bench overlooking a lake, Therese told him a little bit more of her story in carefully measured words. "Ron, I can't tell you what he did to me. I don't want to sicken you. I feel dirty. I feel guilty for what he did to me. I didn't know how to stop him. I'm watching our own girls grow up, and I can't keep this inside anymore."

Ron had no idea how to counsel his wife through her pain. But he knew it was a crisis they could face together. He knew how to hold his hurting wife. And he knew how to find help.

Obtaining a referral from his pastor, Ron persuaded Therese to see a Christian counselor who had worked with dozens of women dealing with sexual abuse issues from their past. For weeks Ron faithfully sat in the waiting room while his wife met with the therapist. One day Therese invited him into the session. She was ready to bring Ron into the healing process, a process that might never have begun without Ron's help and encouragement.

Husbands and wives, you will face trials that are too big for you to handle, problems you can't begin to address in your own strength and wisdom. As spouses, your roles are simple: Be the best help you can be. But also commit yourselves to finding help beyond what you can offer.

A fourth key to building a love that endures involves seeing God's perspective of our trials. Barb will discuss this important key.

## Rest in the Truth That God Has a Purpose for Trials

If it were up to Gary and me, we would choose to navigate through life with as few problems as possible. God doesn't see things our way, however. He has allowed trials in our lives to teach us persevering love, to help Gary and me bond together as best friends for life. We can't say the trials have been fun, but we do appreciate what God is building in us in the process.

The trial of Gary's depression was excruciating for both of us. But our experience in that trial has provided us with a foundation to weather other storms God may allow us to face. We have experienced the truth of Romans 5:3-4: "We can rejoice, too, when we run into problems and trials, for we know that they are good for us—they help us learn to endure. And endurance develops strength of character in us, and character strengthens our confident expectation of salvation."

If your confidence is only in your own ability as a couple to make it through life's hardest moments, you are woefully unprepared. But when you acknowledge that God is sovereign over all of life, that nothing can touch you except what he allows, that his purpose in trials is to build your endurance and character, then you are ready to weather any storm. These are truths you can rest in now and forever.

Early one morning during Gary's crisis, I wept uncontrollably through my prayer time. Memories of our happy, love-filled home washed over me. I desperately wanted to go back in time to the way things had always been. "Oh God, I want my home back!" I sobbed. In my private agony, I pleaded, "Please, God, strengthen my husband!"

In that moment, God's unfathomable love embraced me. I sensed that he was my close companion in the midst of the battle. I transferred my needs to the one who promised to carry all of my burdens. Matthew 11:28-29 reminds us so clearly: "Come to me, all of you who are weary and carry heavy burdens, and I will give you rest. Take my yoke upon you. Let me teach you, because I am humble and gentle, and you will find rest for your souls."

As God began to heal Gary of depression, I sensed greater passion and deepened love for God. I began to enjoy closer fellowship with Jesus, an intimacy that I may have missed had the hurricane of Gary's depression not driven me to utter dependence on God.

My perspective on trials has changed since then. I'm not as fearful to face them now because I know they actually produce something good in my life. People continually ask Gary and me where we get our joy. If you didn't know us well, you might think we didn't have any burdens. Well, now you know. Like you, we do have burdens, trials, and storms. But we have much joy as well! It's because, just like you, we have a heavenly Father who provides shelter through the storms, a haven so safe and strong that no power on earth can conquer it!

Lasting love is often forged through difficult trials. Whatever you may be facing in your marriage right now, let the words of James 1:2-4 be both instruction and comfort: "Dear brothers and sisters, whenever trouble comes your way, let it be an opportunity for joy. For when your faith is tested, your endurance has a chance to grow. So let it grow, for when your endurance is fully developed, you will be strong in character and ready for anything."

Someone may be saying, "What? Consider our child's illness, my spouse's unemployment, and the termites in our basement as an opportunity for joy? Are you kidding?" No, we're not kidding. It's not always easy, but God desires that we take joy in our trials—not because they are joyful, but because he is using those experiences to strengthen our faith and make us mature.

Gary has one more key for building a love that endures.

## Decide to Tackle Trouble Together—Wherever It Takes You

Tyrone was a young, successful foreign service officer. Serena was an artist. They were different in a lot of ways, but they had in common a deep love for God and a keen wit. They instantly became best friends. When they married one bright summer day, Serena had no clue that she would be back in the same church less than a year later—for Tyrone's funeral.

Soon after the wedding, sudden vision difficulties sent Tyrone first to an optometrist and then to an ophthalmologist. Further tests revealed he had an aggressive, inoperable brain tumor.

As radiation and chemotherapy treatment began, Tyrone regretted that he had "dragged Serena into this," as he put it. Serena reassured him that she hadn't been dragged into anything. She was with him because she loved him. And she would stay with him for the same reason, no matter what happened.

One day, when the situation looked grim, Serena held Tyrone's hand through another round of radiation treatments and chemotherapy cocktails. Suddenly she grinned at him, and he looked at her as if she had gone mad. "I love you," she said. "You throw quite a party. I wouldn't miss this for the world."

It soon became clear that Tyrone wasn't going to get better. They quietly acknowledged that they would never realize many of their dreams for their life together. But they also realized that they had each other for as long as God allowed it, and that was what they really wanted.

One bright winter afternoon, shortly before Tyrone began to lose his mental faculties, he asked Serena if she wished she had married someone else. "Never once," she whispered. "I promised I would be with you. And I will be . . . 'till death do us part.' " Even after Tyrone slipped into a coma, Serena kept her promise. At his bedside she did the only thing she could do: stay beside him until their trial was over.

Barb and I have found that our love for each other is glorious in the good times—the vacations on the beach, the memory-making experiences with the kids, the times of deep intimacy together with Jesus Christ. It's easy to love in the good times. But when our marriage comes under intense testing, we still have in our possession what really matters. We relish a love that won't quit. We know a friendship that only gets stronger as life gets tougher. We find acceptance in our neediness. We have a hand to hold in our pain. In short, no matter where our trials take us, we have each other.

In your times of crisis and unbearable stress, you may secretly wonder if your spouse will draw closer to you and stand with you, no matter what, or turn away and let you battle the storm alone. You may also wonder if you have the strength to hang in there with your spouse or if you will be tempted to walk away. Now is the time to decide and agree together: Together we will tackle anything that comes our way, and we will stay together in it no matter where it goes.

When you commit to this level of persevering love, you are deciding to stick around through the suffering, to walk through pain, and to stay devoted through difficult times—until you are parted by death. You are offering your spouse the assurance that he or she will never be alone when trials come. Persevering love gains you the privilege of walking through every storm with your best friend.

It is a sobering reality that some trials, like that of Tyrone and Serena, end in the death of a spouse. Even then there is joy and triumph. Our spouses who go on to glory gain the presence of Jesus Christ and the end of all trial and pain. Those of us left behind have one of life's most treasured possessions: memories of a love that endured to the end.

We all need persevering love to keep our marriages intimate and rooted, regardless of what happens in life. You can take steps to insure that your love will endure. Commit yourself to making sure that your relationship is a safe place, that communication lines are open, and that you view the storms in your life from God's perspective.

# Guarding Love

*Guarding love protects from threats
and helps spouses feel safe and secure*

# 9

## The Castle of Your Heart

"If you lined up five million women," Michelle began her letter to Barb and me, "I'd be the last one you would suspect to have an affair. I was a *pure* woman. My eyes never looked at another man."

Michelle's sad story is one of vulnerability and carelessness. Read it for yourself:

> I helped lead a Bible study for women facing marital struggles. I saw these women through pain in their marriages and even separations. But I was different. I was faithful and true.
>
> When we finally purchased a computer, I found that the Internet contained so many interesting places. I could look up vacation spots, read newspapers. These were all good things, nothing evil. I never realized that I was only a click away from destruction.
>
> One day I signed up for a chat room. I chose a clean one, not a porn room. I wanted to just go in and see what was going on. Almost immediately a man began

talking to me. He paid attention to me and had an insightful response to every word I wrote.

I continued to meet this man in the chat room, even though I knew it was wrong. The relationship seemed innocent. We just talked about family and life. Soon we progressed to phone calls. I loved communicating with him. He cared so much.

After some time, we decided to meet. We were in love, or so we thought. After telling my husband I was meeting some girlfriends, I took off and hooked up with this man for what I thought would be a romantic weekend getaway. It wasn't at all what I expected, and suddenly everything came crashing down. I had betrayed my husband and my family.

My careless involvement with the Internet nearly destroyed my marriage. I became addicted, and it eventually led to an affair. I have regretted the day when, with one click on the mouse, I entered a downward spiral of sin and deception. I failed to build a fence of protection around my marriage. I didn't guard my heart.

## THE STATE OF THE HEART

Notice Michelle's closing line. She admitted that she had tumbled into an affair with an online stranger because she didn't guard her heart. That poignant insight reflects both her condition and its cause. Whenever a marriage self-destructs, the *heart* is the heart of the matter.

Your heart, simply put, is the core of who you are. It's everything. It's the source of all life. In our culture, we have neglected this truth while declaring that the mind is the center of our being. Any Hebrew scholar in biblical times would have countered, "No way. Life flows from the heart. Everything we do and everything we are—our very destiny—bubbles up from that deep inner spring." Used in a literal, concrete sense, the Hebrew word for *heart* means the internal, blood-pumping organ buried in our chest. In metaphorical use, however, *heart* became the richest biblical term for the whole of our inner or immaterial nature, encompassing emotion, conscience, thought, and will.

The heart is where your life meets your world. It's the gateway to your emotions and relationships. It's where you feel deep joy and experience deep pain. And where your heart leads, your eyes, mouth, and feet naturally follow.

In Proverbs 4:23, wise King Solomon offers a vivid picture of the importance of your heart to the state of your whole being. He calls the heart "the wellspring of life" (NIV). What is a wellspring? It is the fountainhead or source of a spring, stream, or river. More broadly, a wellspring refers to a seemingly endless supply of something. When Solomon identified the heart as the wellspring of life, he meant that our very selves bubble up continuously from this central, inner source.

Think about an artesian well for a moment. If the source of the well—the wellspring—is good, you will get good, life-giving drinking water. But if something is wrong at the source, if the wellspring is contaminated by poison or parasites, the bad water that flows from that source has the power to kill.

No wonder Solomon admonished in the first part of Proverbs 4:23, "Above all else, guard your heart" (NIV). When you read "above all else" in Scripture, you know the message must be important. Guarding our hearts is *very* important. If we fail to keep our hearts free from contaminants—ungodly thoughts, desires, and choices—our entire lives will be negatively affected. Your heart is supposed to be a wellspring of life. Left unprotected, it can become a source of destruction and death, as Michelle found out.

The instruction to "guard your heart" means to purposely place a protective shield around the center of your life. The word *guard* suggests exercising great care over or posting a watch. When you guard your hearts, you are guarding all that is truly valuable in life. And the love that identifies and stands against real-life dangers to a marriage is *guarding love.* When you practice this fourth secret, you protect your hearts from both internal and external threats. When guarding love is in operation, you and your spouse will enjoy a heightened sense of safety and security in your relationship. And without guarding love, your love will not last.

## SAFE WITHIN THE CASTLE WALLS

Once upon a time, defending your family from danger and death required something concrete and visible. If you wanted the ultimate in protection for your family, you built a castle. You may hold the romantic notion of a castle as a "tower of love," where the beautiful princess met the dashing prince. But in reality, castles were fortresses designed to keep the bad guys out and the good guys safe.

Castles first appeared in northwest Europe in the ninth century. Many of them were built so well that they still exist more than a thousand years later. One authority catalogs the remains of at least fifteen hundred castles in England alone.

Ever wonder who lived in castles? Besides the lord and his family, the inhabitants of a castle included knights, squires, men-at-arms, a porter who kept the outer door, and watchmen. Other ministerial and domestic staff members, stewards, and servants kept the estate running well. The larger the landholdings, of course, the larger the staff. But one thing was always true: The castle was built to protect them all.

If you study about castles, you will discover a history of warfare. These family strongholds were typically built on high ground, positioned to command the view of the lord's landholdings and a major thoroughfare. Medieval military science basically boiled down to the attack and defense of castles. Castles were constructed to defend the inhabitants from thieves and plunderers. The stronger the castle, the more the attackers schemed to break through its defenses.

Invaders knew they could attack the castle in one of two ways. In a *frontal assault,* the attackers marched up in plain sight and started hammering away with catapults, battering rams, flaming arrows, and hordes of invaders scrambling up long ladders. The head-on approach was an attempt to break into the castle by brute force.

A second approach could be called a *sneak attack.* A few attackers would try to slip into the castle undetected—by night over the wall, through an underground passageway, or by other means. Once inside, the infiltrators could disarm the guards and throw open the castle gates for the army concealed outside. And the castle would fall from within.

We can see a clear parallel between ancient castles and the defense of our marriages and families. Let's face it: Marriages are objects of attack in this country. Our godless culture is attacking marriage and the family on every side. We see the frontal assault of the media: movies, TV programs, music lyrics, and Internet Web sites that mock sexual purity, abstinence, marital fidelity, and family values. We also feel the sneak attack, Satan's subtle attempts to twist our minds and our hearts away from God's plan for marriage and family.

We must be well prepared to stand against this onslaught and protect those dearest to us. If we are going to fight the battle, we must understand both the nature of the assault and the weapons of defense at our disposal.

You may say, "I'm really not that vulnerable to attack. After all, I'm a Sunday school teacher and choir member at our church. I don't rent R-rated videos or visit pornographic Web sites. You must be talking to husbands who spend a lot of time away from home on business or to wives who are always bemoaning the lack of fulfillment in their marriages."

Holding such a casual attitude is like leaving the castle gate wide open at night. Don't underestimate the enemy of your soul. We are all at-risk, all vulnerable to attack. Ask Michelle. We must heed Solomon's advice to build a secure castle around our hearts. To lose our hearts is to lose everything.

## THE FATE OF UNGUARDED HEARTS

Michelle isn't the only Christian whose unguarded heart became contaminated and whose marriage suffered the consequences. Compromised hearts come in all shapes and sizes:

- Jim seeks out tough assignments, extra hours, and long trips at work as his way of leaving his mark on the world. Feeling abandoned by her husband, his wife, Angela, strikes back by furnishing their house well beyond their means, and hosting lavish parties. Her latest find? A throw rug for the back entry "that can get dirty when the kids track in mud." The cost? A mere three hundred dollars. Jim and Angela's hearts have been contaminated by the drive to look good.

- Acting on her lifelong dream, Sheila tells Ray she is quitting her day job to join a band. She buys high-end sound equipment, putting the couple deeply in debt. Then she leaves Ray for the manager of the band. Sheila's heart has been stolen by the fantasy of fame and then by another man.

- When David was a boy, he found stacks of pornographic magazines in his dad's workshop. As an adult, David feels that his wife isn't meeting his sexual needs. So, like his father, David turns to pornography. He tells himself that viewing hardcore porn on the Internet is better than having an affair. David's heart has been poisoned by sexual temptation.

❧ When April first dated Joe, she loved how he pulled her onto the back of his motorcycle for rides that terrified her parents. Now married, April mocks everything about Joe—his "biker" behavior, his clothes, and the beat-up truck he drives to a dead-end job. April's heart is dominated by a critical attitude.

❧ Jerry frequently claims that he doesn't have time for his wife or kids. Yet every fall he disappears for at least four weeks during hunting season. Where is he? Crouched in a stand of trees with his bow, poised to skewer a deer. Jerry's heart has been taken over by a hobby.

❧ Jill won't let her children play with any of the neighbor kids, whom she fears may say or do something that will corrupt her kids' morals. When her husband watches TV, opens a magazine, or reads a newspaper, she goes on and on about her disapproval. She is making everyone's life miserable. Jill's heart has capitulated to fear.

The Bible reminds us that "the human heart is most deceitful and desperately wicked. Who really knows how bad it is?" (Jeremiah 17:9). We all have an inclination to minimize the vulnerability, weakness, and sinfulness of our own hearts. And Barb and I don't claim to be exempt! Until we were confronted by our daughter's family picture (see chapter 1), we did not realize that our marriage was under siege. We had convinced ourselves that our marriage was utterly secure. It was not. The enemy was on the offensive. In many ways, our hearts had been left unguarded.

This is why we are compelled to constantly guard our own hearts—and to urge you to do the same.

## ARE YOU PREPARED FOR THE BATTLE?

Guarding love will serve your marriage the way ancient castles served their inhabitants. Guarding love will help you fend off attacks on your marriage from without and within. Guarding love will keep your focus where it belongs—fixed on your first love. Without guarding love, you risk disconnecting from each other and connecting to other people, things, or activities that will pull you away from your spouse and send you on the slide away from your dream marriage.

When you guard your hearts, you are protecting everything that is most important to you in life. You are guarding the love you have always dreamed of. What more do you want than a spouse who loves God, who loves you more than anything on this earth, who is wholeheartedly committed to you, and whose heart is pure and true? Isn't this your dream for your marriage? Wouldn't you do anything to protect it? Of course you would. That's why you need the fortress of guarding love around your hearts and your relationship.

Satan's agenda is to draw you and your spouse away from each other. He is subtly at work to accomplish his goal at this very moment! Although failing to guard your hearts may not lead you into a full-blown extramarital affair, it always leads to trouble. If you intend to foil the enemy's agenda, you need a plan to nurture guarding love. If you want a lasting love, you must take charge of your own heart and help guard your partner's heart.

It is important to know that the threats to a man's heart are somewhat different from the threats to a woman's heart. And Satan knows where we are most vulnerable, so our defenses must be fortified in those areas. In this chapter we will identify these specific areas of potential weakness, and in the next chapter we will discuss how to counter these threats to men and women.

# MEN UNDER ATTACK

Let's look first at the points where men are most vulnerable to attack, starting with external threats, Satan's frontal assault through our culture. Then we will look at areas where women are most vulnerable.

*Career pressures.* God created all of us to be involved in meaningful work. Most men, and many women, work outside the home. But when a man allows the world's formula for success to capture his heart, he is playing with dynamite! How many men do you know who have lost their wives and children because their job was more important to them? The pressure from supervisors or peers to make a man's work his life can be a serious threat to his marriage relationship.

*Worldly distractions.* In a man's most inspired moments, he may set godly goals for growth in Christ, family enrichment, and job success—usually in that order of priority. But the daily grind and hourly interruptions sometimes blur or bury those goals. Distractions may come in the form of pleasure (recreation, entertainment, etc.), power or position (influence at work, at church, in the community, etc.), or paychecks. Although all of these elements are fine in their place, if they distract a man from the primary values of faith and family, his heart is left dangerously unguarded.

*Relationship pressures.* Some days a man feels that everybody wants a piece of him, and most of the time he wants to comply in a loving, helpful, godly way. The boss wants him to work a little later or come in for evening meetings. The neighbors want him to help them roof their house or move furniture. The Sunday school superintendent is in desperate need of more teachers. The missions committee needs a chairman. And the guys keep bugging him to spend more Saturdays with them out on the lake. If a husband allows these relationship pressures to dominate his life, if he is trying to please everybody who needs something from him, his marriage and family will suffer.

*Sexual temptation.* Here's an obvious one—and it's a deadly peril. Barb and I can't even count the marriages we know about that have been shattered by sexual sin. For every ten guys on your softball team or in your Sunday school class, four or five have fallen in some way—an emotional affair, a physical affair, addiction to pornography, some sexual sin. These flaming arrows fly at men from every direction in our culture. A husband cannot let his guard down for a moment.

In addition to threats launched at us from outside, we can also fall prey to internal threats.

*The search for significance.* What man doesn't want to make his mark on the world? Properly directed, a husband works to use the gifts God has given him to become part of God's great plan for the world. His greatest significance is bringing glory to God. But some men can become so sold out to "I am what I do" that they lose all sense of balance. They claw their way up the corporate ladder and develop their careers while sacrificing their families. Success can take over a man's heart when it becomes his primary purpose in life.

*Passivity.* As Barb and I speak across the country, the number one lament we hear from wives is that their husbands are passive. A passive man backs off and does little or nothing to nurture the relationship. A passive man has the attitude, "Hey, I work hard to make a living for the family. My wife should take care of the responsibilities at home—including the health of our marriage." A passive man stops running hard and fast after God's best for his family.

*Control.* Let's face it: Most men like to be in charge. But God never intended for a husband to control his family. Rather he is called to love and serve his family as Christ loves and serves the church. Control is going all-out to get things your way, and it can be the result of fear, insecurity, aggression, or low self-esteem. Whatever the source, a controlling husband and father can be poison to a family relationship.

*Competition.* Most men love to compete. Competition in balance is called a sport; competition out of balance is a war. If a man's priorities are not firmly in place, the drive to compete can unravel what matters most to him: his family.

A woman's heart is just as vulnerable to attack as a man's heart. Yet these attacks are often different. Barb will help us understand the ways Satan tries to capture a woman's heart.

## WOMEN UNDER ATTACK

Ann met Rusty at work. Like Rusty, Ann was a Christian. Both were married. She was attracted to his big heart, which in her mind was surely an outgrowth of his Christian faith. Ann noticed how Rusty truly cared about the people he worked with. He seemed like such a dedicated Christian. One day Rusty found Ann crying. He put his arm around her, consoled her, and prayed for her. He had no idea that her husband wasn't doing a good job of meeting her emotional needs. At that moment, Rusty touched Ann's vulnerable heart.

After that incident, Ann felt spiritually and emotionally connected to Rusty. She began thinking about Rusty a lot. She dressed to impress him and sought him out at work. Until Ann started reaching out to him, Rusty thought that he could not be tempted by another woman. He and Ann were just friends, after all, and he was just ministering to her.

Can you see how inadvertently Ann and Rusty developed an emotional bond? It was a bond that ravaged both their marriages. Even as Christians they were not exempt from a heart-poisoning relationship.

Let's look at some of the dangers women need to guard against. Here are some of the more obvious, external temptations:

*Relationships with other men.* As Ann discovered, wives must protect themselves when interacting with men other than their husbands. Even though a woman may be attracted by a man's physical attributes, she is many times more likely to be lured by an emotional connection. Wives must not allow themselves to be emotionally dependent on other men—or vice versa.

*Preoccupation with children.* When a wife continually puts the children before her husband, the marriage becomes unbalanced. True, she can't ignore the runny noses or the homework that's due tomorrow morning. But a wife must do whatever it takes to manage her children's needs in a way that doesn't ignore her husband's needs.

*Failing to meet personal needs.* Women often spend their time meeting the needs of everyone around them and then fail to refill their own tanks. That leaves wives vulnerable to many threats that can disconnect them from their husbands, including bitterness and anger. If these threats are not addressed, they lead women to be vulnerable to the attention of other men. Take care of yourself. Get the rest you need. Spend time with female friends who encourage and energize you. Refresh yourself daily by spending time in prayer and in God's Word.

Wives, you might not get drawn into an emotional or physical affair. But your hearts may be drawn away by something seemingly as innocent as some of these internal threats:

*Worry.* It's natural to be concerned for the people you care about. But all-consuming worry pulls you away from trust in God. Worry is a distrust of God's resources and an attempt to live by your own devices.

*Critical attitude.* Most women hold an ideal for their marriage and family life. When a wife feels that her husband doesn't support these needs and wishes, she may develop a critical attitude, especially toward him and her children. A critical spirit is a real love killer.

*Comparison.* Some women tend to compare themselves to others on everything from the intelligence of their children to the address and square footage of their homes. This unhealthy habit can lead to dissatisfaction with themselves and their relationships—especially the people they may hold responsible for any shortcomings: their husbands.

*Control.* It is the nature of many women to take charge, to coordinate their families, and to make things happen. But God's plan for marriage involves family leadership from the husband. Women who assert unreasonable control may cause great discomfort to their husbands. It is a sure way to push them even farther away than they may already be.

## TREASURES WORTH GUARDING

Gary and I want to strongly admonish you to continually pursue guarding love for your relationship. We need to be vigilant in guarding the love of our lives. Any of the external and internal threats we have mentioned can pollute an unguarded heart and poison your marriage. No matter how positive your legacy as a couple may be at this point, the enemy will continue to pound at your gate, attempting to steal your dream and nullify your example to others. He knows that *in one single unguarded moment* you can lose your testimony, your platform for counsel, and your positive influence as role models of a loving marriage. What a frightening thought! It's like spilling a bottle of black ink across the carefully written pages of a beautiful life story.

You may find it hard to believe that your heart could ever drift from devotion to your husband or wife or become poisoned by other loves. Relational ruin happens to other people, not you. Don't be lulled into a false sense of security. You are wise to heed the caution of 1 Corinthians 10:12: "If you think you are standing strong, be careful, for you, too, may fall into the same sin." Or as Proverbs 16:18 pointedly teaches: "Pride goes before destruction, and haughtiness before a fall." Your success at developing guarding love depends on recognizing that your hearts and your marriage *are* vulnerable to devastating attack.

It is likely that you have already experienced the pain resulting from severe attacks on your heart. Perhaps you have even tasted the humiliation of a major defeat in your marriage. Is there still hope for plundered hearts that were left unguarded?

We want to assure you that there is always hope. Take courage from the good news at the end of Michelle's Internet affair. Eventually she was confronted with her behavior and confessed her sin. Although she had not intended to hurt anyone, she hurt a lot of people. Even her children knew what she had done. Yet in spite of all the lies and hurt, God has given Michelle and her husband the courage and strength to rebuild their marriage and recapture their dream. "We are taking back our home and telling Satan to get out," she writes. "We have a lot of work to do, but I know it will be worth it." Michelle and her husband have discovered the great worth of guarding love.

In the next chapter, you will learn how you can put guarding love into action. We will share with you how to protect your heart and the heart of your spouse. The result will be a greater sense of safety and security in your relationship than you have ever known.

# 10

## *Building Walls of Protection*

Six years ago, Conner landed the position of junior vice president in a Fortune 100 company. With a dozen years of experience in the industry, an MBA from a prestigious business school, and a no-holds-barred work ethic, Conner knew he had the tools to do his job and do it well.

After a few steps up the corporate ladder, his momentum stalled. He went two years without a promotion, and by his mid-thirties Conner feared that he had topped out with the company. Whichever way he pushed to expand his responsibilities, he met resistance. His personal, cynical motto became, "I work for idiots." He knew that his judgmental attitude was neither charitable nor Christian, but he felt it captured the reality of his situation.

When he was passed over for the job of president of his division, Conner was more than a little rattled. Frustrated by his inability to advance, he went to visit a career coach, who signed him up for a group seminar on finding meaning in work. The first exercise was to think through a list of a hundred items such as honesty, balance, generosity, and security, with the goal of determining the half dozen or so qualities that mattered most to him in life. Conner rapidly narrowed his list down to five: personal growth, achievement, competence, challenge, and advancement.

For several moments, Conner sat and pondered the five words he had chosen. Slowly he began to realize that he had excluded family relationships from his list. That stark insight slashed through his heart like a knife. He might as well have pushed his wife, Sasha, and two small sons out the front door of his heart, slammed the door, and thrown the dead bolt. Unable to face this reality, he bolted from the room. One of the seminar trainers found him sitting alone in a stairwell, staring down at the floor, tears staining his shirt. He was a broken man.

When Conner returned to the seminar room, he redid his list to reflect the values he *wanted* to have—with his family coming ahead of his work goals. With the fresh certainty of what really mattered to him, he wrote that his new mission in life was to put his family first and to guard against anything that would rob his family of its rightful place in his priorities.

"That was a turning point in my life and in our marriage," Conner says. "As I sat in that stairwell, I thought about everything I had to lose if I didn't do something different with my life. I knew Sasha was slipping away from me because I had left her behind in my business pursuits. I decided that day to stop clawing my way to the top and to be content with my position. I have mastered my current job, which is really an advantage at this stage of my life. I can do my job and still have energy left for Sasha and the boys. We're on our way to healing the wounds I caused. A promotion right now would put them back at the bottom of my list. And I don't ever want to hurt them again. I think I am finally realizing that significance is more important than success. I *can* win in the marketplace, but I *have* to win at home."

# GUARDING YOUR OWN HEART

Barb and I are encouraged by Conner's decision to take a stand against the enemies of his heart and his family. We have witnessed scores of couples who have made the same decision to build a protective castle around their relationship. If they can do it, so can you. In fact, you *must* commit yourselves to guarding love if you want to recapture your dream and build a lasting love.

Guarding your heart isn't a one-person job. It won't do to send a husband scurrying out of the castle to defeat the ravaging hordes single-handedly. It isn't a wife's job just to stay behind in the castle and worry about her husband. Your relationship is a partnership in every way, including the defense of your marriage.

We will look first at how you as husband and wife can post guards over your own hearts. Then we will share how you can help guard each other's heart. Your marriage and your legacy depend on winning this crucial battle.

## Be Committed to the Task

The Bible has some strong words about the task of guarding our hearts. In addition to the admonition in Proverbs 4:23, "Guard your heart," the Bible tells us how seriously God wants us to take our job. Jesus repeatedly coached his disciples to be on guard against hypocrisy (see Matthew 16:6-12), greed (see Luke 12:15), persecution from others (see Matthew 10:17), false teaching (see Mark 13:22), and above all, spiritual negligence and lack of preparation for the Lord's return (see Mark 13:32-37).

More cautions echo throughout the Scriptures.[1] "*Be careful* that you don't fall" (1 Corinthians 10:12). "*Be careful* to do what is right" (Romans 12:17). "*Be very careful*, then, how you live" (Ephesians 5:15). "*Be careful* that none of you be found to have fallen short" (Hebrews 4:1). "*Be careful* to do what the Lord your

God has commanded you" (Deuteronomy 5:32). *"Give careful thought* to your ways" (Haggai 1:5).

Barb and I say the same thing to you. Be careful!

Don't let down your guard. The threats to your marriage are real. The dangers are even more dire for those who don't realize they are under attack.

If you think you are wavering in your commitment to the task of guarding your heart, take a moment to catalog everything you stand to lose if you fail to protect your innermost heart. Like Conner, you will find that nothing is as valuable as the priceless treasure of your family's love.

## Ask the Lord to Protect Your Heart

Roger and Sharon are not millionaires, and they don't have jobs in a Fortune 100 company. But they feel amply protected in life. They have a decent bank account, paid-up life insurance, a service contract on the furnace, and an extended warranty on their vehicles.

These are good things. But there is only one totally trustworthy source of protection for a marriage: God himself. David said it well in Psalm 61:1-4, when he cried out to the Lord:

O GOD, LISTEN TO MY CRY!
    HEAR MY PRAYER!
FROM THE ENDS OF THE EARTH,
    I WILL CRY TO YOU FOR HELP,
    FOR MY HEART IS OVERWHELMED.
LEAD ME TO THE TOWERING ROCK OF SAFETY,
    FOR YOU ARE MY SAFE REFUGE,
    A FORTRESS WHERE MY ENEMIES CANNOT REACH ME.
LET ME LIVE FOREVER IN YOUR SANCTUARY,
    SAFE BENEATH THE SHELTER OF YOUR WINGS!

When you realize that the internal and external threats to your hearts are real, you can pray as David prayed. Maybe you have never "prayed Scripture" with your spouse. But you can use Psalm 61 as your script.

Tell God, "I will cry to you alone for help. You are my safe refuge, a fortress where my enemies cannot reach me."

Plead with God, "Hear my cry. Listen to my prayer. Lead me to the towering rock of safety. Let me live forever close to you. Shelter me beneath your wings."

Jesus invited us to trust God to safeguard our hearts when he taught his disciples to pray, "And don't let us yield to temptation, but deliver us from the evil one" (Matthew 6:13).

Spending time daily in God's Word and in prayer is vital to keeping your connection to Christ. And by protecting your relationship with Christ first, you can avoid falling into traps. Daily obedience to Christ is the best defense you have against the enemy of your heart and your marriage.

## Establish Openness with God

I don't like going to the cardiologist. I don't enjoy having electrodes taped to my chest and running on a treadmill until my lungs burn and my stomach churns. And that's only part of why I don't like going to the heart doctor. My ego doesn't like the possibility that there might be something wrong with my ticker. But in reality, learning what may be wrong with me—and as soon as possible—is the more direct route to getting well. So an occasional heart checkup is a good thing.

Even more important is a spiritual checkup, a *real* heart checkup. We need to be open and honest with God about what is going on at the wellspring of our lives. Few of us, men or women, are eager for our weaknesses to be exposed. But allowing God to probe us helps detect any areas of the heart that may be weak and in need of spiritual repair.

God, the Great Physician, wants to see us more than once a year, however. He can keep our hearts strong by seeing us daily. Psalm 139:23-24 shows us how we can come to God and let him do a heart exam. It's another passage of Scripture you and your spouse can pray together in order to guard your hearts:

SEARCH ME, O GOD, AND KNOW MY HEART;
   TEST ME AND KNOW MY THOUGHTS.
POINT OUT ANYTHING IN ME THAT OFFENDS YOU,
   AND LEAD ME ALONG THE PATH OF EVERLASTING LIFE.

As you expose your heart to God on a daily basis, he will show you what you need to do to keep the wellspring of life healthy and flourishing. He will help you guard your heart.

Our deepest fear in facing any doctor is that he or she might uncover a problem for which there is no cure. However, there is no inner heart problem that cannot be completely healed. Through the death of Christ, God has provided a way to cleanse us from our sins. Here is his prescription for getting rid of sin once and for all: "If we say we have no sin, we are only fooling ourselves and refusing to accept the truth. But if we confess our sins to him, he is faithful and just to forgive us and to cleanse us from every wrong" (1 John 1:8-9).

Do you invite God to examine your heart and point out where it needs to be guarded? When you allow God to search your life for wrongdoing and when you confess and turn from that wrong as soon as you see it, you establish a habit that offers powerful protection to your heart.

## Keep Short Accounts with Each Other

In the chapters about forgiving love, Barb and I shared that it is crucial to close the loop and resolve all the hurts and anger we cause each other in marriage. When we hang on to hurt and withhold forgiveness, it makes us bitter people, and the hearts of bitter people are very vulnerable to attack.

Several years ago I spoke at a conference with a couple named Jim and Renee Keller. During his talk, Jim described the pattern of communication he and Renee have used since the first day of their marriage.

Before they were married, Jim explained, he realized that both he and Renee were a little headstrong. So he knew they needed a plan for dealing with the inevitable conflicts they would face. He promised Renee that whenever they had a conflict, he would initiate the resolution of the problem and the process of forgiveness, no matter who was at fault.

I sat in the back row of the auditorium waiting for the punch line. But he had already delivered it. Jim had committed to initiate conflict resolution and forgiveness—even when Renee was the offender. I was in awe.

Later that afternoon I took Renee aside and said, "Okay, Renee, this is just between the two of us. You have been married well over a dozen years. How many times has he violated that promise?"

"Never, Gary," she replied with a smile and a twinkle in her eye. "He has initiated forgiveness every time."

Again I was awestruck. Renee admitted that there are times when Jim is 100 percent right and she is 100 percent wrong. Yet he still takes the first step toward forgiveness and reconciliation.

Jim is determined to douse any coals of resentment before they burst into flame. He is a peacemaker. He is also reflecting incredible servantlike male leadership. Keeping short accounts with Renee is more important to him than his pride and ego. Just think how such an approach would keep the air clear in your marriage, especially if both you and your spouse adopted Jim's attitude.

## Stay Accountable

I have a close relationship with six men who ask me the tough questions. I have met with the same small group of men (Jerry, Mike, and Tim) since 1979. These three guys, along with my buddy Steve Farrar and my sons-in-law (Scott and Cooper), have carte blanche to ask me anything they want about my life. My accountability partners can pelt me with honest questions about guarding my heart in every area of life, including marriage. The questions can be brutal: "What has been dominating your thoughts this week?" or "Have you put yourself in a compromising position with another woman this past week?" or "Have you been studying the Bible?" or "What issues are you and your wife dealing with this week?" or "Are you in your kids' lives?" or "Are you shooting straight with me, or are you blowing smoke?"

I don't get together with my small group or connect with Steve, Scott, or Cooper to talk about Barb's flaws. I focus on my faults and struggle points, not hers. These guys are trusted advisors. They encourage me to follow God's best. In addition to accountability, we experience deep friendship and healthy male intimacy. We spur each other on toward growth in Jesus and in turn sharpen each other's ability to serve.

Why do I do this? Because I'm convinced of the truth of Proverbs 27:17: "As iron sharpens iron, a friend sharpens a friend." We need each other! Think about it, men. When we were boys, we had buddies to play with. We built forts and tree houses, played baseball, or—if you're a little younger than I am—video games. Oh sure, sometimes we got into arguments and fights, but those guys were our pals and were in our lives day in, day out.

But then something happened in adolescence. We discovered girls. We stopped hanging out with the guys. We headed off for college or work, and we met some new friends. But by the time we settled down and got married, a lot of us had lost our best male friends. Not having close male friends leaves a gaping hole in a man's heart. We all need other men who will help us guard our hearts.

Accountability is a pressing need for women as well. Barb will share the feminine perspective of staying accountable.

When Gary talks about men's accountability groups, all I can picture is a serious meeting of the president's cabinet. Various officials offer status reports on the state of the nation. Men get down to business and deal with issues and events. Yet women need accountability as much as men do, first to our husbands and then to a few Christian female friends. But our accountability sessions may look quite different.

My accountability meetings involve people as varied as my daughters to women from church to other solid Christian female friends. Our times of open sharing, Bible study, and prayer encourage me. Sometimes my sisters in Christ challenge my attitudes and behavior. But more often we need support.

Women, be honest. How many of your girlfriends support you in your marriages—unfailingly prod you toward faithfulness and friendship in body, soul, and spirit with your husbands? And how many of your friends get together just to have a gripe session? You need women to step close to you and risk saying something that may be hard to hear, to point out a mistake so you may grow deeper in Christ, and to help you guard your hearts. But you need a group that doesn't spend its first fifty-nine minutes taking "prayer requests" (sometimes another term for gossip) before devoting its final minute to prayer. Find women who share your devotion and love for God.

In addition to guarding your own hearts, you can do several positive things to guard the hearts of your spouses. First, I will share some helpful ways that wives can help their husbands guard their hearts, then Gary will do the same for men.

## SEVEN KEYS TO GUARDING YOUR HUSBANDS' HEARTS

Men's hearts are precious and private things. Men are less likely than women to bare their souls or communicate every thought. Their hearts are often locked up and protected, great treasures stored in a secure vault. This inner wealth represents their identities as men.

As their wives, you hold the key to your husbands' hearts. You are the people who know their deepest needs, the quiet longings of their souls, their search and struggle for significance, their God-given strengths, and even the weaknesses they can hide from others but not from you.

Make no mistake: You have significant influence in your husbands' lives. I believe a great deal of men's personal success and right choices can be traced back to the women who whisper affirmation and encouragement in their ear at night.

A woman was walking down the street with her husband, who was the mayor of a small town. As they passed a construction site, she stopped to say hello to a worker, who happened to be one of her old high school boyfriends. As they walked on, her husband commented, "Aren't you glad you're married to a mayor and not a construction worker?" His wife replied, "If I had married him, *he* would be the mayor."

Yes, as women, you hold the power to help or to hurt your husbands. The pastor who officiated at our wedding ceremony said a bad woman can break her husband and a good woman can make him better. Here are ways you can demonstrate guarding love and make your husbands better men.

*1. Honor them and their world.* Most men would admit that deep inside every man is a boy and his dreams. Close your eyes for a moment, and envision your husbands as energetic, clear-thinking, bright-eyed ten-year-olds shooting baskets—totally in love with life! Their futures at that point were all promise.

They had great dreams and plans, perhaps to be basketball stars, global adventurers, or presidents of the United States.

Now think about your husbands as they are today. Have they quit dreaming? If so, when did it happen, and why?

Men need their wives to dream with them, to envision the possibilities and walk courageously into change. Often women can be so preoccupied with the security of their husbands' jobs that they can't even consider the great things that may await them in a different company or a new career field. Men long for the freedom to be fully who they are, assured that their wives will stand beside them through it all.

*2. Avoid sabotage.* I trust you would never intentionally mean to do harm to your husbands, but you can inadvertently sabotage them without realizing you are doing so. How? By misusing power.

Do you have any idea how influential you are in your husbands' lives? It's your voice that whispers into their ears at night. Your beliefs, behaviors, and decisions have as great an impact on them as most other forces. They listen to you and trust in your advice and counsel. This incredible influence carries with it great responsibility. Make sure you do not mismanage your power in their lives and end up wounding them.

"How could I be wounding my husband?" you may be asking. Many of us women like to be in charge, and sometimes we like it too much. I love being efficient! I'm good with organizing our household, family schedules, time with our grandchildren, appointments, my daily workload. It takes a concerted effort and control to maintain order and stay on task. But I create a problem when I begin thinking that my control extends to others, especially to Gary.

At times I've been guilty of questioning or doubting my husband, and in the process I have undermined his God-given leadership and personhood. To avoid sabotaging our marriage,

I have learned to guard our relationship by surrendering my need to be in charge.

*3. Love them unconditionally.* A wise older woman once explained the difference between love and infatuation in this way: "Infatuation is when you think he's as sexy as Tom Cruise, as smart as Albert Einstein, as witty as David Letterman, and as athletic as Kurt Warner. Love is when you realize he's as sexy as Albert Einstein, as athletic as David Letterman, as witty as Kurt Warner, and nothing like Tom Cruise . . . but you'll take him anyway!"

Every one of us longs to be loved with no strings attached. Do you love your husbands for who they are—right now, with all their imperfections? Or do you watch their every move with a critical eye? Do you place your expectations for them so high that disaster is inevitable?

You can measure your own love for your husbands by comparing it to the standard described in 1 Corinthians 13. Are you patient and kind? Or are you envious and proud? Do you keep records of your husbands' wrongs, then drag them out when they might be advantageous for you? Do you continue bringing up things that should have been dealt with and forgotten long ago?

Guarding love is deeply and passionately proud of the men you married. If you do not love your husbands for all they are, you are leaving them vulnerable and your marriages unguarded.

*4. Understand your differences.* Yes, men and women are different. One of the most reckless things a woman can do is insist that her husband wants what she wants, feels the way she feels, behaves as she behaves, thinks as she thinks. I don't know a woman who would want her husband to insist that she want, feel, behave, and think the way he does. A husband is 100 percent male; a wife is 100 percent female. Your husband isn't your girlfriend any more than you are his buddy. Respect the gender differences by encouraging him to be all the man God created him to be!

You can learn about your husband's uniqueness only as you

study him. Listen carefully to him. Communicate by opening up and sharing with him. And when you talk to him, tell him honestly what you think and feel. But always be tender. The more you understand and respect your husband's male characteristics, the more you can intimately meet his need for you—and help guard his heart in the process.

5. *Honor their friendships.* Can you remember some of the guys your husband hung around with when you first met—the ones who resented you for stealing their buddy away? Well, some of those guys have grown up. Your husband needs like-minded Christian men to reinforce his character qualities. He needs to be around guys who want to follow Jesus Christ regardless of the cost. Give him space to connect with other men who will sharpen him as iron sharpens iron (see Proverbs 27:17).

6. *Clarify your family roles.* When God created Eve, he made her in his image, with qualities not found in Adam. He gave the woman an incredible title of honor and strength, calling her "helper" (see Genesis 2:18, NIV). The Hebrew word translated *helper* can also be translated as one who brings unique strengths and qualities to the other; these qualities, found only in the woman, complete the union between man and woman.

Elsewhere in the Old Testament, this word is used in reference to God himself. In Psalm 54:4 David tells us that God is our "helper." It is a title of honor and great worth.

By understanding the meaning of your role as helper, you can be encouraged to use your distinctive strengths to build up your husbands and contribute to their lives. Your very uniqueness can offer your husbands qualities that fully complete them—as no one else can!

You can complete your husbands and guard their hearts by working with them, not against them. How? If your husbands are struggling in an area, pray for them. Talk to them if they are open to that. Listen to what they are saying and *not* saying. And then get out of the way, and let God work in their hearts. God will open their spiritual eyes as you obey the scriptural command to win them by a "gentle and quiet spirit" (see 1 Peter 3:4). You are a major part of the equation to help your husbands understand their roles in the family. But you can't do it alone or by nagging. You have to let God do it in his good timing.

7. *Commit yourselves to them and to God.* Wives may feel that they made a commitment once and for all to their husbands on their wedding day. And in a way, they did. But they need to renew that commitment every day.

Similarly, your lifetime commitment to God should be renewed daily as you seek to follow Christ moment by moment. Without a doubt, the most lasting gift you can give your husbands is your rock-solid faith in Jesus Christ. I want to live my life with God as my first love. When I experience God's unconditional love, he fills me to overflowing. And after me, who benefits the most from my walk with God? Gary, of course. He benefits from the overflow of my dependence on Christ.

Don't make the mistake of putting your husbands on a throne that only God should occupy. God alone is God, and your ultimate source of strength is found in him. But after God, your next allegiance is to your husbands. These are your two primary, daily commitments.

Gary will now share tips for how men can express guarding love to their wives.

## SEVEN KEYS TO GUARDING YOUR WIVES' HEARTS

Men, if your goal is to maintain a heart-to-heart connection with your wives, here are seven ways you can guard their hearts:

1. *Listen!* I remember a weekend some years ago when our daughter Missy was a high school senior. It was homecoming weekend, and she was on homecoming court. This was a big

deal for my three women—Barb, Missy, and Sarah. To put it mildly, the emotional tide in our home was at flood stage. Insecurity and anxiety over the event pushed Barb to tears. Missy and her big sister experienced their fill of emotional swings too. It was a classic woman thing.

What did I do? I reminded myself, *Okay, Gary, Barb says that both short-term and long-term marital success depends on a husband's ability to meet his wife's emotional needs.* I knew that with a word, a look, or an attitude I could either tune in to or turn off these women who are so important to me. My wife and daughters needed my soft side during this time, not my logical, hard side. So I listened. I exercised compassion in the midst of their emotional stirrings.

The way my best female friends in the world reacted to the homecoming thing was an issue of "heavenly wiring," not a character flaw on their parts. That's the way God made them. When that wiring trips a breaker and the emotions bubble over, men are tempted to fix it, to tell their wives what to do. At that point, however, wives don't want to know what to do. They just need their husbands to be with them through the range of feelings they are experiencing. Save the advice until they have had a chance to express their hearts—and then think hard about saving it until they ask!

Guys, have you ever just held your wives when they were struggling with something? I tried it recently when Barb was stressed. I just looked at her and said, "May I just hold you?" She melted in my arms. I couldn't believe it. After several minutes and a few tissues, she looked at me and said, "Thanks, Gary, for supporting me." I was stunned. It worked!

Trust me, men: Supported wives are guarded wives.

*2. Offer practical help.* If you have children, you know how your wives notice the kids' needs, which you sometimes overlook. Often our wives are present when the kids have needs, and they do what it takes to keep the children safe and content.

God gave children two parents for a reason. It's tough for moms to go one-on-one with an energetic child, much less get double- or triple-teamed by other kids in need. You can protect your wives' hearts from heaps of bitterness and resentment if you pitch in and help with the kids. Dying to selfishness is lived out by serving your wives in the day-to-day things. Don't save your practical help only for special occasions; make it an every-day occurrence. There is wisdom in the familiar kitchen motto informing us that the secret passageway to women's hearts runs right through the daily chores: "I like hugs, and I like kisses, but what I need right now is help with the dishes."

3. *Make time just for your wives.* Have you noticed what draws women to men who are not their husbands? It usually doesn't have anything to do with brains, bucks, or brawn. It's what won them in the first place: men's time and undivided attention.

If you don't meet your wives' need for friendship and emotional intimacy, you will leave them vulnerable. They may withdraw from you, or they may not feel free to respond to you sexually. Worst-case scenario, they may begin to look elsewhere to have their needs met.

Men, when you sense that your wives are withdrawing, it's probably not because they have decided you were right and they should "stop nagging." They have given up on connecting with you. Something is very wrong. From the women's perspective, it means you are not a harbor of safety to them but a threat. If you do not address this pattern of withdrawal, you may end up as two strangers coexisting under the same roof, sharing meals and the same bed but walled off from each other emotionally.

4. *Give them time for themselves.* Many women who work so hard to meet the needs of their husbands and children fail to meet their own needs. Wise, guarding husbands will make sure their wives have time and opportunity to rejuvenate themselves

through spiritual growth, physical exercise, or emotional interchange with female friends.

This is not as simple as choosing to baby-sit and watch a ball game on TV for a couple hours while they're out. Wives are recharged when they know their duties at home are being done—not just delayed—while they're gone. For example, yesterday, while Barb and I were working on this book, I took intermittent breaks to throw a load of clothes into the washer, fold some laundry, and empty the dishwasher. These small acts of service took just a few minutes, but they allowed Barb extra time for her writing and filled her love tank.

If your wives need just a temporary respite, step up and take over some of the chores. But if they feel constantly behind, you probably need to completely rethink the division of labor at your house. It may cost you some time and effort, but it also may get them thinking and feeling more positively about you.

5. *Love them unconditionally.* I hope you regard your wives as the most wonderful women in the world. I hope you are their greatest encouragers. But you are also the people who see their faults most clearly—not because you are critical of them but because you know them better than any other people do. What should you do with what you know about their weaknesses?

Women's acceptance of themselves hinges on so many things. Seeing themselves through your eyes is perhaps the biggest of them. You are their mirror. They see themselves most clearly in how you respond to them. You guard their hearts by loving them despite their flaws. You protect them by loving them even if they don't change. When they look at you and see unconditional love and acceptance shining back at them, they will more readily accept themselves. Let them know through your words of affirmation, your supportive prayers, and your positive body language that they are very important to you.

6. *Demonstrate spiritual leadership.* The apostle Peter wrote,

"In the same way, you husbands must give honor to your wives. Treat her with understanding as you live together. She may be weaker than you are, but she is your equal partner in God's gift of new life. If you don't treat her as you should, your prayers will not be heard" (1 Peter 3:7). The point about your wives' being "weaker" does not mean they are morally or mentally inferior to you. Rather, it most likely refers to relative physical strength between the sexes.

God has called you to devote yourself to honoring, understanding, and accepting your wives as your equal partners in life. He is asking a lot of you! But you have chosen to accept this mission. And know that your wives long to experience the fulfillment that comes from knowing that you love God and are willing to serve him by being effective husbands and fathers. So as you strengthen *your* relationship with God, you will help your wives strengthen *their* relationship with God and with you.

When I see guys struggling with their wives' response to their leadership, I help them focus on their relationship with Jesus. Bottom line: When they get their relationship with God in sync, their wives' positive response will invariably skyrocket.

Barb and I both read *The One Year Bible* (Tyndale House) each year. I read it each morning, before I even look at the sports page. This discipline took some time to develop, but I know that it not only enriches my life spiritually but also gives Barb incredible security to see me leading by studying the Bible consistently. When I tell her what I am learning in the Word, her trust in me grows because she knows Christ is working in my life.

7. *Pray for and with your wives.* Husbands who pray with their wives will find them more trusting. In turn, wives will be motivated to be one in mind and spirit with their husbands. If you want a biblical family, then you must initiate prayer with your wives. God has promised to bless that kind of spiritual investment.

Before Scott married our daughter Sarah, I took him aside and said, "Scott, you have the opportunity to base your marriage on prayer and spiritual intimacy with Sarah. Start your marriage relationship by loving Sarah as Christ loved the church. Every morning when you wake up or at night right before you go to sleep, take Sarah's hands and pray out loud together. I'm not legalistic. If you miss a day occasionally, it's no big deal. But how about being one of the few guys in America who commits to pray daily with his wife?"

Every so often I check with Scott to see how he is doing. I am thankful to say that he is on target in this vital area.

As much as Barb and I pray together now, we didn't always have a good track record. I didn't start as strongly as I wished in our marriage, but I am hitting the mark now. I'm not perfect, but I am enthusiastic about my role as the servant leader of our home. Your record may not be perfect either. But praying with your wives consistently will draw the two of you together in spiritual intimacy. Nothing will make your wives feel more safe, secure, and protected than your prayers *for* them and *with* them.

We have shared with you what we have learned about the areas where men and women are most vulnerable to attack. We have also shared how you can help guard your heart and the heart of your spouse. We encourage you to take the next step and form your own group for loving support and accountability, if you are not already participating in one. If you want more help in guarding your hearts, read *Guard Your Heart* and the *Guarding Love* workbook. By systematically working through the biblically based content and following through on proven marital exercises, you will find that the various facets of guarding love will provide the safety and security your marriage needs in order to last forever.

# Celebrating Love

*Celebrating love rejoices in the marriage relationship
and helps spouses feel cherished and captivated*

# 11

## *Rekindle the Joy of Being Married*

Men, do you remember how you felt when you brought home the first love of your life? You couldn't wait to show her off to your family and friends. You fawned over her. You expected a wink of approval from those whose opinions you trusted most. She was the apple of your eye.

We're not talking about bringing your *girlfriend* home to meet your mom and dad. We're talking about your love affair with your first *car*.

Chances are your first set of wheels cost you plenty. Whatever it looked like, you were thrilled to drive it home. Whether it was brand-new or just new to you, you carefully parked it away from other cars to avoid those ugly parking-lot dings. You kept it spotless inside and out. You may have spent your Saturday afternoons waxing and buffing it to a blinding sheen.

Eventually, however, your first car's beauty began to dim. You couldn't prevent the dings from accumulating, the carpet from wearing thin, or the vinyl from cracking. And if you had the bad luck of crunching your car in an accident, your love affair may have ended even sooner. You couldn't wait to trade in your old clunker for a pretty, new model.

Your marriage is a lifelong commitment, not something you can trade in when it has lost some of its just-married luster. Yet Barb and I know of countless men and women who "swap out" a spouse for something newer, nicer, prettier, or more exciting—either through divorce or by attaching themselves to an object or activity that seems more appealing.

Why do they do it? Because one or both spouses lose sight of the infinite value of the love they already have. They need a love that remains fresh and vibrant as the years roll by.

## ARE THE MILES SHOWING ON YOUR MARRIAGE?

On your wedding day you were flooded with joy over your spouses, and you gladly proclaimed your undying commitment to each other in front of family and friends. It was a moment when all the emotion of King Solomon's love poem came fully alive: "I am my lover's, and my lover is mine" (Song of Songs 6:3).

But maintaining the I'm-rejoicing-over-you attitude isn't automatic once your relationships have logged some miles and picked up a few dents and dings. It's even worse if you carry around lots of unresolved disappointments. What if your wives look more like their aunts than the women you married? What if your husbands wear the same size pants they wore in high school—with forty added pounds hanging over their belt? What if the sparkling extrovert you married has turned into a couch potato? Where did the magic go? Is there any way to get it back?

As married couples grow older, they lose some of their showroom luster. Some of us have been around for a few years and are showing a whole lot of wear and tear. Many couples grow apart over the years, and their marriages are marked by everything from ho-hum to hatred. Feelings of boredom, disappointment, or disdain can make couples slide a long way away from the dreams they had for their marriage.

If this is the case, what will you get excited about as the years go by? What do you have to celebrate? Can you really expect your marriages to get better with age? Or do you just have to make the best of it with the same old model?

Marriages hold no joy for those who feel stuck. But they hold infinite happiness for couples who learn to celebrate their one-of-a-kind love. The fifth secret to a lasting love is what Barb and I call *celebrating love*.

## LOVE WORTH CELEBRATING

Celebrating love revels in the emotional, physical, and spiritual connections that bond you to your spouses. It's a love that protects you and your spouses from drifting apart and enables you to fall in love and feel discovered all over again. Celebrating love rejoices daily in the marriages you have and helps you feel cherished and captivated by each other.

Celebration is an inescapable element of God's love. Maybe you have never thought about God's enthusiastic love for us. The Bible tells us that "the Lord . . . is a mighty savior. He will rejoice over you with great gladness. With his love, he will calm all your fears. He will exult over you by singing a happy song" (Zephaniah 3:17). God is so excited about his relationship with us that he celebrates his love by bursting into song! And Solomon's biblical love poem, Song of Songs, is a romantic celebration of marital love and sex. No doubt about it: God celebrates us!

Let us share one example of what celebrating love looks like in today's world. Barb and I received this e-mail from a friend.

> *While waiting to pick up a friend at the Portland, Oregon, airport, I had one of those life-changing experiences that you hear other people talk about—the kind that sneaks up on you unexpectedly. This one occurred merely two feet from me.*
>
> *Straining to locate my friend coming off the jetway, I*

noticed a man coming toward me. He stopped right next to me to greet his family. First, he motioned to his younger son (about six years old) as he laid down his bags. They gave each other a long, loving hug. As they separated enough to look into each other's face, I heard the father say, "It's so good to see you, Son, I missed you so much!" His son smiled somewhat shyly, averted his eyes, and replied softly, "Me too, Dad!"

Then the man stood up, gazed into the eyes of his older son (about nine), and while cupping his son's face in his hands, he said, "You're already quite the young man. I love you very much, Zach!" They too hugged a most loving, tender hug.

While this was happening, a toddler (about two years old) was squirming in her mom's arms, never once taking her eyes off her dad. The man said, "Hi, baby girl!" as he gently took the child from her mother. He kissed her face all over and then held her close to his chest while rocking her from side to side. The little girl instantly relaxed and simply laid her head on his shoulder, motionless in pure contentment.

After several moments he handed his daughter to his older son and declared, "I've saved the best for last," and proceeded to give his wife the longest, most passionate kiss I've ever seen. He gazed into her eyes for several seconds and then silently mouthed, "I love you so much!" They gazed into each other's eyes, beaming big smiles at one another, while holding both hands. For an instant they reminded me of newlyweds, but I knew by the age of their kids that they couldn't possibly be.

I puzzled about it for a moment then realized how totally engrossed I was in the wonderful display of love not more than an arm's length away from me. I suddenly felt uncomfortable, as if I were invading something sacred. I was amazed to hear my own voice nervously ask, "Wow! How long have you two been married?"

"Been together fourteen years total, married twelve of those," he replied without breaking the gaze from his wife's face.

*"Well, then, how long have you been away?" I asked. The man finally turned and looked at me, still beaming his joyous smile. "Two whole days!"*

*"Two days?" I said, stunned. By the intensity of the greeting, I had assumed he had been gone for at least several weeks, if not months.*

*Wanting to end my intrusion, I said, "I hope my marriage is still that passionate after twelve years!"*

*The man suddenly stopped smiling. He looked me straight in the eye with a force that burned right into my soul. Then he told me something that left me a different person. He simply said, "Don't hope, friend. Decide!"*

*He flashed his wonderful smile again, shook my hand, and said, "God bless!" With that, he and his family turned and strolled away together.*

*I was still watching that exceptional man and his family walk out of sight when my friend came up to me and asked, "What are you looking at?"*

*Without hesitating, and with a curious sense of certainty, I replied, "My future!"*

That's the power of celebrating love. It's not just a dream. It's a facet of love that we all have experienced and can recapture in our marriages. It produces great joy—and it will help you build a lasting love. If you stumbled onto the airport scene our friend did, we suspect you would stare with just as much amazement. Who wouldn't want a relationship like that? Who would ever think of walking away from that kind of love?

## RECAPTURING THE JOY

Without celebrating love, your relationship will stagnate—or worse. But when you cultivate celebrating love in your marriage, you will reconnect with the heartfelt love you discovered when you first fell head over heels for each other—and better. Celebrating love allows you to grow deeper in love year after year, rediscovering what you almost forgot about each other, appreciating again what may have lost its shine, and displaying affection and appreciation for all that you find in each other.

If we asked you to give three reasons for celebrating your love, what would you say? Or would you come up empty? You may feel you have nothing to celebrate. You may think that the days of passion, joy, and excitement in your marriage ended when the babies began arriving and you took out a second mortgage. "The party's over," you glumly report.

The Bible offers strong guidance on how we can recapture the celebrating aspect of love, which may have grown cold through the years. We see the solution in the book of Revelation, where Jesus scolded the believers in Ephesus for forsaking their deep love for him and for one another: "But I have this complaint against you. You don't love me or each other as you did at first!" (Revelation 2:4).

Then the Lord immediately tells them two things they must do to correct the problem: "Look how far you have fallen from your first love! Turn back to me again and work as you did at first" (2:5). Jesus doesn't tell them to wait for the old, warm feelings of love to well up again. He commands them to act by *recalling* their former love for him and *returning* to their former habits of devotion to God.

This passage coaches us to all-out commitment to the Lord. But the same principle applies to your relationship with your spouse. If you think back to the early days of your relationship, even to the days before you got married, what do you recall? How great was your love at that point? How did you demonstrate that love to one another? What kinds of loving attitudes and habits did you practice? If you have lost the sparkle and intensity of your love for each other, how can you return to those expressions? How can you return to the excitement you once sensed for each other?

# FIVE KEYS TO CELEBRATING LOVE

The words spoken by the man at the airport—"Don't hope, decide!"—have stuck with Barb and me from the moment we first read that e-mail. In marriage, every day is cause for celebration, and enjoying each other is a choice just like any other secret to lasting love. Let's look at five ways you can practice celebrating love in your marriage.

## 1. Put Each Other at the Top of the List

Fred was a workaholic. Fifteen-hour days as a consultant in the tech industry consumed him, and he thrived on conquest, whether beating people in games of one-upmanship or closing a deal and nailing the competition. He was proud of the lifestyle he had provided for his wife, Peg. After all, he had achieved the American dream of having it all: a large home with a three-car garage, pricey cars, a plump stock portfolio, a four-season cabin complete with a shed full of snowmobiles, and a boat so sleek it looked like a spaceship. Peg felt as if she had everything—except her husband.

A severe downturn in the tech sector left Fred scrambling for work. The months of joblessness stretched on and wiped out most of Fred and Peg's assets, leaving them struggling to pay their bills. When bankruptcy was unavoidable, Fred hit bottom.

Peg had a different outlook. She was confident they could start afresh, just as they had when they were young. And she was secretly glad to be rid of many of the things they had lost. She gently told Fred that she didn't need all the things he had worked so hard to accumulate. What she really wanted and needed was him.

The first key to celebrating love is to move each other to

the top of your to-do lists, just below your love for Jesus. You must make spending time together a priority, just as you did when you were first dating. Barb and I are amazed at how many people buy into the idea that "quality time" with our spouses and children is sufficient. Quality time is a myth. I am ashamed of how many people in my field of counseling have perpetuated that myth.

You need hundreds of hours of *quantity* time before you can enjoy real *quality* time. You need frequent periods of time away from the kids and other responsibilities. Find enjoyable activities to do together—everything from hobbies to foreplay to conversation—activities that will rekindle intimacy of the heart and spirit. Give your spouse priority time instead of just the leftovers. Here are several ideas to help you elevate celebrating love in your schedule.

*Put family second, right after your relationship with God.* Plan the together times you need, and write them on your calendar—in ink. That means not only date nights and getaway weekends but also smaller time slots each day, like dinner together, time with the children, and time to talk, play a game, or watch a favorite TV program together after the kids are in bed.

*Be cautious when making commitments outside your family.* Ask yourself: Do I really have the time, energy, and resources to make this happen without compromising my commitment to make my family a priority?

*Cultivate enriching relationships.* All of us deal with people who sap our strength. These are the people who always seem to be in crisis, people who mostly take from us and are unable to give of themselves. In addition to these "ministry opportunities," you need friendships with people who energize you instead of drain you.

*Make communication a priority in your relationships.* Take advantage of time in the car and around the dinner table to promote meaningful conversation. Don't clutter your life with the noise of constantly droning TV or radio.

*Let your body language demonstrate that your spouses are your priority.* When you talk together, put down the newspaper and turn off the television. Make eye contact. Give undivided attention. Ask God to give you the ability to focus directly on your spouses. When you walk together, hold hands. When you are together with other people, touch each other or make eye contact across the room in ways that say to each other and to people around you, "This person is the love of my life."

Instead of evaluating your daily success by how many tasks you check off your to-do list, ask whether they are the *right* tasks, those that properly balance God time, personal time, and family time. Your attention to the Bible, prayer, and fellowship with God will give you access to the only power source that will ultimately satisfy, allowing you to properly honor your family.

## 2. Confess to Each Other

We're back to this important point of closing the loop through forgiveness.

When Fred's work as a consultant dried up, he and Peg had to deal with issues that were even bigger than their financial problems. Peg was hurting from years of not being at the top of Fred's priority list and from their lack of emotional connection. She didn't know where to take all these issues, so she stuffed them inside, buried her pain alive.

After declaring bankruptcy, Fred finally found work at one of the few surviving tech companies in his area. He began to contemplate what Peg had said about getting along just fine without "all that stuff." He asked her how she felt about their old life and how he had wounded her. In short, he became teachable. As he began to understand all the hurt he had caused Peg, he confessed how wrong he had been and asked for her forgiveness. For the first time in their marriage, Fred began to factor Peg's thoughts and feelings into his career decisions.

Unresolved offenses block all kinds of intimacy—emotional, physical, and spiritual. Barb and I know this from our own experience and from talking to countless couples whose love has grown cold. Trying to get close while those hurts remain is like trying to jump over a hundred-foot wall. It won't happen.

When you sense a wall between you and your spouses, something is very wrong. Husbands, why not take the lead to address the pain, close the loop, and restore intimacy? Become responsible for the tone of the relationship and get your marriages back on course, especially if you are guilty of contributing to the pain.

Barb is going to discuss another key to celebrating love, the importance of getting to know one another deeply.

## 3. Get to Know Each Other Again

Most men tell Gary and me that they were far more successful at connecting with their wives before marriage or before children. And many women report to us that as family responsibilities and challenges mount, they lose track of their husbands' most heartfelt needs. Recapturing the joy of celebrating love in your relationships requires that you get to know your spouses all over again.

How? Demonstrate your love by showing that you are deeply interested. It takes effort to rediscover your wives' strengths, personal interests, and uniqueness. It requires focus to rediscover things that you have overlooked about your husbands for years. Yet detecting these deep, hidden qualities will bring new excitement into your marriages. Here are some tips for getting started.

*Study your spouses.* Watch closely to discover what makes your spouses' eyes brighten. Men, make it your goal to know your wives better than they know themselves. Women, do the same. You will learn what your spouses are thinking about, what is important to them, and what energizes them. The more you study your spouses, the better prepared you will be to serve them.

*Really listen to each other.* Give your spouses your complete attention, even if you don't have a clue what they are talking about. Ask questions. Notice what your spouses get excited about in conversation and what causes them to slow down and reflect. Pay attention to your spouses' choice of words when talking about a subject close to their hearts.

*Work alongside each other.* You may have devised a tidy division of labor to keep your household humming along smoothly: Husbands always fuel the car, wives do everything in the kitchen; husbands handle outside chores, wives do homework with the kids. It may be efficient and orderly, but it isn't much fun doing your chores and tasks alone. And in a busy household, it can mean constant separation. Try flip-flopping some of the roles and responsibilities, or better yet, team up with your spouses to do them together.

*Try some of your old favorites again.* What are some of the things you and your spouses did when you first met and married? You know the things I mean: hobbies, sports, shopping, cheap dates, even parking beside the lake. Your spouses' interests don't have to be your favorite things to do, but you can take turns participating in each others' favorites. Honor your spouses by sacrificing some of your own agenda to please them.

*Get away together.* Go on a picnic. Go for a walk. Send the kids to their grandma's or a friend's house for the weekend, and take off for your favorite bed-and-breakfast. Or spend the weekend at home. Take a minivacation each year without the kids. And during a normal, busy week at home, spend a part of every day or evening with each other, just the two of you. Your getaways don't have to cost a lot of money, but the effort to be together will pay significant dividends in your marriages.

*Be captivated by the love of your life.* A few years ago Barb and

I spoke to hundreds of students at our daughter Missy's college campus. We delighted in seeing these young men and women thirsty for biblical truth about godly relationships. As I was coaching the guys, I taught them what Solomon wrote: "Why be captivated, my son, with an immoral woman, or embrace the breasts of an adulterous woman?" (Proverbs 5: 20). In this Scripture passage Solomon confronts us by describing the futility in seeking pleasure from someone other than the love of our lives: wives—or for that matter, husbands. To really bring this teaching alive, read verses 18-19 and capture the king's instruction: "Let your wife be a fountain of blessing for you. Rejoice in the wife of your youth. She is a loving doe, a graceful deer. Let her breasts satisfy you always. May you always be *captivated* by her love" (emphasis added).

You should have seen the eyes of these eager young men bulge as I described being *captivated* by the wife of my youth. Being captivated by Barb isn't being trapped or stuck. To the contrary, being captivated means celebrating the reality that I am enthralled with Barb. It is being caught up and bound to each other. It is the experience of not seeing another woman in the room because I have eyes only for the woman with whom I am sharing my life. Captivating love celebrates God's design for marriage. And it doesn't get any better than that!

### 4. Rethink Your Thinking

Gary and I know a lot of people like Dale, who always sees the dark side of everything. Whether the subject is work, church, or his wife, he notices flaws and failures everywhere. By constantly focusing on the negative, Dale misses the brighter side of life, especially in his attitudes toward his wife, Katie. His mind endlessly cycles a negative commentary about her, like a looped tape recording. If Dale doesn't break this gloomy pattern, he and Katie are doomed to a marriage devoid of celebration.

What tapes are you playing about your spouses? Can you change the way you think? Absolutely. We believe it is possible to learn to fall in love again, and we have two simple coaching tips to get you started:

1. *Be willing to fall in love with your spouses again.* Being in love begins in your mind with the choice to surrender to feelings of love. Celebration is a learned response to the way your partners look and feel, to the things your partners say and do, and to the emotional experiences you share. Only when you have made this basic choice can you train yourselves to look for the good in your spouses and be glad for it.

2. *Control your thoughts.* The New Testament encourages us to control our thoughts, to take them captive and make them obedient to Christ (see 2 Corinthians 10:5, NIV). We can do that in our marriages. When a negative thought about your spouses comes along, arrest it, lock it behind bars, and throw away the key! When you see a positive trait in your spouses, embrace it, think about it, comment on it, and enjoy it. Change the focus of your thinking to the qualities that caused you to fall in love with your spouses in the first place.

The next time you are with your spouses, look closely at them. Look at their hands. Do you remember when just holding hands made you tingle? Look into their eyes. What makes those eyes sparkle? Think about your spouses' passions and dreams. What makes them excited to be alive?

Then tell your spouses what you see. Give words to your love. Express your love aloud, and do it often.

Ask God to refresh your love for your spouses. Even if you currently complain to yourselves about them a hundred times a day, even if you genuinely feel your marriages have gone bad, even if many days you don't feel in love anymore, you can change. God can still help you develop a celebrating love.

## 5. Rekindle Romance and Physical Intimacy

Romance and sex may be the first thing you associate with celebrating love. Gary and I are as glad as anyone that celebrating love includes this special kind of husband-wife closeness!

But sex isn't all there is to celebrating love; there is more to feeling cherished and captivated than what happens in your most private and intimate moments together. Let's look for a moment at the full extent of captivating love. Men, I have found that as a husband demonstrates being captivated by his wife, she flourishes and revels in his love. Captivating love is reflected when a man is mesmerized by his wife. He connects to her and is entranced by her. His eyes light up when he is in her presence and reflect warmth and tenderness when he speaks of her in her absence. He is charmed by her, and others can see something special about the kind of love that reflects celebration. Captivating love leads to the expression of sexual intimacy in the marriage relationship.

As we discuss the component of sexual intimacy in celebrating love, let's start with a foundational truth: God created men and women to be different. "So God created people in his own image; God patterned them after himself; male and female he created them" (Genesis 1:27). In addition to the obvious differences in physical anatomy, have you noticed how this difference works out in everyday life? For example, while women are thinking about a dirty kitchen floor or errands or bathing the kids, their husbands may be thinking about sex. And when husbands are in the garage rebuilding a carburetor or refinishing a piece of furniture with a ball game blaring on the radio, their wives may be thinking about quiet conversations over a cup of tea.

Back in chapter 6 we said that most men spell intimacy S-E-X and most women spell it T-A-L-K. This basic difference can lead to enormous confusion and outright conflict. But here's the good news: The difference was God's idea, his design. He created women with all the incredible, unique gifts and needs they bring to their relationship with their husbands—including women's need for emotional connection through talk. And he created men with all of their wonderful, unique gifts and needs—including men's needs for sexual intimacy.

How do husbands and wives bridge these differences so that both thoroughly enjoy the sexual intimacy of celebrating love? It happens when we understand and lovingly accommodate the unique intimacy needs of our spouses. First, I will coach the husbands on how to meet wives' intimacy needs. Then Gary will coach the wives on meeting husbands' unique needs.

## UNDERSTANDING YOUR WIVES' INTIMACY NEEDS

Shared emotional arousal between husbands and wives is a catalyst in the development of a passionate physical love. What husbands must realize is how their seemingly nonsexual activities help to satisfy their wives' hunger for physical intimacy. At the heart of these nonsexual actions is the emotional bond of being friends. "The determining factor in whether wives feel satisfied with the sex, romance, and passion in the marriage is, by 70 percent, the quality of the couple's friendship," says marriage expert John Gottman, and "for men, the determining factor is, by 70 percent, the quality of the couple's friendship. So men and women come from the same planet after all."[1]

A key quality in married friendship, for men and women alike, is staying interested in their spouses and keeping their partners interested in them. No gimmick—flowers, candy, or a candlelight dinner—works unless your partners are genuinely interested in you and their faces light up when you enter the room. Especially for wives, the pathway to sexual intimacy is *emotional* intimacy.

Husbands, don't underestimate the power of the small signs

of affection that communicate to your wives all day long that they are loved. This is vital to your wives' sexual fulfillment. Susan gives a personal example:

> For years I have tried to encourage my husband to show affection outside the bedroom. He just can't seem to say anything nice or touch me without wanting sex in the next five minutes.
>
> One day we got together with another couple, Matt and Leann. Matt was a high school friend—not a boyfriend, but he could have been. The four of us spread out a picnic. I watched Matt throughout the afternoon as he held Leann's hand. He said kind things about how much he appreciated her. He carried everything from the vans and helped serve lunch to the children. He even kissed Leann good-bye when she and I took the kids for a trip to the rest rooms.
>
> Watching Matt love his wife hit me hard. He's someone I've thought about a lot over the years, wondering if I missed something by not dating him when we were younger. Seeing his minute-by-minute connection with Leann sure didn't help me feel content with my husband. I really had to give my attitude to the Lord and ask him to help me be patient with my husband. He's a great guy in so many other ways.

Wives starved for emotional intimacy and nonsexual affection may withdraw from their husbands physically. They may seem distracted and distant, spending more than the usual time at work or in other activities. They could be "too busy" or "too tired" for sex and avoid spending time with their husbands. And husbands might notice that the children are a higher priority for their wives than they are. These are all warning signs that their wives' needs for friendship and nonsexual affection are not being met. They do not feel that you cherish them. They do not feel captivated. Celebrating love is not part of their experience.

Husbands reading this book are married to walking, talking marriage manuals. You will be amazed at what you can learn about your wives' needs if you just watch them and ask them. Women tend to be naturally gifted with the ability to show their husbands the keys that will emotionally strengthen their marriages. Husbands, your wives are your greatest guide to discerning how to be tender, tuned in, and teachable. But you won't learn anything if you don't pay attention to them.

Wives, Gary has a few important paragraphs to help you cherish and captivate your husbands.

## UNDERSTANDING YOUR HUSBANDS' INTIMACY NEEDS

Men talk to Barb and me all the time about their frustrations regarding sexual intimacy in their marriages. Few women understand the depth of anguish husbands feel when their need for sexual intimacy is not fully met.

"I felt that I was meeting Olivia's emotional needs," Owen says. "She even said I was. I was doing everything I knew to do, and she told me how much she appreciated how we talked and how I treated her. But when it came to my desire for sex, it was completely up to what kind of mood she was in. Some days she was preoccupied, as if I was last on her list, not worth her attention. Other days she just didn't feel like it. When I told her I wanted to get close to her, I felt as if I was begging. It was humiliating."

With his one legitimate, God-appointed outlet for sexual intimacy cut off, Owen retaliated by shutting down the emotional connection Olivia so enjoyed. His tactic backfired when his wife pushed him away and started a relationship with a man at work.

Sexual frustrations can lead to more serious marital problems. Husbands whose wives ignore their drive for sexual intimacy feel rejected as people and as men. They often shut down or pull away, perhaps turning to pornography or affairs to meet their needs. We do not condone or excuse these activities no matter who is at fault. Men or women who step away from God's moral guidelines are personally responsible for the painful consequences. However, such actions can be averted if wives are attuned to the depth of their husbands' need for physical intimacy.

Wives, you can view your husbands' strong need for sexual intimacy as a negative thing—a problem to manage—or you can delight in the fact that they have such a deep hunger for you. If sexual intimacy is a struggle for you, begin by taking the issue of your sexual relationship to God: Ask him, "What is blocking me from enjoying the sexual aspect of our marriage? Is it unresolved hurt? Do we need to deal with conflict or forgive each other? Am I bringing past pain from other relationships into our marriage bed?"

Until you resolve your own issues, it will be nearly impossible for you to enjoy a healthy, active sexual relationship with your husbands. Women with unresolved emotional pain have difficulty taking the risk and opening their hearts and bodies to their husbands.

If you want to maximize your sexual relationship, follow these coaching tips:

*Don't stay angry.* Anger robs you of intimacy, and unresolved tension brings a frosty chill to your bedroom. Confess your offenses, forgive your husbands' offenses, and be done with it!

*Exchange tips with your husbands.* Outside the bedroom, in the calm light of day, ask your husbands how they would like you to give them pleasure the next time you are together sexually. Ask them to make a list of things you can do to please them. Then create your own list of three to five ways they can give you sexual pleasure. Exchange your lists, and take turns treating each other to the new ideas.

*Confront the darkness.* More and more women confide to us that their husbands bring pornography into the bedroom for erotic stimulation, whether in the form of sexually explicit magazines or videos. If it's happening in your relationship, put a stop to it. Keep your marriage bed pure.

*Pray about your sex life.* God isn't intimidated or embarrassed by your sex life. He invented it! Invite the originator of sex into this arena of your marriage, and let him guide you in cherishing and captivating your husbands.

## LITTLE THINGS MEAN A LOT

You can do much to rekindle celebrating love in your marriage by paying attention to the little things. Small acts of love can ignite a bonfire of passion in your spouses' hearts. Barb and I have listed a number of ideas below. You may recognize some of them from the early days of your courtship and marriage. Select a few to put into practice. As you do, feelings of being cherished and captivated will follow.

## IDEAS FOR CELEBRATING YOUR HUSBAND

- Send him off and welcome him home with a smile and a kiss.
- Let him know you're glad he's home just because you love him, not because the sink is clogged or you need to get away from the kids.
- If you arrive home after your husband does, find him before you do anything else and tell him how glad you are to be home.

- Let him know you care. Buy a mushy card, and send it to his office, hide it in his briefcase, or slip it into the book he's reading at bedtime.
- Write down a list of reasons why you love him, then share the list with him over a romantic dinner.
- Leave him a surprise note with an encouraging Bible verse.
- Buy attractive new nightwear for yourself—and hide his!
- Give him massages.
- Pray for him before he leaves for work.
- Join him in his favorite activity even if you aren't crazy about it. Try doing with him some of the things he enjoys doing with his buddies.
- Say, "I'm sorry" when you are wrong, and forgive him when he is wrong.
- Initiate sexual intimacy.
- Listen to his opinions on spiritual issues. Ask him what type of activities would fuel his spiritual growth. Don't impose your ideas on him.
- Leave him a voice-mail message saying you love him and are praying for him.
- Eat breakfast with him, and enter his world at the start of the day.
- Accept your body, and enjoy experimenting with him sexually.

## IDEAS FOR CELEBRATING YOUR WIFE

- Be accessible to her—always! Tell her where you will be and how long you will be gone.
- Let your coworkers know you can always be interrupted when she calls.

- Repeat your wedding vows often. Tell her that if you had it to do all over again, you would choose her again—and again, and again.
- Continually promise and reassure her that your love for her and faithfulness to her is "till death do us part."
- Invite her to tell you how she desires to be loved, then seek to love her in that way.
- Give her a head-to-toe massage.
- Compliment her, especially for the little things.
- Send flowers or chocolates or whatever little gifts she likes.
- Attend a marriage conference together. Take the initiative to locate one, make all the arrangements, including a baby-sitter if that is necessary. Join us at one of our conferences. Check our Web site (www.afclive.com) to see if we are going to be in your community this year!
- Lavish her with nonsexual touch.
- Call her during the day just to say hello.
- Put your arm around her or hold her hand in public.
- Say "I love you" before she does. Begin and end each day with encouraging words.
- Write notes to her regularly telling her how proud you are of her.
- Hold her hands, and pray for her.
- Send her cards or love letters.
- Bring her breakfast in bed.

Celebrating love doesn't need to be extravagant or showy. It can be expressed by a hand-in-hand walk, a single rose, a carefully placed note, and the creative thoughtfulness that comes from the heart. Start with affirmation and compliments because a lack of appreciation for your spouse will kill anything else you try.

One more component of celebrating love is so important that it requires its own chapter. Let's consider what spiritual intimacy can do to help you and your spouse feel cherished and captivated.

$$— 12 —$$

## Building Spiritual Intimacy

The following letter is from a woman we will call Nicole. She wrote in after listening to our radio program. Barb and I often hear sad stories like this from our listeners and conference attendees. They remind us of the critical nature of spiritual intimacy in building a lasting love.

*Dear Gary and Barb,*

*My husband and I listen to your radio program daily, and we have attended your marriage conference and read your books. I'm glad my husband has been involved in your material. But there is also a problem with him. It's like there are two men in my life. The public side of Trent goes to church and does all the acceptable Christian things. But at home, where it really counts, Trent lives a private life that doesn't match his profession. I know I sound critical, and perhaps I am. It's because the man I thought I was marrying is not the man I live with. Let me explain.*

*Trent grew up in a Christian home. He went to Sunday school as a boy and was taught Christian principles. When we dated, he appeared to have a relationship with Jesus. But soon*

after our wedding, he fell away from what little faith he had.
I saw it in his business dealings, as he moved into gray areas
financially and violated biblical principles. I saw it in his
personal habits. He would stay up late at night watching TV,
and if he heard me coming into the room, he would quickly
switch the channel.

The Internet became an obsession with Trent. I went online
once to check out a plane fare and found that he had logged a
string of visits to a porn site that made me gag.

But it wasn't only the money and sexual things that
bothered me. It was the heart things. Trent would attend men's
conferences, buy the books, and appear to be seeking spiritual
things, but he wouldn't share anything with me. Sometimes I
would see him talking to his small-group buddies in the church
hallway, laughing and enjoying rich fellowship. But I was crying
on the inside because he never shared this kind of joy with me.

I heard you say to one radio listener that a hurting wife
should express her heart to her husband. I did that to Trent.
I heard you encourage another listener to pray. I have prayed,
over and over again. And then I heard you tell one caller to
get out of the way and let God work. That's the only thing
I haven't done. I am afraid that if I do move out of the way,
Trent will never move closer to me or to God.

I long for Trent to pray with me. I long for him to say,
"Nicole, look what I just read in the Word." I long for him to
initiate spiritual discussions with me. I see other women growing
spiritually with their husbands, but on the inside I feel as if
I am dying. I want to love Trent unconditionally. I want to encourage him, and most of the time I do. But more than anything,
I long for the "marriage of three" you two talk about on the
radio—a marriage of Jesus, Trent, and me. I don't want more
stuff, I want more of my husband—his thoughts and feelings.
Most of all I want more of his spiritual heart.

> *I won't leave Trent. I am committed to him. I also know*
> *that I am part of the problem. I expect things too quickly, get*
> *short with him, and get critical at times. Please pray for us:*
> *Trent and Nicole. Pray that I won't get discouraged and that*
> *somehow we will experience a breakthrough without facing*
> *a big crisis. I've heard you say so often that pain is the precursor*
> *to growth. I am fearful of what could happen, what God could*
> *allow, to lead us to that growth. But I am willing to surrender*
> *if God would take his rightful place in our home.*
>
> *Thanks for being there. I am praying for you two.*
>
> *Nicole*

These kinds of letters break our hearts. Sadly, this isn't the only Christian home in which a spouse has subtly or deliberately allowed the spiritual underpinnings of the marriage to crumble. We find so many couples living in a daze, wondering what piece of the marriage puzzle is missing. Often it is spiritual intimacy.

As the result of our listening to couples, we have identified several telltale signs that suggest a marriage may be languishing in spiritual impotence. Read the following signs, and see if any of them describes your marriage.

*Sign #1: You may experience conflict in many areas.* The spiritual dimension provides the foundation for how the game of life is to be played. It's tough to play well in marriage if you and your spouse don't equally value God and Scripture. You wouldn't want to play a game of baseball if people didn't agree on the rules. It's true of marriages as well.

*Sign #2: You may feel incomplete.* You may be on top of your game in every other area of your relationships, but if you don't connect spiritually, you will always feel as if something is missing—because the most important element *is* missing! Without a spiritual connection, you miss out on the closeness and joy God intends. The deepest part of your spouse will go unexplored, leaving the greatest joys of your marriage untapped.

*Sign #3: You may lack a firm foundation for your marriage commitment.* The Bible declares marriage to be a sacred, unbreakable union. But without that biblical foundation in your life, it is easy to see marriage as an arrangement of convenience rather than commitment. And when it is no longer convenient, you want out.

*Sign #4: You may lack boundaries for guarding your marriage.* The Bible provides absolute standards for right and wrong. God's people enjoy confidence that the boundaries they live by were erected by a kind and loving God. But without the spiritual dimension, your marriage lacks God's protection and provision.

Many of these signs are evident in Trent and Nicole's marriage. But there is great hope for this couple and others who are struggling in the area of spiritual intimacy. Developing and enriching spiritual intimacy in marriage is a vital element of the celebrating love that helps husbands and wives feel cherished and captivated.

## A MARRIAGE OF THREE

It is relatively easy to understand the *emotional intimacy* that creates a heart-to-heart bond as well as the *physical intimacy* that brings a couple together body-to-body. But every couple also needs soul-to-soul closeness. If you want to enjoy the deepest level of connection and celebration, you need to develop *spiritual intimacy* in your relationship.

Bonding spiritually can be a puzzling area for husbands and wives. Even if you both set a goal to grow together spiritually, you may have difficulty deciding how to get there. And if only one of you wants to pursue spiritual depth in your relationship, you will face additional struggles.

So what is spiritual intimacy? There is nothing weird or

mystical about it. Spiritual intimacy occurs when you as husband and wife surrender your lives and relationship to the Lord. You grow together spiritually when you live out your marriage relationship according to God's ways and aim to please him in all things.

Spiritual intimacy is an ingredient available only to those who have a personal relationship with God through Jesus Christ and who live to please him. When you are joined with another Christian in marriage, you have the wonderful privilege of seeking spiritual intimacy in your marriage. When husbands and wives are growing in their vertical relationships (individually with God), their horizontal relationship (between the two of them) comes together as well.

Barb and I believe that spiritual intimacy in a marriage is a "God thing." It's a marriage of three—an intimate relationship between God, a husband, and a wife. Profound intimacy happens when two hearts, two bodies, two souls connect with the God who created them and designed marriage. Picture a triangle with you, your spouse, and God positioned at the three corners. As you and your spouse draw closer to God, you naturally draw closer to each other.

Most of our world doesn't understand spiritual intimacy in marriage. Sadly, many Christian couples haven't grasped this profound truth either. But when husbands and wives truly begin to understand the significance of marriage of three, their relationships begin to flourish. In the Old Testament, King Solomon offers a great picture of what we mean by this intimacy of three. "A person standing alone can be attacked and defeated, but two can stand back-to-back and conquer. Three are even better, for a triple-braided cord is not easily broken" (Ecclesiastes 4:12).

Later in this chapter we will look at practical ways you can make spiritual intimacy a reality in your relationship. But first we want to explain exactly what working toward spiritual intimacy can accomplish in your marriage. And we want to speak frankly about the harm that can come to marriages missing this all-important foundation.

## THE BENEFITS OF SPIRITUAL INTIMACY

You may not realize the power of spiritual intimacy in creating celebrating love in your relationship. Barb and I often describe it this way. Emotional and physical intimacy ignite the rocket in your marriage, but spiritual intimacy fires the afterburners and gets you into orbit. Emotional and physical attraction is what drew you together, but the spiritual connection is what *keeps* you together. Spiritual intimacy is indispensable to achieving the marriage of your dreams and forging a lasting love.

Spiritual intimacy will be the source of your greatest joy as husbands and wives. It is also the source of the strength you need to build marriages that will last. In fact, we can't limit the role of spiritual intimacy to celebrating love. It is the foundation for all six key kinds of love we present in this book. Your vital relationship with God through Christ empowers

- the grace in forgiving love
- the humility in serving love
- the patience in persevering love
- the wisdom in guarding love
- the joy in celebrating love
- the power in renewing love

You, your spouse, and God are an unbeatable team. No matter what life throws at you, no matter how the enemy tries to thwart you, no matter what mistakes you or your spouse may make, a marriage of three not only can get you through it but can also help you go deeper. The closeness that comes from spiritual intimacy is the greatest connection of all. Here are just a few key benefits of spiritual intimacy:

*Spiritual intimacy empowers celebrating love.* A spiritual connection won't make your marriage perfect, but it will keep you in touch with God, the author of marriage and the one who has the answers to your deepest marriage problems. Bonding spiritually enables you to accept each other as people whom God has forgiven. And as God reminds you of the true nature of your union—that your love isn't between two persons but three—you will experience the depths of uniting body, soul, and spirit. It is impossible to keep such a connection from igniting into feelings of being cherished and captivated.

*Spiritual intimacy allows you to connect at the deepest level.* God designed husbands and wives to join together emotionally and physically. And these connections are electric! But he also created you to come together at the deepest level of your being—soul and spirit. If you want the deepest possible connection with your spouse, this is it. As you seek God together, your hunger for wholeness will be satisfied.

*Spiritual intimacy links you with God's purposes and plans for you.* In the Old Testament, God told his people, "'For I know the plans I have for you,' says the Lord. 'They are plans for good and not for disaster, to give you a future and a hope'" (Jeremiah 29:11). This promise is for you today too. God has good plans for your marriages. He guarantees to make your marriages adventures as you trust him to guide you together through life.

*Spiritual intimacy allows you to bless each other with God's love.* In the Bible, God often uses the intimacy of marriage relationships as a metaphor for his love for humankind. As husbands or wives, you can demonstrate what God's love for your spouses looks like. You can be God's voice and arms of love and care. What a privilege! As you meet your spouses' needs, you are God's love "with skin on."

*Spiritual intimacy brings your deepest values and desires into agreement.* Barb and I believe that the Bible not only communicates how you can know God and connect with your spouses but also lays out principles for what is right and important in life. As you and your spouses grow spiritually intimate and submit to the teachings of Scripture, your biggest goals and beliefs will be in harmony.

*Spiritual intimacy opens the door to the deepest levels of communication.* One of the fundamentals of intimacy is being honest about who you are—warts and all. As you grow in spiritual intimacy and transparency, your communication will expand from the physical and emotional levels to include the spiritual element of your lives and relationships. Spiritual intimacy permits profound sharing you cannot enjoy at any other level.

*Spiritual intimacy empowers your marriage to survive.* All couples encounter circumstances in which they feel overwhelmed. The power of God is bigger than any situation you will ever face, and he can enable you to stand firm in the storm. Barb and I have seen a number of Christian couples collapse under trials and conflicts. But these collapses happened only after one or both partners compromised or abandoned their core spiritual values.

*Spiritual intimacy connects you to a supportive body of fellow disciples.* Husbands are the strength of their wives, and wives are the strength of their husbands. But no marriage survives or thrives by itself. God has given you his people, the church, to stand with you when you struggle and celebrate with you when you triumph. If you are not connected with a local body of believers who support your marriage, make that connection! It is a benefit God doesn't want you to live without.

## WHAT SPIRITUAL INTIMACY LOOKS LIKE

Spiritual intimacy is more than going to church together and holding hands during the service, as nice as that may be. Carl and Danielle's story gives us a peek into what spiritual intimacy looks like in a marriage relationship.

"Danielle and I met at the state university," Carl explains. "All I knew was that I couldn't stop staring at the young woman across the room in my sophomore literature class. I had no shortage of physical attraction to her, and I found out later that she had no shortage for me.

"When I approached Danielle about starting a study group, she agreed, provided we met in a place like a restaurant or the library—not the dorms. She also insisted that other people be in the group. I had no idea where all these 'rules' were coming from. But I was willing to jump through some big hoops to get to know her."

"To me," Danielle interrupts, "they weren't just rules. I was a Christian, and these boundaries made sense. I had no idea who this guy was, other than that he was smart—and cute. The 'rules' protected our long-term good."

"The big change," continues Carl, "came when I asked her out on a date. Danielle turned me down flat. By that time, our studies had touched on some spiritual topics, and she and I both knew I wasn't a Christian. She said that if I wanted to get closer to her, a good place to start would be joining her at church."

"You have to imagine how I felt at that point," Danielle says. "Carl was a great guy. But he was clueless about God. I knew one of God's boundaries for me was not dating a non-Christian. I didn't want to let my heart get attached to a guy if he didn't trust in Christ, but I also didn't want him to fake a spiritual awakening just to get a date. He had to realize the truth of the Bible for himself—and for real. And he did."

Carl explains, "Not only did Danielle make me wait until I became a Christian before we dated, she made me wait most of another year to 'make sure it stuck.' She said her older sister married a guy who always nodded when she talked about spiritual issues. He is a really compassionate guy who works with kids in the city. But faith in Christ isn't real for him, and they have struggled ever since. Danielle wasn't going to go there.

"Danielle didn't allow physical attraction to drive our relationship. In fact, she told me to keep my hands to myself—another one of those boundaries. She said she wanted her body to be a gift to her husband. But I got to unwrap the package later, after we got married.

"Meeting Danielle and meeting God revolutionized my life—not so much in *what* I did but *why*. Before I became a Christian, I was a good, moral person, but I didn't have a relationship with God. When I learned that Christ died for me, and that his death made me acceptable to God, I realized that I needed God and I wanted to live for him. The real change in me took some time—almost six months. It didn't happen overnight."

"That was fifteen years ago," Danielle says. "We married knowing that our lives were fully committed to God. Our strong and growing faith has helped us stay close to God individually and support each other's growth. And our spiritual life together has had a huge impact on how we bring up our children and what we teach them about faith and life.

"I think one of the ways we are different from non-Christian couples is that we make decisions God's way. First, we always pray and tell God that we want to follow his will for our lives. Then we look hard at the Bible to see what it says about our situation. We don't argue about what *I* want or *he* wants. Sometimes we can't agree on what *God* wants, but we leave it up to God to show us through the Bible or through the other ways he can guide us, like prayer and wise Christian counsel."

Carl adds one last point. "When I became a Christian, this was all a mystery to me. But it's not a mystery anymore. I have a close relationship with Christ and with my wife, loving each of them with all my heart."

# ROADBLOCKS TO SPIRITUAL INTIMACY

Maybe your response is, "That's a wonderful story, but I can't see it happening in our marriage. I already have a hard time maintaining a spiritual focus in my own life, let alone worrying about developing spiritual intimacy with my spouse. How can I cram more into life?" Or maybe you're saying, "My spouse just isn't interested in spiritual things. What can I do?"

Barb will walk you through three major hurdles to spiritual intimacy and how you can overcome them.

*"I don't have time for spiritual things. We have more pressing issues right now."* If I walked out to the garage tomorrow morning and found that my car wouldn't start, I would investigate. (Actually, I would ask Gary to investigate!) He would first check to see if the battery had somehow drained overnight. He would double-check that the car had adequate fuel. But the problem might run deeper than the obvious. There is no substitute for keeping your battery charged and putting gas into the tank, but sometimes the engine needs an overhaul. Surface fixes won't do the job.

That's the situation with our lives. Smaller concerns are pressing and urgent, but none is as important as developing spiritual intimacy. Even if your life is in shambles, the most important thing you can do is make room for God.

*"I'm afraid God will expect more than we can do."* Maybe you're afraid that God will force you to give up something you like or lead you down a painful path. Yes, giving yourselves to God often involves making hard choices regarding your activities and possessions. But remember that his purpose is to "give life in all its fullness" (John 10:10). And you can trust him to do that as he shapes you into a couple who lives close to him.

*"My spouse isn't interested in spiritual matters."* If your spouses are struggling with this whole area, pray for them. Share your own convictions if your spouses will listen, and then let God work in their hearts. God will gradually open your husbands'

spiritual eyes as you obey the scriptural command to win them by a "gentle and quiet spirit" (1 Peter 3:4). Or God will work in your wives' hearts as you treat them "with understanding" (1 Peter 3:7). You can be God's instrument in reaching your spouses. But you must let God do it in his good time.

The truth is, the only person you can change is you. So let God do his work in you. Open your heart to him, and continue to pursue a faithful, obedient relationship with him, giving him your whole heart, soul, and mind. At the same time, pray faithfully for your spouses. You might even want to ask some of your trusted friends and prayer partners to join you in praying that God will work in your spouses' lives. Then be patient. Don't give up, ever.

Back in the early days of our marriage, both Gary and I were growing in our faith—with a lot of maturing yet to do. I remember a conflict that had spiritual implications. One summer our house needed painting. Gary decided that since he couldn't paint during the week because of work, he would stay home from church for four Sundays and paint one side of the house each week.

I didn't think that was a good idea. I was excited about going to church and didn't want to miss out. And I was afraid that four weeks away from church would have a negative effect on Gary's growth and on our marriage. I could have nagged, complained, or even enabled his behavior by staying home with him. But I decided to surrender the issue to God, keep up my own relationship with God, and let God handle Gary. So I went to church that month while my husband painted the house.

It turned out to be a pivotal time in Gary's growth. After missing church four weeks in a row, he realized more than ever the value of the worship, teaching, and fellowship he missed. When I got out of the way, God, in his time, had his way with Gary.

## GETTING STARTED ON YOUR SPIRITUAL JOURNEY TOGETHER

Maybe you are looking at the possibilities more than the roadblocks. "I like what you're talking about," you say, "but I don't know where to start." That's an attitude Gary and I enjoy working with. It's the place we all find ourselves at some point.

How do we go deeper with God? How do we make a spiritual connection with our spouses? Let us coach you on some tips for getting started on your spiritual journey.

As an accountant in a rapidly expanding business, Denise is exhausted most of the time. Each night she carries home a laptop full of work and continues to answer e-mail and phone calls late into the evening from clients across the country. Her job was once enjoyable and challenging. Now she feels like quitting. But she can't because she and her husband, Ken, need the double income.

Ken knows that Denise's needs run deeper than what he can meet himself. He knows she is making the best of a difficult situation at work, but she has been ignoring her own spiritual needs. When Ken suggests that she join a Monday evening Bible study for working moms, Denise scoffs. Then Ken explains that he will clear his own schedule on Monday evenings so he can take care of the kids. Denise deeply appreciates his sacrifice and accepts his offer. Within a few days she has notified key clients that she won't be available on Monday evenings. With her husband's loving assistance, Denise finally gets some much-needed soul nourishment.

You and your spouses need to be growing spiritually. And although you are not ultimately responsible for your husbands' or wives' growth, you can help or hinder that growth in significant ways. Encourage each other into settings where you can grow in your relationship with Christ: Bible studies, prayer groups, accountability groups, conferences. And then do what you can—such as providing child care—to allow your spouses to take advantage of these opportunities.

Here are a number of specific ways to encourage spiritual intimacy and celebrating love in your marriages:

*Encourage personal time in prayer and Bible study.* One time Gary opened the door to our walk-in closet and found me there in the dark, on my knees. I was a bit surprised but not any more than he was! That's when Gary discovered that I truly do have a "prayer closet" and how precious that time is to my spiritual growth. If I neglect prayer or focus on my worries instead of praying about them, my heart can quickly become hard. So one way I commune with God is by going into a secluded place to pray. Now that Gary knows how vital this private prayer time is for me, he does everything he can to make sure nothing interferes with it.

So what do you pray for when you get alone with God? Wives, pray for your husbands; pray daily that God would give them wisdom, strength, knowledge, and power to overcome temptation. Pray for areas where they need help and guidance. Pray for areas where you disagree, and ask God to reveal his plan to both of you.

Husbands, pray for God's help. Ask God to reveal ways you can create more meaning and value for your wives. Earnestly seek God's insight and leadership as you learn new ways to express your love to them. Tell your wives you are praying for them, and encourage them by sharing what you are learning.

You should study the Bible daily for yourselves. But you can double your insight by sharing what you learn with your spouses. You may both want to use something like *The One Year Bible* (Tyndale House), which divides the Bible into 365 daily readings. When you're each reading the same passage every day, you can talk about what you learned from it. Or you can read the same devotional book or study guide in your individual devotional time, sharing insights with each other at another time.

*Encourage participation in fellowship and worship.* Beth and Steve had always been committed to regular Sunday church attendance. They loved to meet with their Christian friends, to worship, and to hear the teaching. When Steve's schedule changed, he was forced to work some weekends. Even though Beth preferred going to church on Sunday, she understood Steve's need for flexibility in getting to church. She held her husband accountable for his need for active involvement in church. Some weeks they were able to worship together on Sunday mornings. Other weeks they attended the Thursday-night service. And when Steve's schedule kept him from all services, Beth gently encouraged Steve to attend an early morning men's study on Wednesdays.

Weekly involvement with a body of believers is what Christian community is all about. You and your spouses need to have regular contact with people whom you can know and who can know you. Hebrews 10:25 says: "Let us not neglect our meeting together, as some people do, but encourage and warn each other." Make sure you and your spouses stay involved, even if it requires some creative scheduling.

*Encourage expression of spiritual gifts.* Thad found great fulfillment in being part of a ministry that installed and maintained a tiny-tot playground at church. His wife, Lisa, wasn't so mechanically inclined, but she enjoyed teaching Sunday school for the toddlers' class. Thad was no teacher, but he and Lisa had a great time leading singing and games together for the little ones. They were committed to using their gifts individually when needed and together whenever possible.

The gifts of the Spirit are the special abilities God gives all believers to do his work in the world (see Romans 12:4-8; 1 Corinthians 12 and 14; and Ephesians 4:11-16). God has chosen to involve us in the building of his kingdom. "We are God's masterpiece. He has created us anew in Christ Jesus, so that we can do the good things he planned for us long ago" (Ephesians 2:10). Each of us should use our unique gifts for the Kingdom of God, and we should encourage our spouses to do the same.

It's great fun to discover a shared ministry. You may not be drawn to the same interest, but if you find a place where you and your spouses can minister as a team, you will experience wonderful spiritual harmony.

## TIPS FOR GROWING SPIRITUALLY TOGETHER

Spiritual growth is the job of both husbands and wives as individuals. But spiritual intimacy happens when you experience God together and share what you have learned. Here are some ideas Gary and I recommend for growing spiritually as a couple:

1. *Read the Bible.* Schedule daily times to read God's Word. Make an appointment with God, and keep it.
2. *Share the Word.* Talk together about what God is teaching you.
3. *Pray aloud together.* You can't get any more intimate than praying together as a couple. If you haven't prayed with your spouses before, start slowly—but start today.
4. *Hold hands and pray.* Joining your hands as well as your hearts and voices as you pray is a great way to draw close.
5. *Study together.* Do a Bible study or devotional book together, or work through a study independently and then discuss it together. Our book *Renewing Your Love* is a thirty-day devotional designed to help couples study a passage together, reflect on its meaning for their marriages, pray together, and practice ways to love each other more deeply.
6. *Make Sundays relaxed.* Plan ahead so that going to church is not a hectic event. Replace the race to church with relaxation and heart preparation. If you have children, you

and your spouses can share the responsibility for getting them ready and in their classes before you sit down for worship.

7. *Be accountable to each other.* Your spiritual relationship will grow deep if you allow yourselves to share and receive correction from each other.

8. *Encourage accountability to others.* Help each other find an accountability group—men for him, women for her—that will serve as a sounding board and spiritual support. Choose groups that will ultimately strengthen your commitment to each other, not weaken it.

9. *Spend time with other couples.* Choose wisely. Link up with couples who are intent on developing strong marriages and have boundaries.

10. *Find mentors.* Ask a mature Christian couple with a healthy marriage to mentor you as a couple.

11. *Speak up.* When you see your spouses take steps of spiritual growth, compliment him or her about it. Cheer your spouses on to more of the same.

12. *Seek God's will for your life.* Start by telling God that you want to do life his way. Read Scripture, and heed the advice of more mature Christians in discovering what it means to live out God's will.

13. *Teach your children to follow God.* One of the greatest responsibilities of your shared commitment to Christ is passing on your faith to your children. Strategize together about how to make faith vital for each of them, and act on your plans.

14. *Count your blessings.* Set aside time to thank God for everything he has done for you.

Don't ever stop working toward spiritual intimacy. One of the greatest gifts you can give your lifelong partners is a lifelong commitment to spiritual growth.

But don't put off getting started. As Gary will share, ignoring or delaying your spiritual journey together does not work in favor of celebrating love.

## START NOW

Many Christian couples Barb and I talk to wish they had a deeper spiritual life together. They know how important it is, but somehow they just never get around to making it happen. Their intentions are good, but their excuses take precedence. Just think how powerfully God could work in your marriage if you would allow him to get started.

You can learn from the experience of Alex and Karla, who recently visited my office for counseling. Alex had broken his wife's heart—again. He had distanced himself from her and the kids, worked too many hours, and disconnected from her and the Lord. He had caved in to temptations. Karla had responded with bitterness that was demoralizing Alex and exacerbating the problem. Trust had broken down. Neither of them was seeking the Lord, and their relationship was in danger.

Karla pleaded, "Gary, I don't know how to get through to him. I want our marriage to be rich in Christ. I miss the quiet times with Alex, the prayer times we used to experience. They are distant memories now. Help!"

I saw the couple five times and tried to break through some of the pain. Nothing seemed to click. When they arrived for their sixth appointment, I could tell right away that something had really changed. Alex was more responsive. Karla was more gentle. I looked at them and said, "What happened? You two look like completely different people!" They shared their story.

"Gary," Alex began, "last week at work I was so angry with Karla that I decided to write a letter to you. It was five pages long. I pointed out everything she had done to hurt me recently. I was just plain hot. I ragged on her sloppy housekeeping. I blasted her coolness in the bedroom. I hammered on her flagrant money mismanagement. I went on and on.

"I felt a little better after getting all that off my chest, so I decided to write a letter to Karla. I had the pen in hand, ready to pour out all the poison I had written in my letter to you. Then a lightning bolt hit me. I just thought, *What am I doing? I want so much for my wife to connect to me. I want so much to experience God the way I used to. I want so much for our two kids to grow up in a healthy Christian home, and here I am just messing it up.* It's as if my desire to be connected to Karla is somehow blocked by my not connecting to God first. I hadn't prayed. I hadn't read the Bible. I was just playing church on Sundays. I realized in that moment that as I confessed my hard-heartedness toward God and truly sensed his forgiveness, I could then deal with my hard heart toward Karla. I realized that what you said is true: a marriage really is a marriage of three."

As I listened to Alex pour out his heart, Karla was captivated by his words. She was looking at him as if he had just conquered Mount Everest. In a way, he had.

"Instead of lambasting her," Alex continued, "I started to pour out my hurt in that letter. I confessed to her that I wasn't the man I knew she needed me to be. I asked her to forgive me. I prayed for another chance from God and from her. I prayed for another opportunity to connect to my wife and kids. I prayed that Karla would really listen to me.

"When I got home, I read Karla the letter. Gary, it was unbelievable. She started to cry and open her heart to me. We just sat on our sofa holding each other. Our two-year-old son came up to us and patted us both on the backs. It was as if I had my family back. And I don't ever want to lose my wife again."

What happened to this family? Alex and Karla reconnected, but not before Alex reconnected with God, experiencing his grace and mercy. As the Lord convicted his heart and as Alex restored his vertical relationship with God, the horizontal relationship with his wife opened up again. As Karla saw the work God was doing in her husband's life, it bolstered her trust in God to restore their relationship. She still had to rebuild her trust in Alex. But her trust in God allowed her to take the first steps to reconnect with her husband.

Alex and Karla still have some distance to travel in rebuilding their marriage, but they are on the right path. Their two hard hearts, broken before Christ, are healing through his power. The celebration is returning to their relationship. They are feeling cherished and captivated once again.

Karla is experiencing being Alex's "one and only." They are reveling in their oneness with God and each other. She is experiencing a captivating love that is endearing them to each other. Theirs is becoming a marriage that not only will last but also will experience a cherishing and captivating love along the way.

This couple is discovering the joy and fulfillment of spiritual intimacy. The same discovery—or rediscovery—awaits you. And there is no better time than now to start on the journey.

# Renewing Love

Renewing love refreshes and supports the marriage bond
and helps spouses feel confident and rooted

# 13

## A Love That Is Fresh Day after Day

One of the favorite parts of the radio call-in broadcast that Barb and I do is meeting and talking with couples who have been married fifty years or more. In fact, we regularly invite golden-anniversary couples to join us on the program just to drink in their wisdom. We can't help but admire love that has endured a lifetime.

We have searched for clues as to why these marriages have remained strong through the years while others have crumbled. One of the things we ask the couples who have been married for five decades is this: "What do you have to say to those of us who aren't as far along on the journey? What works? How have you done it?" Here are the kinds of things we hear:

"Gary and Barb, we take time daily to listen to each other and learn what the other has experienced that day."

"We love to spend time with each other. We just enjoy being each other's best friend."

"It's a little embarrassing to say on radio, but Barney taught me a long time ago that when I meet his sexual needs, he feels valued. When I listen to him and encourage him, he feels respected.

When he prays with me, I feel so safe. When I spend time with him, he makes me feel like a million bucks!"

"Mildred reminds me often that my words of belief in her are the only words—next to God's—she really needs to hear. So I learned to speak up. Yes, we have been married fifty-four years, and I think the marriage is going to take, don't you, Barb and Gary?"

At the other end of the marriage timeline from the golden-anniversary couples are people like our daughter and son-in-law. It seems like only yesterday that Barb and I picked up Sarah and Scott at the airport after their honeymoon. We were overjoyed to hear Sarah say from the backseat, "Oh, we're so happily married." They had that just-married sparkle about them. Do you remember it? Do you recall how hard you worked day in, day out to keep love alive and growing?

So where are you now? You may be at the beginning of your marriage or near its end. You may have babies on your hip or teenagers in your hair. Or perhaps you are alone together in an empty nest. Will your marriage flourish to the end, "till death do us part"? Will the two of you still be glowing on your golden anniversary? What is your plan to keep your relationships fresh, vital, and fulfilling for the long haul?

Wherever you are in your marriage journey, you have the opportunity each day to strengthen your relationship with the men or women with whom you are spending the rest of your lives.

## LOVE THAT GOES THE DISTANCE

Barb and I were twenty-one and twenty-three respectively when we got married. At that young age we had no way to wrap our minds around the meaning of a lifelong relationship. Yes, we had watched our parents' love sustain them for decades. But only after logging more than three decades together have we gained enough firsthand experience to understand what a lifetime commitment means.

We have discovered that married love is more like a potted plant than cut flowers. The stunning brilliance of a bouquet of cut flowers lasts for only a few days. Then the blossoms dry up and crumble. A blooming plant lasts much longer. The flowers can blossom again and again. What we all need is a love that allows our relationship to grow continually and blossom repeatedly. We need a dimension of love that refreshes and supports our bond as a married couple, one that helps each partner feel deeply confident and rooted in the relationship.

The sixth secret to a lasting love is what Barb and I call *renewing love*. Renewing love keeps the marriage commitment alive. It continually refreshes the solemn, heartfelt pledge of undying love we made to each other before God, our families, and our friends.

What was that commitment about, really? It may seem like a silly question, but we know plenty of people who assume that their marriage commitment was simply about sexual fidelity or not ever getting divorced. But the marriage commitment is so much more than that. The real heart of renewing love is a commitment to keep growing together. It's an ongoing promise to love to the utmost of your ability—never to leave. It's a commitment sealed by the unbreakable bond God formed between you and your spouse when you made that one-of-a-kind promise. It's a living commitment powered by God.

Renewing love refreshes and supports that unbreakable bond and helps you and your spouse feel confident and rooted. Look at some of the profound benefits you will enjoy. Renewing love

- provides an environment in which the deepest level of human trust can form;
- supplies the security that allows intimacy to fully develop;

- protects you and your spouse from the fear of broken promises;
- helps you rediscover the roots of your relationship and stay vitally attached to the love of your life;
- provides security for the children raised in your home;
- undergirds all the other loves and allows them to flourish.

## WAYS TO NURTURE RENEWING LOVE

We all know couples who fully intended to keep the promises they uttered on their wedding day but whose marriages have dried up and died. They neglected the living bond between a husband and wife, a bond that must be tended daily and enthusiastically. They didn't refresh and renew their love, so when trouble developed, their marriage could not endure. It came up by the roots.

Barb and I want to share with you five keys to renewing love, specific ways you can refresh and support your marriage commitment.

### 1. Decide to Pursue the Dream

We hope you realize that the dream marriage we described at the beginning of this book isn't a mirage. It's a real place on the marriage map—just as real as disappointment, distance, disconnect, discord, and emotional divorce.

But remember: When we talk about the dream marriage, we are not talking about a marriage in which we love each other perfectly and never wound each other. We're not saying that you will be immune to difficult circumstances or that you won't have to work at intimacy and communication. The dream describes the *quality of your relationship* to each other, not the *quality of your circumstances*. As you put into practice the secrets to a lasting love, you recapture your dream and have a vibrant marriage even in the midst of stress and struggles. Working hard on your relationship is the normal state of a healthy marriage, even when you're living the dream!

The dream is the kind of marriage we were all hoping for when we committed our lives to each other at the altar. It is a marriage in which husbands and wives are diligent to forgive each other; meet each other's needs; conquer difficulties together; guard each other from threats and temptations; enjoy ongoing emotional, physical, and spiritual closeness; and commit to keeping the marriage fresh and alive.

God wants this kind of marriage for you even more than you do. And he has the resources to get you there. But there's a prerequisite: You have to decide that you will pursue the dream. If you want your marriage bond to grow strong, it won't happen by accident. If you want your union to be everything it can be, you can't leave it to chance. We believe that without a basic commitment to pursue the best for your marriage, your efforts to implement the six secrets will fail. The first step of renewing love is to decide in your hearts that you want to pursue the dream. It takes commitment to propel you toward the dream and the qualities that will make your relationships flourish.

## 2. Commit to Christ

Barb and I are doing our best to help couples strengthen their marriages. We urge you and your spouse to settle for nothing less than God's best in your relationship. This is not our idea; marriages that last are God's idea. These high standards for marriage—the six secrets we have presented—are rooted in Scripture. So the attitude you must have as you seek renewing love in your marriage is the same attitude of humility and service that Jesus had (see Philippians 2:1-11).

Once you commit to pursue God's dream for your marriage, you need to draw on his power to make it happen. Your commitment to pursue the dream starts with a commitment to Christ. Only by staying connected to Christ will you find the resources for the journey God has for you. Jesus said, "I am the vine; you are the branches. Those who remain in me, and I in them, will produce much fruit. For apart from me you can do nothing" (John 15:5). This is as true for our marriages as for our individual lives of service to God. We need Jesus.

But beware: The enemy will do whatever he can to lure you away from the life-giving sustenance that is yours through your connection to Christ. As one couple discovered, the disconnect is not always the result of flagrant disobedience or rebellion. The enemy can lure you away from your dependency on Christ in very subtle ways.

When Paul and Tasha moved to the West Coast for Paul's new job, they enjoyed visiting a number of large, high-profile churches. Yet every Sunday they felt like two lonely spectators among the throngs. After months of church shopping, they still hadn't found a place where they thought they fit. So the couple decided to take a break from the teaching and fellowship that had nurtured their relationship up to that point. Paul had been in church every Sunday of his life. Missing a few Sundays surely wouldn't hurt. And Tasha thought it would be great to sleep in on Sunday and head to the beach by noon. Because they were away from family and friends, they had no one to check up on them and lay a guilt trip on them for skipping church.

The couple soon realized that their decision was not the best for their marriage. "After a few months of sleeping in," Tasha explains, "we noticed that our spiritual passion was sliding away. We seemed never to have time to pray or to share any spiritual insight with each other. But what really prompted us to take notice was that we started fighting over all sorts of things. We were being selfish in ways we had been giving before.

"Looking back at that time, Paul and I feel as if we missed a turn in our lives and drove off the road. God had led us to our new home, but we neglected to ask him where *he* wanted us to attend church. As soon as Paul and I asked God where we should go, we were able to find a church that suited us. We called it 'the little church under the freeway.' The people there welcomed us. They even remembered us from the first time we visited. We felt surrounded by caring people for the first time since we moved west, and once we got a fresh dose of God's love for us, we had more love for each other. We were surprised at how much a simple step like making a connection with a group of Christians could get our marriage back on track."

God doesn't want a commitment to him to be a chore. He wants to strengthen your commitment to each other, and having you stay close to him is his way of making that happen.

Barb had an experience that introduces another key to building a foundation of renewing love in your marriage. She'll share it with you.

### 3. Enter Your Spouses' World

I was having lunch with some of my female friends when one of the women started complaining that her husband played golf far too much.

"Why don't you go with him?" I asked.

"I can't stand to golf!" my friend exclaimed.

"But you love your husband, Stacey. Go out and play with him. Join him. Enter into his world."

At first she brushed me off, but by the end of our lunch she decided to sign up for a beginners' golf class. She didn't tell her husband about the class because she wanted to surprise him.

Several weeks later Stacey showed up on the golf course when her husband was scheduled to play. He was a bit puzzled, but when she announced that she was part of his foursome, he was delighted. Since then they have enjoyed playing many rounds of golf together, and they even have a standing date for an evening game each week during the summer months.

When husbands and wives commit to entering each other's worlds, they are often in for a real eye-opener. Your spouses may live in a world you seldom explore. Getting firsthand experience in their interests and activities—ranging from jobs to hobbies to favorite books and TV programs to family members and friends—can be a rich source of understanding for you. Entering your spouses' world is a great way to renew your bond of love.

Women, you don't have to be good at everything your husbands do, and you don't have to be as enthusiastic about their interests as other guys are. But if you want to bond deeply with your husbands, you need to validate their interests and join in some of their activities. If they bowl, go along sometimes to watch, cheer on, or roll a few strikes—or gutter balls. If they watch *Monday Night Football* religiously, microwave a bowl of popcorn and watch with them. If they putter in the garage, spend some time there watching, asking questions, and handing them tools.

The same holds true for men. Husbands, open your eyes to the experiences that make up your wives' worlds. Most women lead interesting and busy lives. Have you ever noticed the effort, the planning, and the intricacy that goes into their daily schedules? Whether their days revolve around jobs or caring for children or juggling both, spend a day or two in their shoes every month or so. What can you do so they can enjoy some downtime and make room for recreation each day?

We're not suggesting that you force your way into your husbands' golf foursome or that you barge in on your wives' book clubs. Look for fun things the two of you can do together. Enter your spouses' worlds. Wives, take your husbands to the pro shop or the home-improvement store to pick out their birthday presents six months early. Husbands, go with your wives to the store to discover their favorite fragrances or their favorite book. Don't just hand your spouses a gift certificate. Enter their worlds, and get the gift yourselves!

You can also explore the more serious facets of your spouses' lives. How much do you know about your partners' jobs, whether inside or outside the home? If it's appropriate, visit their work sites. Get to know the people your spouses interact with forty or more hours a week. If you can't visit work sites, flip through trade publications to learn more about the job. Attend a business conference or trade show together. If one of you is a stay-at-home spouse, it's only fair for the other partner to take that job for a day now and then. Learn the scheduling complexities, the social world that the stay-at-home spouse relates to.

Enter your spouses' worlds by asking questions: "What did you do today at work [home]?" "How did things go?" "What victories did you have?" "What were your major struggles?" "How did you handle them?" "What one thing do you wish you could change about today?"

The more time and energy you invest in experiencing your spouses' worlds, the stronger the bond between you will be.

## 4. Keep Cheering Each Other On

Gary is my number one cheerleader, and I am his. You need to understand two things about being a cheerleader. First, support from the sidelines can turn a game around. Knowing that someone has confidence in you when you no longer believe in yourself is an incredibly powerful motivator. Second, cheerleaders always stick around. Unlike the fans, who file out of the stadium early when the game appears to be lost, the cheerleaders stay to the end. And they always show up for the next game, even if the home team got walloped the last time.

It is hard to imagine anything more encouraging than having your husbands or wives cheer you on while the battles of life rage around you. Sometimes your spouses can even motivate others around you to join in. Broadway and screen actress Celeste Holm once said, "We live by encouragement and die without it. Slowly, sadly, and angrily." Her words are never more true than in a marriage. It saddens Gary and me that authentic encouragement is rare in many homes today. Both men and women need encouragement. When we surveyed men and women on their top needs in marriage, we found that *both* men and women ranked encouragement as their number four need.

Because men and women are different, your encouragement for each other will take different forms. Notice how similar needs are fulfilled differently between husbands and wives.

| Husbands Need | Wives Need |
|---|---|
| 1. A card once or twice a year to tell them they are loved | 1. Daily doses of "I love you" (cards and flowers work well too!) |
| 2. An evening out every so often | 2. One evening every week with just the two of you |
| 3. A golfing (or sailing, or bowling) buddy | 3. A female friend in whom they can confide |
| 4. A new challenge every five years to keep life interesting | 4. Frequent time-outs from their routines to recharge their batteries |
| 5. A slap on the back from the guys on the basketball court | 5. Supportive hugs from their female friends |

One of the most refreshing and renewing things you can do for your marriage is to offer continual support to your spouses. That's the way you stir up team spirit. When Gary and I run into a problem, it's never me against Gary or Gary against me; it's both of us against the problem. Sure, strife and anger sometimes flare up in our home, just as they do in yours. Yet Gary and I agree that for the sake of our marriage, we will humble our-selves and honor each other through every word we say to each other.

Husbands, complaining and arguing can be devastating to women. When you speak harsh words to your wives, it's as if you are throwing stones at them. Wives, when you don't sup-port and encourage your husbands, it's as if you are jeering at them instead of cheering for them.

You will also be a great source of encouragement and sup-port when your spouses hear you praying aloud for them. For example, how would you feel if your spouses held your hands at the breakfast table and prayed, "Dear Lord, help me to be the most loving and supportive wife [husband] I can be today. Help me to love my husband [wife] as you love both of us. Change my heart and correct my faults where I am wrong. And bless my husband [wife] with a joyful, fulfilling day."

How encouraging is it to know that your spouses care enough to invoke God's best for you? How blessed do you feel knowing that your spouses are asking God to change them to be the best possible partners? You can provide that kind of daily encourage-ment as you pray together for each other.

Since Gary and I work together as well as live together, we deal with potential conflict situations all day long. You can't imagine how many couples have told us that they couldn't work with their spouses. But we wouldn't trade our situation for any-thing, even though we do have our rough spots.

One day after a round of heated debate and decision making at the office, one of our newer staff members pulled me aside. She was taken aback by how Gary and I handled the situation on which we didn't agree. "Even when you're in conflict," she said, "you honor each other."

That's what being your spouses' cheerleaders is all about. That's what it means to be on the same team, urging each other on toward a common goal. We need to be able to face off on important issues, but we must commit to love, honor, and cherish each other in the process. Help your spouses know that they are more important to you than any issue and that your relationships are never at-risk, even when you argue. Always be encouraging and supportive. It will renew the bond of love between you.

We have one more tip for renewing love. Gary will share the importance of hanging in there when other couples are bailing out.

## 5. Commit to Keeping Your Covenant

Some people have gotten married in unusual ceremonies. People can get married riding on horseback, sailing aboard a cruise ship, bungee jumping, skydiving, scuba diving, flying in a helicopter, paddling in a canoe, soaking in a hot tub, perching atop a speedway winner's stand, floating in a hot-air balloon, or galloping into a ghost town. A woman who calls herself Reverend Karyl "I'll Marry Anybody" Miller offers "sweet, lighthearted personalized ceremonies" ranging from "way-cool cheapo weddings" to "your-daddy's-rich weddings." You can get "linked at a rink" or "tie the knot on a yacht." She'll even do the ceremony on a roller coaster "as long as you provide an airsickness bag."

Although Barb and I have nothing against creative, personally meaningful ceremonies, we suspect that for the couple who gets married while parachuting, the real significance of marriage might hit the ground without a chute.

Sadly, the undoing of marriages is often treated just as casually as a novelty wedding. We live in the land of prenuptial agreements and no-fault divorce. Having talked with thousands of couples, Barb and I have found that divorce is contagious, kind of like the flu or a cold. When couples come to us and announce that they are getting a divorce, the first question we often ask is, "Who else do you know is getting divorced?" Often it's a close friend or relative of the person. A divorce creates an atmosphere of acceptability for others around that couple to abandon their marriage as well.

At the heart of renewing love is the continually reaffirmed commitment to the permanency of marriage—to love to the utmost of your ability and never to leave. This commitment is much more solemn than most people understand. It's so far beyond a run-of-the-mill commitment that we need a different word for it. It's a *covenant*. That's a term we don't use much anymore. A covenant is a binding, unbreakable agreement between two people.

You can understand the significance of the term when you consider its usage in the Bible. God made a covenant with Abraham when he promised to make his descendants a mighty people. God made a covenant with Moses and the Israelites when he gave them the Ten Commandments. God made a covenant with David when he swore that his throne would last forever. God made a covenant with us when Christ died for our sins and opened our way to God through faith in him.

These biblical covenants are serious, permanent, and irrevocable. Your marriage is also a covenant, and it should be regarded just as solemnly. God's covenant of grace moved Jesus Christ willingly and unflinchingly to the cross. Your marriage covenant should move you to any lengths necessary to love, honor, and cherish your spouse for life.

Daily living out your covenant of marriage is what brings a sense of confidence and rootedness to your relationships. You don't need to wonder whether or not you will stay together; the decision has already been made. And when you affirm that decision day by day through loving service and commitment, even during the tough times, you will feel confident and rooted in your unbreakable bond.

Hudson Taylor, the great missionary to China, once said that when stress comes down on a relationship, it either drives a wedge between two people, pushing them into isolation, or it comes down at their sides, pushing them closer together. When we are in a covenant relationship, we allow no room for stress to divide us; it can only push us closer together. Such a commitment gives us the ability to say confidently, "We're going to persevere. We're going to make it. We're going to paddle upstream in a culture that doesn't applaud commitment. We have a love that would say 'I do' all over again."

## DIVORCE IS NOT AN OPTION

The very survival of your marriage depends on your recognizing the scope of the covenant you made on your wedding day. Renewing love says with absolute conviction, "Divorce is not an option. We are married for life." Without this firm pledge to God and to each other, your marriage is vulnerable to defeat from every angle. But when you take a stand on your lifetime promise, your marriage can survive anything.

Here is what one of our conference participants wrote to us about the permanence of marriage:

> *My husband and I attended an "I Still Do" conference where you spoke. We have been married for eight years, and we've had our normal ups and downs, like any couple. But our first year or so was extremely difficult. Although I was filled with joy all through our engagement and wedding, from the moment I stepped out of the church to go on our honeymoon, I became increasingly disillusioned with married life.*
>
> *From that very day, a thought was planted in my head that I allowed to remain—the thought that we would probably get a divorce someday. Now, my parents never divorced, and neither did my husband's parents. But my marriage never seemed "right"*

*to me. We just weren't meant for each other. I felt we had both made an awful mistake (and I'm sure he felt that way too). Each of us thought we'd married a monster.*

*By God's grace, we made it through those first few years. But thoughts of divorce still had a foothold in me. However, at the same time God was beginning to teach me something I'd never realized or understood before: Our marriage was not a mistake. I was married to the right person. I began to change my attitude to be the wife God wants me to be.*

*At the conference someone said that marriage is for life. I realized then that I had never rejected that little thought of divorce in my mind. But, praise God, I have now made a conscious choice. My husband is my husband for life. I am committed to him as long as I live. He is God's perfect gift to me.*

We need to forever banish the idea of divorce from our thinking. Our marriages will last only when we commit to never using the "*d* word"—*divorce*. Before we can ever know the deep security and confidence God intends for us to enjoy as a couple, we need to be certain in our heart of hearts that our relationship is rooted in a love that will never give up.

Renewing your commitment to your spouses is so essential to building a lasting love that we want to explain in the next chapter how you and your spouses can keep your commitment in the forefront of your minds and at the center of your marriages.

# — 14 —

## *Nurturing a Lifetime Marriage*

Seventeen-year-old Mike was a goal-oriented young man. He had noticed Cheryl around school and decided he wanted to get to know her, even though she already had a boyfriend. So when he found Cheryl working the counter at the local McDonald's that summer, Mike strolled up and asked if she would ever date someone other than her current boyfriend. Cheryl said, "Sure, sometime."

During a school football game that fall, Mike spotted an opportunity to make his move. While Cheryl's jock boyfriend was out on the field, Mike found her in the stands. She said yes to a date.

By the next summer, Mike had turned eighteen and graduated. Cheryl was seventeen, getting ready for her senior year.

And she was pregnant with Mike's baby.

The young couple's family and friends told them they were crazy to get married. Mike and Cheryl were also pressured to get an abortion. But they were in love and wanted to raise their baby together. So they married that summer, mere kids themselves about to raise a kid of their own.

Mike took on the situation as a challenge. He came from a

successful family and knew he would probably be part of the family business someday. In the fall he started college full-time while working sixty-five hours a week delivering milk for the family's dairy.

Cheryl, a brand-new mother, stayed at home in their tiny house every day while Mike immersed himself in school and work. "It was a struggle from the beginning," she says. "I had no idea what my role was or what my commitment to Mike entailed. I made a lot of mistakes, bad choices. We had a new baby, but we didn't work on our relationship at all."

Instead, they spent their nights and weekends drinking and partying with friends, running wild. Cheryl knew she wasn't bonding with either their son, Michael, or her husband the way she should. "I was just a little girl looking for love and having a good time. I didn't know how to be a mom."

"I wasn't an alcoholic back then," Mike insists, "but I was a heavy drinker. And when I was under the influence, my aggression and anger kicked in. I punched holes in walls, and I once smashed a kitchen chair on the floor. I also lashed out at Cheryl, not physically but verbally. We would stand on the front step of the house screaming profanities at each other. In just a short time, we had become enemies."

Mike's behavior was all too familiar to Cheryl. Having grown up in the home of an alcoholic, she had seen it before. What she saw in Mike scared her and made her question whether or not she wanted to deal with his drinking and rage the rest of her life. "Mike was never abusive with me," she says, "but I didn't feel safe around him."

As her relationship with Mike continued to deteriorate, Cheryl agonized over what had become of their storybook romance. "We were really miserable, so I decided to leave Mike. Our divorce was finalized a few months later."

After Mike and Cheryl were divorced, their relationship

remained ugly. "I didn't want anything to do with Mike," Cheryl says. "I blamed him for everything that went wrong between us. We really weren't speaking at all. Our contact was limited to those times when we met to hand off our young son, Michael."

In the meantime, Mike had become a Christian, and Cheryl was on her way back to the Lord. As God began to change Mike's heart, he thought about the young family he had lost. He made up his mind to try to win Cheryl back—and to do it the right way this time.

Cheryl remembers being in the car one day as little Michael sobbed. "Why can't we be with Daddy?" Soon after, Mike called and asked if Cheryl would like to do something together. She agreed. "After I talked with Mike for a while, I knew I would be safe with him," Cheryl says. "He had a peace that wasn't there before. He even sounded different. He must have noticed that Christ was making a difference in my life too."

Following that first evening of being together with their young son, Mike and Cheryl began rebuilding their relationship under the counsel of a wise pastor. They went back to square one. Mike dated and courted his former wife. They had no physical relationship during this time. They wanted to build a love that would last, a love that was spiritual and emotional, not just physical.

A year and a half after their divorce became final, Mike and Cheryl were remarried in the presence of family and friends, many of whom had bitterly taken sides when the couple split up. The healing process in this family feud began that very day when three-year-old Michael stood up during the ceremony and yelled, "Hey, that's my mom and dad!" Hearts softened. Tears flowed. Everyone realized they were witnessing a miracle in the rebirth of Mike and Cheryl's marriage.

But the story doesn't end there. A few years ago Mike and Cheryl celebrated their twenty-first wedding anniversary. Their special anniversary happened to fall on the Day of Marriage and Family proclaimed by the governor of Iowa. Mike and Cheryl stood together before hundreds of people in the rotunda of the Iowa State Capitol building. Their pastor led a service of celebration for a marriage that would not die. The crowd was attentive as Mike and Cheryl shared their story. I had the joy of leading the couple in reciting their marriage recommitment vows and signing a marital covenant—a restatement of their vows that recognized the permanence of the God-designed bond of marriage.

When Mike and Cheryl learned the truth about God's dream for marriage, the truth set them free, and they have a wonderful story of renewal and reconciliation to tell.

Mike and Cheryl Wells have indeed come full circle. Instead of delivering milk, Mike is now an executive in the family business. The couple's painful past is gone, replaced by forgiveness, unselfishness, and unwavering commitment. Mike and Cheryl have four children now, and they can't believe how awesome their marriage is. They see each day as a beginning, another step on the journey. And their story of recapturing their dream marriage, of rebuilding a marriage from the charred ruins of their divorce, is making a difference in marriages across the country.

When they were divorced, Mike and Cheryl honestly thought they could escape each other. Then they came face-to-face with a life-changing reality. Their marriage—the first one—had knit them together in a sacred bond. "From the day of the divorce, I was the most miserable person in the world," Mike says. "The night the divorce was final, I went out drinking with the guys. Someone came up to me and said, 'Wow! You must feel great. You're finally divorced.' I told him that I had never felt more empty in my entire life. Part of me had been taken away. Part of me was missing."

Mike thought that pulling away from Cheryl would make

everything okay. Although the legal papers said they were no longer one, they could not sever the emotional bond that had formed between them. For them, divorce made them feel as if an arm or a leg had been ripped off.

Mike and Cheryl did not understand at the time that when they uttered their first "I do," it was a lifetime promise. God had bonded them to each other on the basis of their commitment, and he wanted them back together. He wasn't going to let them go without a fight, even after the divorce!

This is our message to you: No matter where you are on the marriage map—even if you are languishing in emotional divorce, even if you have initiated separation and legal divorce—good things are possible because a bond exists between you, and God will not let you ignore it. He created the marriage bond—that solemn covenant—to be unbreakable. Renewing love keeps it that way, helping you and your spouse feel confident and rooted in each other's love.

## MARRIAGE IS FOR LIFE

God is serious about the covenant you made on your wedding day. It's clear that he intends marriage to be a lifelong commitment.

Knowing the pain that shattered relationships create, God counsels us in the strongest possible language against divorce. In the last book of the Old Testament, the prophet Malachi wrote:

> You cry out, "Why has the Lord abandoned us?" I'll tell you why! Because the Lord witnessed the vows you and your wife made to each other on your wedding day when you were young. But you have been disloyal to her, though she remained your faithful companion, the wife of your marriage vows. Didn't the Lord make you one with your wife? In body and spirit you are his. And what does he want? Godly children from your union. So guard

yourself; remain loyal to the wife of your youth. "For I hate divorce!" says the Lord, the God of Israel. (2:14-16)

In this brief passage, Malachi teaches us a number of core principles for the covenant marriage:

1. God is a witness to the marriage covenant.
2. The marriage covenant is at the top of God's list of concerns for his people.
3. God makes husbands and wives one in body and spirit.
4. God seeks godly offspring.
5. We are to guard ourselves and not break faith with our spouses.
6. God hates divorce.

Do you see why Barb and I are so passionate about helping couples build lasting marriages? They are God's idea!

God calls us to build strong marriages not only for our good and his glory but also for the benefit of our children. He desires godly offspring. The benefits of a covenant marriage always spill over and bless our children.

Our daughter Missy was ten years old when a man in our neighborhood left his wife and his four young sons. As we passed those boys playing in the street on their bikes, I pulled our car to the curb. I cupped Missy's face in my hands and said, "Missy Rosberg, I'm going to tell you something."

"What, Dad?" she said, wide-eyed.

With my eyes boring into hers, I said forcefully, "I will never, ever, *ever* leave your mother."

Missy smiled. "I know, Dad," she said, "because if you try, I will sew your bodies together so you can't ever pull apart." I think her reply impressed me even more than my proclamation impressed her!

Kids today need to know that marriage is for life. More specifically, your kids need to know that *your* marriage is for life.

We need to build lasting marriages for the sake of the next generation. Don't just tell your kids you are committed for life, *show* them. Demonstrate that your commitment to one another permeates every attitude and action.

In the Malachi passage God didn't just diagnose the problem. He also pointed out the solution; he showed us the way back into the center of his will. "Guard yourself," he said; "remain loyal to the wife of your youth" (v. 15). The New International Version translates "remain loyal" as "do not break faith." This is exactly what we are calling you to do. Be on the alert to anything that could compromise or kill your marriage. Consistently practice forgiving love, serving love, persevering love, guarding love, celebrating love, and renewing love. Never break faith with your husband or wife. That's building a lasting marriage.

## THE STATE OF YOUR UNION

Now it's time for a reality check. Barb and I want to ask you a question: How are you doing in the process of building a lasting love? Exactly where are you on the marriage map? A major part of the rebuilding process for Mike and Cheryl, for Barb and me, and for other couples mentioned in this book was coming to an honest realization of the state of our marriages. What about you?

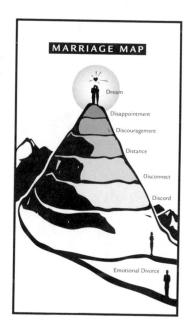

MARRIAGE MAP

Dream

Disappointment

Discouragement

Distance

Disconnect

Discord

Emotional Divorce

## THE STATE OF OUR MARRIAGE

*Review the seven stops on the marriage map as described below, then check one or two that you think most closely describe your marriage today. Realize that your spouse may have a different perspective on the state of your marriage. That being the case, Barb and I recommend that you both complete the exercise independently and then discuss your evaluation together. If it makes you feel too vulnerable to put your responses in the book, make two photocopies of the checklist (see appendix A for a checklist that you can photocopy) and record your responses there.*

**H    W**

### DREAM

☐   ☐   We communicate freely and keep no inappropriate secrets.

☐   ☐   We forgive each other and seek forgiveness.

☐   ☐   We seek to discover and meet each others' needs.

☐   ☐   We face and conquer difficult circumstances.

☐   ☐   We guard our marriage against threats and temptations.

☐   ☐   We enjoy ongoing emotional, physical, and spiritual closeness.

☐   ☐   We are committed "till death do us part."

**H    W**

## DISAPPOINTMENT

☐    ☐    We have difficulty affirming each other.

☐    ☐    We are surprised by each other's flaws.

☐    ☐    We feel let down by each other's imperfections.

☐    ☐    We cause each other hurt and anger.

☐    ☐    We have conflict over our differences.

☐    ☐    We compare each other to other people.

☐    ☐    We wish we could change things in each other.

## DISCOURAGEMENT

☐    ☐    We often wonder if our marriage is missing something.

☐    ☐    We have reasons to be dissatisfied with our marriage.

☐    ☐    We don't understand each other or meet each other's needs.

☐    ☐    We feel unimportant to each other.

☐    ☐    We are not successful at meeting each other's needs.

☐    ☐    We have difficulty expressing our needs to each other.

☐    ☐    We wonder if we chose the wrong partner.

**H    W**

### DISTANCE

☐  ☐    We do not see a letup in our difficulties.

☐  ☐    We do many activities alone, without each other.

☐  ☐    We have given up most expectations for each other.

☐  ☐    We feel little excitement about being married to each other.

☐  ☐    We sometimes feel and act like strangers.

☐  ☐    We keep many of our thoughts and feelings from each other.

☐  ☐    We face a problem that may eventually drive us apart.

### DISCONNECT

☐  ☐    We sometimes feel lonely even when we are together.

☐  ☐    We don't feel an emotional connection to each other.

☐  ☐    We seldom have much to say to each other.

☐  ☐    We often misunderstand and misinterpret each other.

☐  ☐    We direct our attention and activities away from each other.

**H   W**

☐   ☐   We doubt that our marriage can change for the better.

☐   ☐   We are not very interested in each other.

### DISCORD

☐   ☐   We think and act negatively toward each other.

☐   ☐   We lash out and hurt each other verbally.

☐   ☐   We wonder what it would be like if we weren't married.

☐   ☐   We wonder what it would be like to be married to someone else.

☐   ☐   We feel that we are at war.

☐   ☐   We lack tenderness and sexual intimacy.

☐   ☐   We cannot hide from others that our marriage is severely strained.

### EMOTIONAL DIVORCE

☐   ☐   We are staying married for some reason other than love.

☐   ☐   We have no hope that our marriage can be better.

☐   ☐   We pretend that our marriage is okay to keep up appearances.

**H    W**

☐    ☐    We only want to protect ourselves from further pain.

☐    ☐    We have separated or have considered separating.

☐    ☐    We are emotionally attached to someone else.

☐    ☐    We have already walked away from our marriage emotionally.

## YES, IT CAN HAPPEN TO YOU

Being honest about your starting point—the present condition of your marriage—is the first step to recapturing the dream for your marriage. Yet some couples are startlingly *dis*honest about the true state of their marriage. The sheer number of couples who divorce each year should be sufficient to scare us into honesty. Don't beat yourself up by saying your marriage is worse off than it really is. But also don't be fooled into thinking you are immune to the disappointment, discouragement, distance, disconnect, and discord that can lead to emotional divorce. Renewing love begins by seeing it and telling it as it is.

You may say, "Most of the time I am committed to renewing my marriage, but sometimes I don't feel so committed. What's wrong with a marital 'bad-hair day' once in a while?" Unfortunately, even an occasional lag in commitment can lead to more serious marital trouble. Marriage expert and psychology professor John Gottman notes that a creeping dissatisfaction with marriage can reflect a longer season of marital strain experienced by many couples.

Gottman states that every marriage goes through a cycle of hot and cool phases. The first seven years is often a hot, highly committed phase of marriage during which we really try to learn and practice conflict resolution. At times we butt heads and can even become harsh, but we work through it. In the second seven years, we enter a cool phase where we become distant, suppressing our emotions. The cool phases are potentially deadly. If we fail to address our problems, we can wind up in a marriage with no laughter, no love, and no interest in each other.[1]

Gottman also warns against four indicators of imminent danger in a marriage. His methods accurately predict a 94 percent chance of divorce in marriages in which these four indicators are present:

- *Complaining.* Complaining can be *to* your spouse or *about* your spouse, but your husband or wife gets the message.
- *Defensiveness.* A defensive spouse says, "I'm putting my guard up. You are the enemy, and I don't want you near me."
- *Contempt.* When walls of defensiveness go up, there is anger. And anger can breed contempt. This is the discord we talked about.
- *Withdrawal.* This means emotionally or physically removing yourself from the situation. You've checked out.[2]

Have you ever complained to or about your spouses? Do you see where such an "insignificant" lapse in commitment can lead? Barb and I are serious about this. If you are not perpetually experiencing renewing love, your marriage is in danger of heading in the wrong direction.

## THE ROAD BACK TO THE DREAM

Now here's the good news. Wherever you are on the marriage map today, you can find your way back to the dream by practicing the six secrets to lasting love. We have shared the stories with you in this book.

> 🍂 *Forgiving love* reconciled Mark and Shannon after Mark revealed his addiction to pornography.
>
> 🍂 *Serving love* enabled Robertson McQuilkin to minister to Muriel when she fell ill with Alzheimer's disease.
>
> 🍂 *Persevering love* preserved Dan and Jeannie after Dan's paralyzing fall in a construction accident.
>
> 🍂 *Guarding love* erected a new wall of protection for Michelle after her affair with a man she met on the Internet.
>
> 🍂 *Celebrating love* brought Carl and Danielle together in spiritual intimacy.
>
> 🍂 *Renewing love* saw Mike and Cheryl renew their commitment to each other and keep it fresh daily.

Where you are in your marriage is important, but where you're headed is even more crucial. So Barb and I want to ask you a few other questions: What will you do to practice the six secrets in your marriage? Which kind of love do you most need today to begin recapturing your dream? Knowing that you can't tackle every problem at once—and that building a lasting love is a lifelong process anyway—where are you and your spouses going to concentrate your efforts right now?

## GETTING BACK TO THE DREAM

*Look at the list below, and check the loves that you feel will most effectively bring the growth your marriage needs. Then indicate in the blanks to the right which love you feel deserves the highest priority in your strategy to get back on the road to the dream. Identify your top three priorities. Complete the exercise independently and then discuss your evaluation together. If it makes you feel too vulnerable to put your responses in the book, make two photocopies of the checklist (see appendix A for a checklist that you can photocopy) and record your responses there.*

**H   W**

☐   ☐   Forgiving love (priority: _____)

☐   ☐   Serving love (priority: _____)

☐   ☐   Persevering love (priority: _____)

☐   ☐   Guarding love (priority: _____)

☐   ☐   Celebrating love (priority: _____)

☐   ☐   Renewing love (priority: _____)

One word of advice: If you want a rock-solid commitment in your marriage, start with renewing love. It will set all the others in motion. You need the other secrets—forgiving love, serving love, persevering love, guarding love, and celebrating love—to make your marriage last a lifetime. But without a deep commitment to experience—and keep experiencing—these various loves, you will lack the confidence that your marriage can survive the pressures of twenty-first-century culture.

Love may be a choice, but it is more than a decision of the heart and mind. You must commit your full energy to nurture, feed, and care for your spouse.

You see, God's design is that the person to whom you said "I do" will be the love of your life. Your commitment to that person must be renewed with each passing day so that your love will grow and deepen to a level of intimacy beyond your wildest dreams. This is no fantasy. It is a living reality for those who come to understand the meaning of love and who commit to love this way.

## GOING IT ALONE

You may be reading this book and applying its lessons alone because your husband or wife is not interested in strengthening your marriage. Barb and I are praying for you because our hearts ache for you. If we could sit down with you and listen to your personal story of pain and isolation, we would coach you that your commitment is first and foremost to God. Let him be your partner in the process, nurturing your marriage from your side of the relationship. There is no greater place of blessing than to be sheltered by God's love and care.

We also want to offer you reasons to keep at the process of working to build a lasting love even if your spouses don't come along. Do it for the sake of your own faithfulness to God. Do it in the hope that your partners will change. But also do it for the sake of your children and the other people in your life. It may be difficult, but try to think beyond your own pain to those who will benefit from your commitment and example of lasting love. Your children may not look back and say that their parents had an ideal marriage, but they will look back and say that they saw their mom or dad display a commitment to love.

One of the great challenges of going it alone in renewing your marriage is trusting God for the work he will do in the lives of your husbands or wives. The potential for restoration when you as spouses exercise humility and obedience is so significant. Don't stop believing what God can and will do through you.

In the meantime, you may experience pain and disappointment. You need to express your feelings and receive encouragement. The best place to take your pain is to a mature, supportive Christian of the same sex: a pastor, pastor's wife, Bible study leader, counselor, or mature Christian friend. As you do, continue to hold out hope for what our great God can do for your marriage as you maintain the commitment you made on your wedding day.

# CATCH THE VISION

Barb and I hope that as you've read this book, you've been encouraged and inspired to make your marriage all that God wants it to be and all that you want it to be. We hope you understand more clearly what a biblical marriage looks like. It takes work, to be sure, but the benefits are incalculable—not only to you and your spouse, but also to your children, to the world around you, and to God.

How does your marriage benefit your children? Every day in your home, your children see your relationship. What do they see? Two people who forgive and serve and persevere and guard and celebrate and renew? Or two people who argue and disrespect each other, who are disconnected and headed toward emotional divorce? When you are in harmony with each other and your marriage is in harmony with God's plan, your children will feel safe and secure. The quality of your marriage makes a difference to your children.

How does your marriage benefit the world and God? Isn't that an overstatement? We don't think so. God chose the marriage relationship as one of the most effective ways of describing his relationship to people, his "bride." When our marriages reflect a love that forgives, serves, perseveres, guards, celebrates, and renews, we reflect God's character. When our marriages are filled with conflict and disrespect, discord and pain, we tarnish and obscure his reflection. A strong part of our witness as Christians is building marriages that positively reflect the character of God.

You may have grown up with parents who had a healthy marriage, and you are carrying the torch of that positive legacy to the next generation. Then carry it well. Maybe your parents did not model a healthy marriage, or maybe your own first marriage did not work out well. Wherever you are, with the help of the Holy Spirit, you can break the cycle and begin a new legacy. A friend of ours says the best time to plant an oak tree was twenty years ago. But the second best time is today. Let's plant some oak trees of righteousness for the sake of the next generation.

But we can't build lasting marriages alone. We all need God's help to build the kind of marriage that we dream of having. We also need the help of our family and friends. Barb and I can't maintain a godly marriage on our own. We need people to pray for and with us. We need people who will hold us accountable. We need people who will help us to nurture our relationship and to stay faithful to our commitments.

You do too.

Who prays for you? Who asks you the key questions? Who cares if your marriage is strong or deteriorating?

Consider gathering a group of couples—from your church or your circle of friends—and helping each other build godly, lasting marriages. Throughout this book we have referred to a collection of workbooks that will help you build a lasting love in a practical, fulfilling way. We recommend that you start with *Discover the Love of Your Life . . . All Over Again*. This workbook will help you understand just what each of the six loves means to your marriage. It will also help you deepen your commitment to the accountability process of experiencing these loves on a consistent basis. The workbook includes instructions for leaders, so it is easy for you to use.

We also offer a DVD series entitled *Discover the Love of Your Life . . . All Over Again*. Consider hosting this eight-part series in your home, with an adult Bible fellowship, or in a retreat setting. Visit our Web site to learn about other books and small-group studies which can be used by couples, by a small group, or by a church as a whole (see p. 296). We want to be your marriage coaches.

Barb and I are committing our marriage and our ministry to a movement to build lasting marriages. We ask you to partner with us to make a difference in our culture. We are looking for "Marriage Champions," couples who are excited about getting off the bench and helping to strengthen marriages across the country. Visit our Web site to learn how you and your spouse can become Marriage Champions and share this message of building lasting marriages.

In the midst of a culture that has lost its respect for marriage, we who have chosen to walk in God's ways need to draw a line in the sand and declare, "As for me and my household, we will serve the Lord" (Joshua 24:15, NIV). We need to take back what the enemy has stolen: the Christian marriage and family.

Barb and I want to help build lasting marriages. We feel an urgency about this matter. The bottom line is this:

If we don't do it together, who will?

If we don't do it *now*, then when?

If it doesn't start here—with our family and yours—then where?

Barb and I believe that if you take the principles we have shared with you and let them take root and grow in the soil of your marriage, you are well on your way to building a lasting love. But it doesn't stop there. If you—as a couple, a pastor, a small-group leader, an adult Sunday school teacher—share these principles with other couples you care about, you will contribute to the stability of Christian marriages and families. Think of the impact you will have—couple after couple, family after family.

# APPENDIX A

## *Marriage Map Self-Tests*

Each self-test and checklist discussed in this book is included here in a format that is easy to photocopy for use by an individual couple or a small group of couples.

## THE DREAM STOP

*Compare yourself to these indicators, and check any that describe the current state of your marriage:*

**H**   **W**

☐   ☐   I communicate freely with my spouse, and we keep no inappropriate secrets.

☐   ☐   I forgive my spouse when I am wronged and seek forgiveness when I offend. I am loved without strings.

☐   ☐   My spouse and I eagerly seek to discover and meet each other's needs.

☐   ☐   We have faced and conquered difficult circumstances that have undone other marriages.

☐   ☐   I consciously guard myself against threats and temptations that could pull our marriage apart.

☐   ☐   We enjoy ongoing emotional, physical, and spiritual closeness.

☐   ☐   We are committed to keeping our relationship fresh and alive "till death do us part."

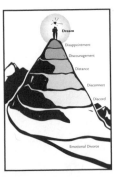

## THE DISAPPOINTMENT STOP

*Compare yourself to these indicators, and check any that describe the current state of your marriage:*

**H    W**

☐    ☐    I have difficulty expressing affirmation to or about my spouse.

☐    ☐    My spouse isn't the flawless person I thought I married.

☐    ☐    I feel surprised and let down when I notice an imperfection in my spouse.

☐    ☐    My spouse and I have caused each other to feel hurt and angry.

☐    ☐    My spouse and I have experienced conflict over personality differences, male-female wiring, or ways of doing things we learned from our families.

☐    ☐    I compare my spouse to other people.

☐    ☐    I have a mental list of things I wish I could change about my spouse.

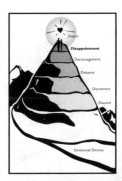

## THE DISCOURAGEMENT STOP

*Compare yourself to these indicators, and check any that describe
the current state of your marriage:*

**H    W**

☐    ☐    I often wonder if I am missing out on
something in my marriage.

☐    ☐    I have a mental list of reasons why I am
dissatisfied with my marriage.

☐    ☐    My spouse implies—or says—that I don't
understand him or her or know how to
meet his or her needs.

☐    ☐    My own needs are not being met in my
marriage. I feel as if my spouse's friends,
work, church involvement, and/or the kids
are more important than I am.

☐    ☐    Even when I recognize my spouse's needs,
I am not successful at meeting them.

☐    ☐    I have a difficult time expressing my needs in
a way my spouse can understand and act on.

☐    ☐    I wonder if my choice of a spouse was a
mistake.

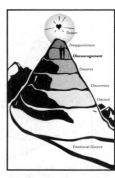

## THE DISTANCE STOP

*Compare yourself to these indicators, and check any that describe the current state of your marriage:*

**H     W**

☐     ☐     I could describe our relationship as "fair to partly cloudy, with no clearing in sight."

☐     ☐     I often fill my free time with activities that don't include my spouse.

☐     ☐     I have given up most of my expectations of my spouse.

☐     ☐     I wonder if my spouse ever feels excited about being married to me.

☐     ☐     My spouse sometimes seems like a stranger to me.

☐     ☐     I keep many of my thoughts and feelings from my spouse.

☐     ☐     I worry that we might someday face a problem bigger than our resolve to stay together.

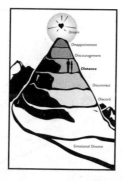

## THE DISCONNECT STOP

*Compare yourself to these indicators, and check any that describe the current state of your marriage:*

**H    W**

☐    ☐    I sometimes feel lonely even when I'm with my spouse.

☐    ☐    It is difficult for me to "feel" that my spouse loves me. I may know it intellectually, but I don't sense an emotional connection.

☐    ☐    When we are together, we seldom have much to say to each other.

☐    ☐    When we do talk to each other, we often misunderstand and misinterpret each other.

☐    ☐    I prefer to devote my time, energy, and money to something or someone other than my spouse.

☐    ☐    I doubt that my marriage can grow or change for the better.

☐    ☐    I don't think my spouse is very interested in who I am or what I want to do.

## THE DISCORD STOP

*Compare yourself to these indicators, and check any that describe the current state of your marriage:*

**H   W**

☐   ☐   Most of my thoughts about my spouse are negative.

☐   ☐   My spouse and I verbally lash out at each other, saying things that are hurtful.

☐   ☐   I often wonder what it would be like not to be married—or to be married to a different person.

☐   ☐   I daydream or fantasize about another person who would make a better spouse.

☐   ☐   I feel as if my spouse and I are at war.

☐   ☐   True tenderness with my spouse is a faded memory. We avoid sexual intimacy.

☐   ☐   Family and close friends notice that our marriage is severely strained.

## THE EMOTIONAL DIVORCE STOP

*Compare yourself to these indicators, and check any that describe the current state of your marriage:*

**H    W**

☐    ☐    I am staying married for some reason other than love for my spouse.

☐    ☐    I have given up hope that my marriage could be better.

☐    ☐    I pretend I'm okay with my marriage to keep up appearances.

☐    ☐    My first goal in my marriage is to protect myself from further pain.

☐    ☐    My spouse and I have separated or considered separating.

☐    ☐    My heart is deeply attached to someone other than my spouse, even if I am not acting on that feeling.

☐    ☐    I know I have already walked away from my marriage emotionally.

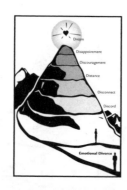

## THE STATE OF OUR MARRIAGE

*Review the seven stops on the marriage map as described below, then check one or two that you think most closely describe your marriage today. Realize that your spouse may have a different perspective on the state of your marriage. That being the case, Barb and I recommend that you both complete the exercise independently and then discuss your evaluation together. If it makes you feel too vulnerable to put your responses in the book, make two photocopies of the checklist and record your responses there.*

**H    W**

### DREAM

☐ ☐ We communicate freely and keep no inappropriate secrets.

☐ ☐ We forgive each other and seek forgiveness.

☐ ☐ We seek to discover and meet each other's needs.

☐ ☐ We face and conquer difficult circumstances.

☐ ☐ We guard our marriage against threats and temptations.

☐ ☐ We enjoy ongoing emotional, physical, and spiritual closeness.

☐ ☐ We are committed "till death do us part."

### DISAPPOINTMENT

☐ ☐ We have difficulty affirming each other.

☐ ☐ We are surprised by each other's flaws.

**H   W**

☐   ☐   We feel let down by each other's imperfections.

☐   ☐   We cause each other hurt and anger.

☐   ☐   We have conflict over our differences.

☐   ☐   We compare each other to other people.

☐   ☐   We wish we could change things in each other.

### DISCOURAGEMENT

☐   ☐   We often wonder if our marriage is missing something.

☐   ☐   We have reasons to be dissatisfied with our marriage.

☐   ☐   We don't understand each other or meet each other's needs.

☐   ☐   We feel unimportant to each other.

☐   ☐   We are not successful at meeting each other's needs.

☐   ☐   We have difficulty expressing our needs to each other.

☐   ☐   We wonder if we chose the wrong partner.

**H   W**

## DISTANCE

☐ ☐ We do not see a letup in our difficulties.

☐ ☐ We do many activities alone, without each other.

☐ ☐ We have given up most expectations for each other.

☐ ☐ We feel little excitement about being married to each other.

☐ ☐ We sometimes feel and act like strangers.

☐ ☐ We keep many of our thoughts and feelings from each other.

☐ ☐ We face a problem that may eventually drive us apart.

## DISCONNECT

☐ ☐ We sometimes feel lonely even when we are together.

☐ ☐ We don't feel an emotional connection to each other.

☐ ☐ We seldom have much to say to each other.

☐ ☐ We often misunderstand and misinterpret each other.

☐ ☐ We direct our attention and activities away from each other.

**H　W**

☐　☐　We doubt that our marriage can change for the better.

☐　☐　We are not very interested in each other.

### DISCORD

☐　☐　We think and act negatively toward each other.

☐　☐　We lash out and hurt each other verbally.

☐　☐　We wonder what it would be like if we weren't married.

☐　☐　We wonder what it would be like to be married to someone else.

☐　☐　We feel that we are at war.

☐　☐　We lack tenderness and sexual intimacy.

☐　☐　We cannot hide from others that our marriage is severely strained.

### EMOTIONAL DIVORCE

☐　☐　We are staying married for some reason other than love.

☐　☐　We have no hope that our marriage can be better.

☐　☐　We pretend that our marriage is okay to keep up appearances.

**H    W**

☐    ☐    We only want to protect ourselves from further pain.

☐    ☐    We have separated or have considered separating.

☐    ☐    We are emotionally attached to someone else.

☐    ☐    We have already walked away from our marriage emotionally.

## GETTING BACK TO THE DREAM

*Look at the list below, and check the loves that you feel will most effectively bring the growth your marriage needs. Then indicate in the blanks to the right which love you feel deserves the highest priority in your strategy to get back on the road to the dream. Identify your top three priorities. Complete the exercise independently and then discuss your evaluation together. If it makes you feel too vulnerable to put your responses in the book, make two photocopies of the checklist and record your responses there.*

**H    W**

☐    ☐    Forgiving love (priority: _____)

☐    ☐    Serving love (priority: _____)

☐    ☐    Persevering love (priority: _____)

☐    ☐    Guarding love (priority: _____)

☐    ☐    Celebrating love (priority: _____)

☐    ☐    Renewing love (priority: _____)

# APPENDIX B

## *Discovering Your Top Five Needs*

The findings here represent the categorical data that emerged from our survey of 700 couples in 8 cities. We gave each husband and each wife a list of 20 needs and asked them to rank them in order of importance. The lists here represent their choices.

How would you have ranked your needs? How would your spouse have ranked his or her needs? Find your top five needs, and share them with your spouse.

| Husbands' Needs | Wives' Needs |
| --- | --- |
| 1. Unconditional love and acceptance | 1. Unconditional love and acceptance |
| 2. Sexual intimacy | 2. Emotional intimacy and communication |
| 3. Companionship | 3. Spiritual intimacy |
| 4. Encouragement and affirmation | 4. Encouragement and affirmation |
| 5. Spiritual intimacy | 5. Companionship |
| 6. Trust | 6. Family relationships |
| 7. Honesty and openness | 7. Honesty and openness |
| 8. Emotional intimacy and communication | 8. Nonsexual touch |
| 9. Family relationships | 9. Security and stability |
| 10. To be desired | 10. Romance |
| 11. Career support | 11. Trust |

| Husbands' Needs | Wives' Needs |
| --- | --- |
| 12. To provide and protect | 12. Understanding and empathy |
| 13. Personal time | 13. Sexual intimacy |
| 14. Understanding and empathy | 14. Personal time |
| 15. Admiration | 15. To be desired |
| 16. Security and stability | 16. Domestic support |
| 17. Significance | 17. To provide and protect |
| 18. Romance | 18. Significance |
| 19. Domestic support | 19. Admiration |
| 20. Nonsexual touch | 20. Career support |

# NOTES

## Chapter 2: Where Are You Headed?
1. William Doherty, "Warning Signs of a Breakup Quiz Can Assess Situation," *USA Today* (July 21, 2001).

## Chapter 3: The Rocky Road of Hurt and Anger
1. Les Carter, *Good 'n' Angry* (Grand Rapids: Baker, 1983), 35.
2. Lewis B. Smedes, *Forgive and Forget* (San Francisco: Harper & Row, 1984), 133.
3. See Matthew 6:14-15.
4. C. S. Lewis, *The Problem of Pain* (New York: Macmillan, 1962), 93.

## Chapter 4: Closing the Loop
1. Bill and Lynne Hybels, *Fit to Be Tied* (Grand Rapids: Zondervan, 1991), 178.
2. David A. Stoop and James Masteller, *Forgiving Our Parents, Forgiving Ourselves* (Ann Arbor, Mich.: Vine Books, 1991), 263.

## Chapter 5: In Honor of Your Spouse
1. Dennis Rainey, *Staying Close* (Dallas: Word, 1992), 31.

## Chapter 6: Communicating Your Needs
1. Robertson McQuilkin, *A Promise Kept* (Wheaton, Ill.: Tyndale, 1998), 22–23.
2. Ibid., 85.
3. Ibid., 64.
4. The five levels are adapted from John J. Powell, *Why Am I Afraid to Tell You Who I Am?* (Chicago: Argus Communications, 1969).

### Chapter 7: Love That Endures Tough Times

1. Glenna Whitley, "George and Laura, Love and Marriage," *Ladies' Home Journal* (February 2002): 56–58.
2. Ibid., 58.
3. Ibid., 144.
4. Ibid.

### Chapter 10: Building Walls of Protection

1. All Scripture quotations in this paragraph are taken from the New International Version. Emphasis is added.

### Chapter 11: Rekindle the Joy of Being Married

1. John M. Gottman and Nan Silver, *The Seven Principles of Making Marriage Work* (New York: Crown, 1999), 17.

### Chapter 14: Nurturing a Lifetime Marriage

1. John Gottman, quoted in Karen S. Peterson, " 'Hot' and 'Cool' Phases Could Predict Divorce," *USA Today* (September 14, 2000).
2. John M. Gottman and Nan Silver, *The Seven Principles of Making Marriage Work* (New York: Crown, 1999), 27–34.

# ABOUT THE ROSBERGS

**Dr. Gary and Barbara Rosberg,** your marriage coaches, are championing marriage for the cause of Christ by coaching husbands and wives to achieve an extraordinary marriage for a lifetime . . . and for the sake of the next generation. Married for more than thirty years, Gary and Barbara have a unique message for couples.

Their book *6 Secrets to a Lasting Love* equips couples to strengthen their marriages by practicing six kinds of love. Other resources by the Rosbergs include these titles: the newly released *The 5 Sex Needs of Men & Women* and *The Great Marriage Q & A Book, The 5 Love Needs of Men and Women* (a Gold Medallion finalist), the *Discover the Love of Your Life All Over Again* DVD series, *Discover the Love of Your Life All Over Again* workbook, *Healing the Hurt in Your Marriage, Renewing Your Love: Devotions for Couples, Connecting with Your Wife, Guard Your Heart* (revised for couples), *Guarding Love* workbook, *Serving Love* workbook, *40 Unforgettable Dates with Your Mate,* and FamilyLife's Homebuilders couples series study guide, *Improving Communication in Your Marriage.*

Together Gary and Barbara host a nationally syndicated weekday radio program, *Dr. Gary and Barb Rosberg . . . Your Marriage Coaches.* On this call-in program, heard in cities all across the country, they coach on many family-related issues. The Rosbergs also host a Saturday radio program that can be heard in the Midwest on the award-winning WHO 1040AM radio station.

The Rosbergs have conducted conferences on marriage and family relationships in more than one hundred cities across the country. Their flagship conference, "Discover the Love of Your Life All Over Again," is having an impact on churches and communities nationwide. They have been on the national speaking team for FamilyLife's "Weekend to Remember" conferences since 1988. Gary has also spoken to thousands of men at Promise Keepers stadium and arena events annually since 1996 and to parents and adolescents at Focus on the Family's "Life on the Edge" tour events.

**Gary,** who earned his Ed.D. from Drake University, has been a marriage and family counselor for more than twenty-five years. He founded and coaches CrossTrainers, a Des Moines ministry that meets weekly and is comprised of more than four hundred men.

**Barbara** earned her B.F.A. from Drake University and has authored *Connecting with Your Wife* and coauthored ten books with Gary. She is also a featured speaker for the *Extraordinary Women* video series produced by the American Association of Christian Counselors.

The Rosbergs live outside Des Moines, Iowa. They have two married daughters and four grandchildren.

For more information on the ministries of America's Family Coaches, contact us at

America's Family Coaches
2540 106th Street, Suite 101
Des Moines, IA 50322
1-888-608-COACH
www.drgaryandbarb.com

# 6 Secrets to a Lasting Love

## Discover the Love of Your Life All Over Again

Everyone wants a marriage that will last a lifetime, and now Gary and Barbara Rosberg have disclosed the 6 secrets that will not only help you create the marriage you've always dreamed of, but one that will last forever. (*Discover the Love of Your Life All Over Again* workbook also available.)

# Healing the Hurt in Your Marriage

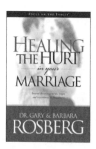

Learn how to forgive past hurts in your marriage, close the loop on unresolved conflict, and restore hope and wholeness in your marriage.

# THE 5 SEX NEEDS
## OF MEN & WOMEN

In this follow-up to the best-selling *The 5 Love Needs of Men & Women*, Gary and Barb Rosberg teach couples how to meet each other's most intimate physical, emotional, and spiritual needs and help them develop a godly view of sexual intimacy. (Audio read by the authors also available.)

# THE 5 LOVE NEEDS
## OF MEN & WOMEN

# SERVING LOVE

Are you meeting all of your spouse's love needs? Do you even know what they are? Discover the deepest yearnings of your spouse's heart as Gary and Barb Rosberg share the groundbreaking research that shows couples how to meet each other's most intimate needs. (*Serving Love* workbook also available.)

# GUARD YOUR HEART

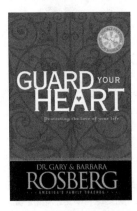

## GUARDING LOVE

We all need to guard our hearts and marriages. In *Guard Your Heart*, Gary and Barb Rosberg outline the dangers and temptations that can devastate a marriage. They also teach couples how to effectively guard their hearts against temptation and strengthen their relationships with each other. (*Guarding Love* workbook also available.)

# RENEWING YOUR LOVE

This thirty-day devotional will help couples focus on Scripture, reflect on their marriage, pray together, and set goals that will renew their love.

# CONNECTING WITH YOUR WIFE

Barb Rosberg writes directly to men about what makes women tick and reveals the best thing a man can do for his marriage—and why it's so important.